JOHN WESTLAKE

INTERNATIONAL LAW

PART II

WAR

Elibron Classics
www.elibron.com

Elibron Classics series.

ISBN 0-543-95335-1 (paperback)
ISBN 0-543-95334-3 (hardcover)

This Elibron Classics Replica Edition is an unabridged facsimile
of the edition published in 1907 by the University Press, Cambridge.

INTERNATIONAL LAW

PART II

WAR

By

JOHN WESTLAKE, K.C., LL.D.,

Vhewell Professor of International Law in the University
of Cambridge;
Late Fellow of Trinity College, Cambridge;
Honorary LL.D. of the University of Edinburgh;
Member and late President of the Institute of
International Law

CAMBRIDGE:
the University Press
1907

PREFACE.

AMONG the causes which have retarded this sequel to the volume of 1904—*International Law, Part I, Peace*—the two principal have been, first, the necessity of bringing out a new edition of my *Private International Law*, and secondly, the imminence of a second Hague Conference, certain to produce important discussions and likely to produce notable amendments of the laws of war. Although the Conference is still sitting while I write, it is now possible to give an account of its work on the laws of war. Obligatory arbitration, a permanent court of arbitration, the Drago doctrine and the limitation of armaments belong to the laws of peace.

Time was gained by printing, before the meeting of the Conference, most of what it was desired to say on the law as it stood, a little however being reserved for treatment in connection with the Conference. In consequence it will be necessary, in order to obtain a complete view of many subjects, to refer as well to the last chapter, in which the proceedings at the Hague are dealt with, as to the former portions of the volume. Perhaps however the balance of convenience is on the side of keeping the old law distinct from discussions and amendments the full effect of which, and even to some extent their general acceptance, time will be required to appreciate.

In reviewing the laws of war for the purpose of this volume, I have been more than ever struck with the differences which exist as to their principles. It is hoped that those differences have been presented and their history sketched without exaggeration or extenuation. One point which it may be worth while to notice here is the author's conviction that the common representation, according to which England early accepted from the Consolat del Mar the immunity of neutral goods in enemy ships, cannot survive Mr Marsden's publication of the *Select Pleas of the Court of Admiralty* for the Selden Society and his *Six Centuries of the Admiralty Court*. See pages 123–127 of the present volume.

J. WESTLAKE.

October 1907.

CONTENTS.

CHAPTER I.

WAR AND FORCIBLE MEASURES SHORT OF WAR.

CHAPTER II.

LEGAL RELATIONS AS AFFECTED BY WAR.

CHAPTER III.

CHAPTER IV.

THE LAWS OF WAR ON LAND, BEING THE HAGUE REGULATIONS WITH A COMMENTARY.

SECTION I. ON BELLIGERENTS.

CHAPTER V.

THE HAGUE REGULATIONS CONSIDERED GENERALLY.

CHAPTER VI.

NAVAL WAR AS BETWEEN BELLIGERENTS.

CHAPTER VII.

NEUTRALITY.

CHAPTER VIII.

DUTIES OF NEUTRAL STATES.

CHAPTER IX.

CHAPTER X.

CHAPTER XI.

TABLE OF CASES.

ERRATA AND ADDENDA.

Page 10, note 1: for "c. Rob." read "C. Rob."

" 11, line 11: for "eighteenth" read "nineteenth."

" 50. To the quotation from Kent, C. J., in *Clarke v. Morey*, add that from Lord Lindley on p. 142.

" 125, line 1. It ought to have been made clearer that "the facts quoted" include the judgment of 1357 mentioned on p. 123.

" 130, line 21: *dele* "men."

" 218, note: for "*Hardricks*" read "*Hendricks.*"

For the last four lines of page 319 read:

Notwithstanding the absence of the ships, she and a German vessel, the *Thea*, similarly sunk, were condemned at Vladivostok. The condemnation of the latter was reversed on appeal, but not on the ground of her destruction being illegal.

CHAPTER I.

WAR AND FORCIBLE MEASURES SHORT OF WAR.

Definition of War.

For the redress of wrongs or the prosecution of claims states may appeal to force either by war or by certain measures—reprisals, embargo or pacific blockade—not inconsistent with peace. The consideration of measures of the latter class will naturally precede the detailed consideration of war, as being more akin to the subject of our preceding volume, but first of all war must be defined or those measures could not be distinguished from it. The definition of war given by Grotius was *status per vim certantium qua tales sunt* (1. 1. 2. 1), which includes, as he intended it should, private quarrels waged by force. But it may well be doubted whether a term becomes more useful by being made so comprehensive, nor does the common employment of the word "war" now extend so far, whatever may have been the case three centuries ago as to *bellum*. We therefore, accepting the definition of Grotius in other respects, will say that *war is the state or condition of governments contending by force*. Governments are here mentioned and not states, because the laws of war belong equally to insurgents not yet recognised as a state but recognised as having belligerent rights, which they could not be if they did not possess a government. Whether and how far individuals can be treated as parties to a war is a question to be discussed in the sequel, and is not prejudiced by the use of the word "government," as indeed it would not have been by the use of the word "state":

if they are treated as parties to a war, that can only be justly done when there is reason for their being identified with their state or government.

The important point of the definition is that war is a state or condition: *non actio sed status eo nomine indicatur* says Grotius (u. s.). As such war is not set up by any mere act of force, whether an act of reprisal, embargo or pacific blockade, or an act of self-defence, or one of unlawful violence. It can be set up only by the will to do so, but that will may be unilateral because the state of peace requires the concurrent wills of two governments to live together in it, and is replaced by the state of war as soon as one of those wills is withdrawn. How the will to set up war may be manifested is a question which we shall have to consider: here attention is called to the fact that acts of force are not war unless either a government does them with the intent of war or the government against which they are done elects to treat them as war. Thus, for example, a pacific blockade may continue long and come to an end without there ever having been war.

It may serve to make our thoughts still clearer if with Grotius's definition of war we contrast an earlier and a later one, both due to writers of great distinction. Albericus Gentilis said that *bellum est publicorum armorum justa contentio: de Jure Belli*, l. 1, c. 2. This does not bring out the cardinal point that war is a state or condition. Also, although the word *publicorum* admits of the meaning necessary to make the definition correct, it would seem that Gentilis regarded it as not war but treason if insurgents not constitutionally having *imperium* fight against their prince (l. 1, c. 3). The truth is that a great insurrection with a real government at its head may have both characters. It will be war for the purpose of the neutrality of the powers which recognise the insurgents as having belligerent rights, and even the government against which it is directed may and ought, for the sake of humanity, to treat it as war while the struggle continues, though if and when it has been put down the internal law of that government will not thereby be prevented from regarding it as treason. Lastly, to define war as a *justa contentio* is correct in the sense in which *justum* means *plenitudo quaedam*, the satisfaction of certain requirements, as in *justæ nuptiæ, justa ætas*; and in fact the common phrase *justum bellum* means only a regular war. Yet although Gentilis gets a glimpse of this (l. 1, c. 2), he does not hold firmly by it as his contemporary Ayala did, but, taking *justum* in the popular sense of consonant with justice, accounts for a war being entitled on both sides to that appellation by there being generally a show of justice on each side, and by the mean in which justice consists being not a point but a space possessing breadth, within which room may be found for each party though one is more just than the other (l. 1, c. 6).

The second writer above referred to is Bynkershoek, who says *bellum est eorum qui suae potestatis sunt juris sui persequendi causa concertatio per vim vel dolum: Observationes Juris Publici*, l. 1, c. 1. Here the sure touch of Grotius is wanting. The character of a state or condition, which when once it had been pointed out ought not to have been forgotten, is omitted, and the mention of *dolus*, which often accompanies force but is neither a necessary nor alone a sufficient ingredient in the constitution of war, gives to the sentence the character of a description rather than a definition. *Juris sui* must be understood and was doubtless intended to include a claim, whether in accordance with *jus* or not.

The Relation of War to International Law.

International law did not institute war, which it found already existing, but regulates it with a view to its greater humanity. War is a piece of savage nature partially reclaimed, and fitted out for the purpose of such reclamation with legal effects, such as the abrogation or suspension of treaties, and legal restrictions, such as what are called the laws of war and neutrality. No force is used in war by agents having an international character, as force is used by agents having a public character in order to secure obedience to the law of the land. That war is often waged by powers which have allied themselves for the purpose by international compacts is no exception to this. If an international government were to arise, either by the authority of the great powers growing into a definite and recognised system or by any other means, the employment of force by such government would be comparable to its employment by the ministers of justice within a state. But that consummation is still far off, and until it shall be reached war cannot be described as an execution. Neither to the claims which furnish the reason or the pretext for war, nor to international law so far as it may pronounce such claims to be just, does war stand in the same relation in which an execution stands to the claim of a plaintiff or to the law of the land under which it is put forward. An attempt is sometimes made to determine in the name of international law the conditions on which a recourse may be had to arms, as that an offer of submitting to arbitration shall have been made, where the case is not one of those supreme ones for which it is generally considered that arbitration is unsuitable. No doubt that is the counsel of morality, and so too is it that much shall be borne rather than that war shall be begun for a slight though just cause, even when there is no other recourse. But these are not rules of law, for they are totally lacking in precision, the principles which they express receive nothing approaching to general observance, and the legal character of a war is the same whether they have been observed or not. The truth is that when war enters on the scene all law that was previously concerned with the dispute retires, and a new law steps in, directed only to secure fair and not too inhuman fighting. This, like the law which during the contest it replaces, consists of rules having the general approval of the society of nations and more or less enforced by the irregular action of that society; but there are great differences in the efficacy of the enforcement.

The rules which lay down the conduct to be observed by neutrals during a war are among those in the elaboration and enforcement of which the action of the society of nations is the most influential. "Let war break out between two powers, and the whole non-belligerent world is at once related to that war as neutral, its political and commercial interests are affected by the views entertained about the mutual rights and duties of neutrals and belligerents, incidents occur which oblige even the remotest state to act on some view about those rights and duties, and a general vigilance is aroused not only as to the observance but even as to the shaping of the rules on the subject." Even what in those circumstances neutrals tolerate on the part of belligerents without expressly sanctioning it easily tends to become clothed with the character of law. But the rules which lay down the mutual rights and duties of belligerents present the action of the society of nations at a low level. "A belligerent may complain that his enemy has violated the laws of war, he may use measures of retorsion, but the discussion which so arises is seldom brought to any clear decision. The victory of one party, or such balance of power as may be reached between the parties, brings to a single comprehensive close the war and every thing connected with it, the disputes which led to the war, the ulterior aims which have been developed in its course, and the recriminations to which its incidents have given rise. In drawing up the treaty of peace what is thought of is the new departure in the relations of the parties," including third powers which may have intervened or made their pressure felt for political reasons—such interference on the ground of the misdeeds of a belligerent in the conduct of the war is scarcely known. "Resentment at an act which he deems to have been a violation of the laws of war may swell the indemnity demanded by the conqueror, but the amount added on that score cannot be distinguished, the vanquished pay the indemnity without admitting the violation, and if they condemn the conduct of the war by the conqueror their remonstrances remain wholly without effect. When in a subsequent war the temptation arises to repeat an act the lawfulness of which has been questioned in a previous war, the records of the latter furnish no pronouncement on its lawfulness which can be appealed to[1]." Since this was written the work of the Hague Conference of 1899 has marked a great advance in the part taken by the society of nations in shaping the laws of war, but the small part which it takes in their enforcement remains open to the same criticism. If on the other hand, with regard to the laws of war, general opinion has less external support than in other parts of international law, it speaks with more authority when it imposes restrictions on violence in the names of humanity and conscience.

[1] The quotations in this paragraph are from *Chapters on the Principles of International Law*, 1894, pp. 232–4.

Reprisals and Embargo.

In the literature of international law there are for modes of self-help several terms which are not always carefully distinguished. The widest is retorsion, which applies whenever action is taken by a state in order to compensate it for some damage suffered through the action of another state, or in order to deter the latter from continuing the action complained of. There may be no breach of law on either side, as when state *A* imposes custom duties which do not contravene any treaty, and state *B*, which believes its interests to be damaged by them, imposes by way of retorsion custom duties from which it also is not debarred by any treaty. These however are matters of policy. As a matter of law there is retorsion when state *A* deems that it has received from state *B* not merely damage but legal injury, exempting it from the duty of a strict observance of law towards the wrongdoer, and replies by another breach of law intended to be compensatory or deterrent. In time of peace such retorsion is not generally justifiable in the forum of conscience unless the complaining state has obtained in its favour the sentence of a court of arbitration, or there are no means of submitting the complaint to arbitration. There may be exceptional cases, as where there is reason to expect that a slight and very clear wrong may be remedied by a not very serious counter wrong, with less expenditure of time and trouble than an arbitration would require; or where, the wrong complained of being greater and very clear, retorsion may fairly be employed concurrently with a demand for arbitration. Such exceptions are especially likely to occur where the complaint is that some provision of a treaty has not been observed, and the retorsion consists in not observing some other provision of that treaty or of another treaty between the same states; but there can be no doubt that in the regular course of things remedies should be sought in arbitration before they are sought in self-help.

Another of the ill distinguished terms to which we have referred is retaliation, which is often used in the wide sense of retorsion of any kind, but is perhaps more properly used only for that kind of retorsion in which the thing done in return is the same as that complained of. "An eye for an eye" is retaliation, but that term would hardly be used of imprisonment for injury to an eye. Thus in war, breaking towards an enemy the particular rule of civilised warfare which you accuse him of breaking would be retaliation, while breaking another rule towards him would best be described as retorsion. And the non-observance of a treaty in one clause in return for its non-observance in another clause might well be called retaliation, the treaty being the same.

Reprisal is another of the terms referred to. Its etymology gives the sense of "taking in return," and its original use was in the plural (reprisals, *repressalia*) as denoting a certain systematised taking by way of self-help which will presently be explained. From that sense it has come to be used in cases where there is no taking because the thing is already in the hands of the power seeking redress, as in that of Frederick the Great's withholding the interest on the Silesian loan in retorsion for what he alleged to be the unjust condemnation of Prussian vessels in English prize courts; and occasionally even still more widely, as equivalent to retorsion generally. But it is not retorsion generally, or even reprisal in the sense of withholding a payment or not observing a treaty provision, that we have to do with in this place. We are not here concerned with self-help in any other form than that of acts of force, because it is only those that are liable to be confused with war. And even among acts of force in time of peace our only concern is with certain classes of them which from various causes have been systematised, and that in modes which make their confusion with war difficult to avoid, although their difference from it cannot be overlooked without undermining the definition of war as a state or condition. Take such an act of force as Russia's occupying the Danubian provinces of Turkey in 1853, with the view of holding them as what she called a material guarantee. We shall see in its place that such an act is not necessarily one of war, but it does not belong to the classified and systematised acts now to be considered.

Reprisals, as a forcible measure employed by states in time of peace, may be defined as the taking possession, at sea or on land, of the ships or other property of a foreign state or its subjects, with a view either to pressure on that state for the redress of a wrong alleged to have been done by it or by one of its subjects, or to the application of such property in compensation of such alleged wrong.

Embargo, as a forcible measure employed by states in time of peace, is a special case of reprisals as above defined, being the detention of such property as mentioned, usually ships in the ports of the embargoing state, with such view as mentioned. Thus embargo and reprisals in the special sense in which they are contrasted with it differ as detention from capture; but when the property embargoed is applied in compensation it is reprisal, and the two terms are not carefully distinguished in practice.

Reprisals (*repressalia*) were based on the solidarity which according to ancient views, still far from having ceased to operate, existed between a prince and his subjects or between a city and its citizens. A wrong done by any of them to a foreign prince, city or person was the wrong of all, and all were answerable for it; the cause of any of them who had suffered a wrong from a foreign prince, city or person was the cause of all, and often in practice all took it up, though perhaps in theory it was only for the wronged one or his prince or city to do so. Together with this there worked another mediæval principle, that of self-help as the primary mode of redress. Even in England the history of our law teaches us that civil procedure at first rather came in aid of self-help than was looked on as being in itself the proper and whole remedy. It is necessary to dwell on this aspect of the case because it must not be supposed that the difference between self-help against the foreigner and war was not well known in the middle ages. War was entered on by *diffidatio*, defiance, severing the tie of faith between him who sent it and him who received it; and this not merely between superior and inferior, in order to discharge the feudal duty of either to the other, but between equals. That tie being severed, the *diffidatio* set up a new relation between the parties, just as we still recognise that of war to be. But self-help neither required nor implied a severance of the tie of faith.

That a person who had a grievance against a foreigner should capture ships and cargoes belonging to him, or to those whom general opinion regarded as being solidary with him, was no more deemed shocking or exceptional in a state of peace, than a man's forcibly retaking his goods from a neighbour who had despoiled him of them was deemed to be inconsistent with the internal peace of a country. Nay, that he should capture and detain the persons of the fellow subjects or fellow citizens of his alleged debtor—for to that extent reprisals went—was a natural conclusion from the principles of solidarity and self-help, applied when imprisonment was deemed the natural remedy for debt.

At least as early as the thirteenth century, however, the practice of reprisals was restrained by the conditions that the license of the self-helper's sovereign was to be first obtained, and that property captured at sea could not be appropriated without a sentence of the admiral. The license was granted by letters of marque or of reprisal, or of marque and reprisal. The former term has been connected by some with *marca*, a boundary, the letters being an authority to make captures outside the boundary of the territory; but it may be derived much more easily from *marcare* or *marchiare*, words which are found in documents of the thirteenth century in connection with *pignorare*, apparently in the sense of marking goods for a claimant's security. If the prince on the other side considered the claim to be unfounded, or the compensation obtained to be excessive, he issued letters of *contre-marque*. The measures which a subject was thus licensed to take for his own redress were called special reprisals. General reprisals were resorted to by princes in pursuance of their own claims, political or pecuniary, or for the redress of their subjects' griefs when they adopted them. The proclamation of general reprisals ordered the subjects to capture the property of the other prince and the persons and property of his subjects, and although not confined to the case of war they became a regular accompaniment of war. In either case they were usually coupled with an embargo on the ships of the other prince or of his subjects which were in the ports of the prince resorting to the measure.

Of all this little now remains. Special reprisals are entirely obsolete: the injured individual is no longer entrusted with his own redress. The liability of enemy property to capture at sea during war, which is still maintained by Great Britain and some other countries, is a survival from the system of general reprisals, but, privateering being abolished, it is enforced only by ships of the national navy. Embargoes and captures at sea even by the national navy, by way of reprisal without there being a state of war at the time, were held by Lord Stowell to justify condemnation of the property seized when war followed, in which case he allowed its outbreak to operate retrospectively[1]—a weaker reason, as Hall observes, than the hostile character which belongs to the property at the time of its condemnation. That decision does not expressly either affirm or deny the right of appropriating the captured or embargoed property to the redress of the wrong complained of, if a long time elapses without the claim being admitted, although war may not have broken out; and the Institute of International Law has expressly affirmed that right[2]. But at least Lord Stowell left untouched the capture or detention of the ships of a foreign government or its subjects as a means of putting pressure on it, whether or not he considered that redress could be reached by their appropriation so long as peace is preserved. This means was employed by the British government in its dispute with Naples about the Sicilian sulphur monopoly in 1840, which was settled without war through the mediation of France, and the ships which had been captured or embargoed were then set free. And the method continues to be applied in substance, though under the name of pacific blockade. Lastly, when a war has not been led up to by reprisals, embargo or pacific blockade, the practice of laying an embargo at its outbreak on ships which find themselves in ports becoming those of an enemy has given way to the practice, now general, of allowing time for the departure of such ships. But when forcible steps taken in time of peace fail to bring about a settlement, they would be stultified if ships detained under them

[1] *The Boedes Lust*, 1803, 5 C. Rob. 245. The case was one of embargo in a port, but it cannot in our opinion be distinguished in principle from one of capture at sea.

[2] Art. 38 of the *Réglement sur le régime légal des navires et de leurs équipages dans les ports étrangers*, 17 *Annuaire* (1898), p. 284. Hall seems to regard Lord Stowell as denying the right to appropriate embargoed property in any case except that of war breaking out, but says: "It is not necessary that vessels or other property seized otherwise than by way of embargo should be treated in a similar manner. They may be confiscated so soon as it appears that their mere seizure will not constrain the wrong-doing state to give proper redress": § 120.

were allowed to depart on the outbreak of the war into which they develop.

Pacific Blockade.

We must here assume that the reader knows enough of the laws of war to be aware that under the name of blockade a belligerent is entitled to cut off all communication by sea with a port or coast of his enemy, whether by his own or enemy subjects or even by neutrals, and to capture and confiscate blockade-runners, the conditions being that his blockade shall be properly notified and shall be substantially effective. In the first half of the eighteenth century the idea occurred that this proceeding might be imported into the laws of peace, the right to make reprisals, as to the propriety of which in the absence of war the general conscience was becoming sensitive, being reinforced by declaring a blockade of the ports or coast off which they took place. Thus a state of quasi-war would arise, to the exigencies of which quasi-neutrals might be required to submit as neutrals submit to those of war; the pressure on the quasi-enemy would be increased by including the quasi-neutrals among those with whom his communication was cut off; and a doubt as to the right to condemn his ships under the law relating to reprisals, instead of only sequestering them to await the pacific or hostile close of the incident, would become less obvious if any condemnation of them were made under the pretext of blockade. Jefferson had already said that some "may to a formal declaration of war prefer general letters of mark and reprisal because, on repeal of their edicts by the belligerents, a revocation of the letters of mark restores peace without the delay, difficulties and ceremonies of a treaty[1]." And if reprisals could be regarded as an informal and more convenient war, why should not they operate as such against all the world as well as against the state deemed to have given occasion for the use of force?

The experiment was first tried in 1827 by Great Britain, France and Russia, who declared a blockade of the coast which not long afterwards became that of the kingdom of Greece, in

[1] Letter to Lt.-Governor Lincoln, 13 November 1808: *Jefferson's Correspondence*, London, 1829, vol. 4, p. 119.

support of their intervention between the insurgent Greeks and the sultan of Turkey, the then sovereign of that coast. It must be observed that neither on this nor on any subsequent occasion has the blockade popularly called "pacific" been so styled officially. The executive orders of the government which applies it only mention blockade, and whether a state of war was intended to be entered on must be gathered from diplomatic or parliamentary statements and from the conduct of operations. If, for instance, a bombardment or any other act of force not within the limits of general reprisals should be added to the blockade, this would be a strong indication that war was understood to have been commenced, while a blockade to which the operations were restricted would easily be regarded as meant to be pacific.

The quasi-neutrals submitted to the blockade of 1827, as was to be expected considering the overwhelming strength at sea of the combination by which it was applied, and none of the vessels taken, whether Turkish or other, were confiscated, unless perhaps, for information on the point is lacking, Russian captures were condemned after war had ensued between Russia and Turkey, which it did not as between Great Britain or France and Turkey. The experiment so successfully tried was repeated, and again only with the sequestration either of quasi-belligerent or of quasi-neutral vessels, in 1831 by France against Portugal, in 1833 by Great Britain and France against the Netherlands, and in 1836 by Great Britain against New Grenada[1]. In 1838 France blockaded some Mexican ports and confiscated quasi-neutral vessels, but since she also seized a Mexican port it may be doubted whether the operation can be classed as a pacific blockade. From 1838 to 1840 and from 1845 to 1848 Great Britain and France jointly blockaded the River Plate against the Argentine republic while professing to be at peace, interfering with quasi-neutral shipping but so far as England was concerned

[1] In 1836 Russia notified a blockade of her own Circassian coast, which was in insurrection, and of course confiscated any vessels belonging to the insurgents that tried to break through, or would have done so if the case had occurred; but a British vessel, the *Vixen*, was only turned back, and our government did not press that of Russia for compensation for the loss of her voyage.

without confiscation. France however set up a prize commission at Montevideo which freely condemned quasi-neutrals. So far as these were Uruguayan they could not have complained, because the Uruguayan authorities had recognised the blockade by a convention concluded with the French commander on 23 April 1839, regulating during it the navigation of the Plate by ships under the Uruguayan flag, and the condemnations were for breaches of that convention. Others were British, and as belonging to a co-blockading power could not have complained. The Argentine authorities answered the blockade by issuing letters of marque, and the French jurists were in doubt whether there was not a war until the minister of foreign affairs stated in a letter that France was not at war with the Argentine republic, whereupon the *conseil d'état* reversed a decision of the commission at Montevideo which had condemned a cargo as contraband of war, while holding that the ship had been rightly released because she had been taken without a special notice of the blockade having previously been entered in her log[1]. The Hansetowns protested against the blockade, and Lord Palmerston desired a formal convention of peace in order, as he said, to legalise the operations retrospectively[2].

[1] This was the case of the *Comte de Thomar,* sentence of 25 March 1848, 1 Pistoye and Duverdy 390. Among other cases before the *conseil d'état* in relation to the same blockade see the *Caïman,* 16 January 1846, *ib.* 383; an Uruguayan ship captured for breach of blockade, then carried off by the Argentines and by them furnished with a letter of marque, and finally recaptured by the French. The *Eliza Cornish,* 17 July 1850, *ib.* 387, and the *Fame,* 12 June 1850, *ib.* 389, were British ships condemned for breach of blockade. The *Aurora,* 14 Nov. 1849, *ib.* 384, was another British-owned ship, but carried no papers.

[2] See his letter of 7 December 1846, in Lord Dalling's *Life of Lord Palmerston,* iii. 327. Palmerston said that "unless you are at war with a state you have no right to prevent ships of other states from communicating with the ports of that state—nay, you cannot prevent your own merchant ships from doing so." On this it is to be observed that the question as to foreign ships is just whether pacific blockade affecting third powers is a recognised institution of international law, but that even should that question be answered in the negative it would remain for a British court of justice, in which a shipowner sued a naval officer for damages, to consider whether the king is not constitutionally entrusted with the power of controlling commerce in foreign parts, so far as it has not been placed

It is needless to detail the numerous instances of pacific blockade which have since occurred, but in all of them except that applied to Greece by Great Britain in 1850 and the blockade of Greece by the powers collectively in 1886 quasi-neutrals were interfered with, while in none did the interference either with their shipping or with that of the quasi-enemy go beyond sequestration. But the remarkable occurrences of 1884 and 1902 require special notice. On 20 October 1884 the French admiral Courbet declared a blockade of a certain part of the island of Formosa, at that time a Chinese possession, neutrals to have three days in which to complete their loading and leave, and this was officially published in the *Moniteur* of the 23rd. Thereupon the British under-secretary of state for foreign affairs stated in the House of Commons, in answer to a question, that the notification of the blockade ought to be regarded by neutrals as a notification of a state of war; and in a note of 11 November to the French ambassador Lord Granville wrote that "the contention of the French government that a pacific blockade confers on the blockading power the right to capture and condemn the ships of third nations for a breach of such a blockade is in conflict with well established principles of international law": *Parl. Papers, France*, no. 1, 1885. It will be observed that mere sequestration is not mentioned. In the Chamber of Deputies, on 26 November, the French prime minister justified pacific blockade and the acts of hostility which may follow from it without a previous declaration of war, as belonging to the policy of material guarantees (*la politique des gages*), and mentioned three advantages which that policy had over a declaration of war: it left the door always open to negotiation, it allowed the rights resulting from previous treaties (*l'état conventionnel antérieur*) to continue, and it did not complicate the conflict by differences or difficulties with neutrals, while a declaration of war would authorise taking measures against (*nous en prendre au*) neutral commerce, and in some sort make it a duty to take them. France however, being challenged by Great Britain either to accept a state of war or to drop the

under the protection of an act of parliament, especially as incidental to the line which he chooses to take in his relations with foreign states.

condemnation of quasi-neutral vessels, made on 3 January 1885 a new notification of the blockade of Formosa, based on "the state of reprisals existing between France and China." And shortly afterwards she took further action at the Chinese port of Foochow, whereupon, the state of war being unmistakable, Great Britain forbade the coaling of French ships of war in her ports.

The operations which Great Britain and Germany took jointly against Venezuela in 1902 were introduced on the British side by instructions for blockade given by the admiralty to Vice-admiral Douglas on 11 December. Vessels under any other than the Venezuelan flag were to be warned, and if afterwards attempting to communicate with any of the blockaded ports were to be handed over to the prize court at Trinidad; vessels sailing under the Venezuelan flag or in the service of the Venezuelan government were to be seized and treated as prize of war; persons not of Venezuelan nationality who wished to leave that country might pass the line of blockade on board ships having no cargo beyond the baggage of *bona fide* travellers. This might be ambiguous in the mouth of any other government, but, as coming from the British government after the position in which the latter had placed itself in 1884, it can only be interpreted as recognising that a state of war was being entered on; and in a proclamation of 22 December the governor and vice-admiral of Trinidad announced that war had broken out between his sovereign and Venezuela. But the protocol of 13 February 1903, which closed the incident, was less outspoken though substantially to the same effect. Its recital ran that "certain differences have arisen between Great Britain and the United States of Venezuela," and Art. 7 was this: "The British and Venezuelan governments agree that, inasmuch as it may be contended that the establishment of a blockade of Venezuelan ports by the British naval forces has *ipso facto* created a state of war between Great Britain and Venezuela, and that any treaty existing between the two countries has been thereby abrogated, it shall be recorded in an exchange of notes between the undersigned that" a certain convention "shall be deemed to be renewed and confirmed, or provisionally renewed and confirmed, pending the conclusion of a new treaty of amity and commerce."

The operations of Germany against Venezuela on this occasion included the bombardment of more than one place on the coast, and it would therefore have been no less difficult than in the case of Great Britain to reconcile them with the absence of an intent of war. But by both powers the captured ships, public and private, neutral as well as Venezuelan, were restored.

The Institute of International Law adopted this declaration in 1887.

The establishment of a blockade without war (*en dehors de l'état de guerre*) cannot be considered as permitted by international law except under the following conditions:

1. Ships under a foreign flag can enter freely notwithstanding the blockade;

2. The pacific blockade must be officially declared and notified, and maintained by a sufficient force;

3. The ships of the blockaded power which do not respect such a blockade may be sequestered. When the blockade has ceased they must be restored to their owners with their cargoes, but without indemnity on any ground[1].

The discussion had been introduced (1) by a report of Perels, the eminent *conseiller rapporteur* of the German admiralty, in which he maintained, as Heffter had done, the right of affecting neutrals by a pacific blockade, but limited it to preventing their passing the line of blockade, while the ships of the quasi-enemy may be sequestered, neither being subject to confiscation: (2) by a counter-report of Geffcken, to whom international law is indebted for the posthumous editions of Heffter's book, and who, avowing the change of his opinion, condemned pacific blockade altogether, even as against the quasi-enemy.

To sum the matter up, pacific blockade as against the quasi-enemy is too well established as a recognised institution to be longer attacked with serious hope of success. So long as war does not result, the only penalty by which it can be enforced is the sequestration of the quasi-enemy's ships, for the institution has been sufficiently differentiated from the reprisals out of which it arose for this affirmation to be made about it, whether or not a right of using the property seized as a real satisfaction

[1] 9 *Annuaire* 300.

is admitted in the case of reprisals or embargo, when redress has been long refused, even though war has not broken out. As against quasi-neutrals the legal position of pacific blockade must be considered as still ambiguous, with the exception that even if interference with them and sequestration of their ships be regarded as lawful, and even also if war results, there can be no condemnation, because in favour of it there is only a minute shred of authority, while on the other side there is the solid argument that as against neutrals war cannot be carried back by relation to a time when it had neither been declared nor clearly existed. The argument which has prevailed in favour of pacific blockade as against the quasi-enemy, and which is urged in its favour up to the point of sequestration as against quasi-neutrals, is that it is a milder remedy than war; but it increases the power of the strong over the weak, and by confusing the bounds of the use of force in time of peace it impairs the certainty which is so important in international relations. The best case for it is when it is employed by the great powers collectively in their new and growing character of the legislature of Europe, but when they employed it against Greece in 1886 they interfered only with Greek ships. As the matter stands it would be difficult to characterise the pacific blockader who sequestrated quasi-neutral ships as a wrongdoer in an opprobrious sense, but it would be equally difficult to deny to the quasi-neutral the right of refusing to submit to the measure.

In conclusion a word must be said as to the occasions on which it is held to be morally justifiable to resort to modes of force short of war. That question was discussed in the remonstrance made by Great Britain in 1751 against the stoppage by the king of Prussia of payment of the interest on the Silesian loan, which was an act differing only in its not being one of force from the reprisals we have dealt with. Reprisals were there allowed to be proper "only in cases of violent injuries directed or supported by the state, and justice absolutely denied by all the tribunals and afterwards by the prince." This limitation has been generally approved, only stress must not be laid in it on the term "violent." It is not doubted that merely civil wrongs for which justice is not obtainable either from the ordinary coints of law, by arbitration or by diplomacy may warrant reprisals, only the wrong must be clear. The point of the limitation is that reprisals are not a proper means of enforcing on a state the line of political conduct which it is desired that it should take, but pacific blockade is employed for that purpose also, as in the cases of 1827 and 1886 which have been mentioned. If however either pacific blockade or reprisals in their older and simpler form should be employed on an occasion which opinion, even general, should pronounce insufficient, that would not affect their legality any more than the legality of a war is affected by the want of justice in the ground for it. So far as any form of force in peace is recognised as an international institution, it is a weapon placed in the hands of states, to be used, so far as law is concerned, in their discretion.

The Commencement of War as between the Belligerents.

It is natural that Grotius, whose definition of war we have found to be the best of those examined, should also be found to lay down a particularly clear doctrine on the mode of commencing it. He has spoken of war as an institution producing legal effects (1. 3. 4. 1, 3. 3. 1. 1), and adds that by the law of nations a declaration of war (*denuntiatio*) is required in every case in order to produce those peculiar effects, but that it is sufficient if this proceeds from one party (3. 3. 6. 3, 3. 3. 7. 3). "The cause," he says, "for which nations have required a declaration for a lawful war was not, as some allege, that they might do nothing secretly or by a clever trick, for that consideration belongs rather to the perfection of gallantry than to law, as we read that some peoples even appointed the day and place of combat, but that it might appear with certainty that the war was not waged by private audacity but by the will of the peoples on either side or their heads; for that is the source of its peculiar effects, which have no place in a contest with brigands or in one between a king and his subjects" (3. 3. 11). It does not however follow that any particular form of declaration is necessary, as by a herald or by sending a bloody spear, or any condition added to the declaration, as the lapse of thirty days before commencing hostilities, for such have often fallen into disuse even among those who once required them (3. 3. 8). "Nor is it true that by the law of nations hostilities cannot be commenced immediately on the declaration of war, for that law requires no intervening time; but by the law of nature"—that is, as we now express it, by justice—"some time may be required by the character of the case, as if redress or the punishment of a guilty person has been demanded and has not been denied. For then so much time must be given as is necessary for doing conveniently what has been asked" (3. 3. 13).

Subsequent practice has ratified the opinion of Grotius as to the indifference of form in public declarations of war. Between 1657, when Sweden declared war against Denmark by a herald-at-arms sent to Copenhagen[1], employing perhaps for the last time the proceeding of the old *diffidatio*, and 1870, when France presented at Berlin a declaration of war against Prussia, it would be difficult to find an instance of war being expressly declared at the court against which it was directed, although notes declaring a rupture of negotiations may have been presented which were so worded as to be substantially declarations of war. During the interval public declarations of war were made by documents bearing that name or that of manifestoes, issued at home by the declaring power, which through the world-wide notoriety ensured them in modern times served every purpose which could have been served by presentation at the other court. They also gave an opportunity of announcing the practice which the declaring power intended to follow in matters concerning neutrals, or even concerning the enemy, for example the treatment of his ships found in its ports. And these declarations of war are still in current use.

But on another point, the necessity that the commencement of hostilities should be preceded or accompanied by a declaration of war in some form or other, it was against a practice which had already begun before his time that the teaching of Grotius was directed. Of this practice the war between Elizabeth and Philip II was a conspicuous example. The depredations of Drake and the other English sea-captains took place without any declaration, but the queen's connivance at and participation in them were not intended as war, except in the limited

[1] Twiss, *Law of Nations—War*, p. 62; quoting Martens, *Précis*, l. 8, § 267, and Holberg, *Danmarkskriges Hist.*, t. 3, p. 241.

and informal sense in which it used to be said in Elizabethan England that there was no peace beyond the line. Neither however was the despatch of the Armada accompanied by a declaration, which on Grotian principles would have been necessary even were it only an acceptance of a state of war declared by it to exist. And the practice continued in spite of Grotius, the first acts of force in the case of naval wars being sometimes done under a formal announcement of general reprisals, as was the case with the Anglo-Dutch war of 1665, which Sir Matthew Hale (1 *Pleas of the Crown* 163) states to have grown, without ever being "solemnly denounced," out of an English "act of council which instituted only a kind of universal reprisal." Thus an institution recognised as distinct from war, which in the middle ages may have served to bring about the settlement of many quarrels without the interruption of the relation of peace, was wrested to a mode of obscuring the demarcation between war and peace; and the Grand Pensionary De Witt was justified, from the point of view of a politician rather than of a jurist, in saying that "he saw no difference between general reprisals and open war[1]." In 1739 George II granted letters of marque and reprisal against Spain on a ground falling within the narrowest view that can be entertained as to the proper occasions for such letters, that of failure to pay a sum of money due by treaty, and deprecated their being considered as an interruption of the peace. But the king of Spain ordered a counter embargo of all British ships in Spanish

[1] Twiss says, it does not appear on what authority, that this remark was not made on the occasion of the reprisals mentioned in the text, but on that of an embargo laid by England on all Dutch vessels in her ports in 1662, for the remedy of a wrong alleged to have been done by the Dutch to the knights of Malta, and removed on its being pointed out that the practice of nations did not justify reprisals being made by a prince on behalf of any but his own subjects—a limitation with which Bynkershoek disagreed, since he regarded reprisals as a remedy to be granted to a complainant in the course of the administration of justice: *De Foro Legatorum*, c. 22. Twiss goes on to suggest that De Witt may only have meant that the embargo, "if not warranted by the law of nations, could only be regarded as an act of open war against the States General": *Law of Nations—War*, § 17. The remark however seems to have a broader meaning, and to refer to the political practice of the time.

harbours, and war was thereupon declared by Great Britain, by the reflex operation of which war Sir Travers Twiss tells us that "the property seized by way of reprisal became subject to condemnation as the property of enemies *ab initio*[1]." The Seven Years' War was not declared as between Great Britain and France till 1756, and general reprisals had not previously been ordered, but French vessels had been captured by the British navy as early as 1754, and their restoration was refused by Lord Chatham in the negotiations for peace in 1761 on the ground that belligerent rights did not result from a formal declaration of war but from the hostilities first offered, which Great Britain laid to the charge of France in respect of the acts of force which had taken place in America and India. In 1778, when Great Britain and France were again fighting without formal declaration, it was represented to Lord Chancellor Thurlow that the case of 1754–6 ought to be taken as one of reprisal, in which captures are only detained as pledges for satisfaction, and it was said that no prizes were then condemned or distributed before the declaration. Thereupon his lordship desired the secretary of the admiralty to order a search to be made as to the course taken in commencing wars by the British government since the revolution[2].

The war of 1778 was never expressly declared on either side. The French ambassador delivered in London a declaration of 15 March, to the effect that the king had recognised the independence of the United States and concluded a treaty of

[1] Twiss: *Law of Nations—War*, § 34. He says that the war, once declared, "reflected back upon the original breach of a treaty an undoubted character of hostility." But the reflex operation cannot be carried further than to the date of the letters of marque and reprisal, the breach of treaty not being an act of force.

[2] See Lord Thurlow's letter to the secretary of the Admiralty, quoted from a MS. source by Twiss, *Law of Nations—War*, p. 67. Thurlow states, apparently not as his own opinion but as the representation made to him, that "declaration is said to be necessary to what writers call a solemn war, but it has been the practice of nations in all ages to begin hostilities otherwise." Grotius however did not make *bellum solenne* a distinct kind of war for which declaration was necessary. He preferred that term to *bellum justum* for all lawful international wars, as carrying no implication of justice, and his *bellum minus solenne* was a contention not international: 1. 3. 4. 1. and 2.

friendship and commerce with them, and was prepared to maintain effectively his treaty rights and the honour of his flag. The British government then recalled its ambassador from Paris and laid an embargo on all French vessels in British ports, whereupon the French ambassador was recalled from London, a French fleet sailed to North America, and a series of naval actions ensued. The war was therefore merely a *de facto* one throughout, unless the French document of 15 March can be considered as a conditional declaration of war, dependent on the attitude of Great Britain on its receipt, and converted by that attitude into an actual one.

The wars between the continental powers in the seventeenth and eighteenth centuries were often commenced in fact before their declaration, and were sometimes carried through without any declaration, quite as a matter of course, without that confused reference to reprisals as a distinct institution which helped to warp the thoughts and the conduct of the maritime powers. Thus on all sides the habit arose of regarding lawful war, that is war with all its legal effects, as commenced no less by fact than by declaration, and dating it from the commencement of hostilities. By that term, if we try to put a definite meaning on it, we must understand the first act of force done with the intent of war and not with that of reprisals or pacific blockade, or the first act of force done with the intent of reprisals or pacific blockade if a war follows, or the first act of force done with whatever intent—self-defence, seizing what is called a material guarantee, or any other—which the state affected by it chooses to regard as one of war. Nor is it possible to refuse its legal effects to a state of war so entered on, or to date its commencement as between the parties otherwise. But from the point of view of political morality it cannot be too strongly maintained that so serious a step as the entrance on a state of war ought not to be taken without the deliberation for which the only security approaching to adequacy is the necessity of expression. No power doing an act of force with the intent of war, nor any power treating as war an act of force done by another, is morally justified in omitting to accompany its conduct by some kind of declaration. Nor again is any power doing an act of force morally justified in not having a clear view whether it intends it as war or not. If an act of force affects third powers and they submit to it, deeming at the same time that it places them in the position of neutrals in war with neutral rights and duties, they can scarcely avoid stating the view which they take of the situation. All this springs from or coincides with the principle that international relations ought to be certain, on which we have seen Grotius basing his demand for a declaration of war in every case; and since the long peace of 1815–1848 the mere *de facto* commencement of hostilities has fallen into desuetude, except so far as pacific blockade tends to obscure the matter as reprisals formerly did, and the commencement of hostilities has been preceded or accompanied by declarations of war.

The demand for an interval of notice, more or less defined, which is sometimes put forward, more by popular or partisan writers than by serious students, we must reject, again in agreement with Grotius. An attack which nothing had foreshadowed would be infamous, and third powers would probably join in resenting and opposing it. But usually claims or complaints are pressed with increasing insistency, the tone of the negotiations becomes more and more acrimonious, preparations are made which cannot altogether be concealed, and the outbreak of war is not really a surprise to anyone. Sometimes the disputant who declares it has delayed doing so until the preparations made by his adversary have convinced him that he can no longer safely delay, and it would be impossible to demand from him a notice which would only give a further advantage to the party which had tried his forbearance so long. In 1187 the emperor Frederick Barbarossa, by a constitution made in a diet at Nuremberg, imposed on the right of anyone to do justice to himself the condition of giving three days' notice to his adversary. This was suitable enough to private war, but not to the contests of the German princes when the weakness of the empire had caused their position to approach that of independence. Accordingly in 1356 the Golden Bull of the emperor Charles IV retained the suspensive interval only as an alternative to declaration, providing that no one should on any pretext invade his neighbour unless he had given him three days' personal notice beforehand, or had publicly signified his intention to make war against him at the place of his usual residence in the presence of competent witnesses. Nor has a necessity for an interval between announcing the intention of hostilities and commencing them ever formed part of the systematic relations between the nations of the world[1].

It will have been noticed that the necessary declaration of war has been spoken of as preceding or accompanying the first act of force, and that the denial by Grotius of the necessity of even the shortest interval between them amounts to permitting the one to accompany and not necessarily to precede the other. That it is necessary not to make everything turn on the declaration's preceding is shown by the case in which a power that has not left its positive insistence on its claims in doubt, and which therefore must be expected to meet force by force, finds itself confronted by preparations which it is no longer safe to disregard. It would be idle to say that a power so circumstanced must let slip an opportunity of hindering the offensive preparations for want of a previous declaration of war, nor can its hindering them be really a surprise, but it will be bound to regularise its action by declaring war as soon as practicable. And this may not be for some days if the incident took place at a distance from the seat of government, so that the term "accompanying" which has been used must not be construed with pedantic strictness. The maxim that the state and legal effects of war must be dated from the commencement of hostilities will apply, but the case will be very different from those which gave birth to that maxim, such as captures being made in distant oceans by commanders acting under instructions to that effect, and war being declared two years afterwards. An example is furnished by the commencement of the war of 1894

[1] Here may be mentioned a clause quoted by Calvo, t. 2, § 1655, from a treaty of 1816 between Portugal and England, and treaties of Brazil with France, 1826, England and Prussia, 1827, and Denmark, 1828: "if a misunderstanding, a cessation of friendship or a rupture should arise between the two crowns (from which may God preserve us) the rupture shall not be deemed to exist until the recall or departure of their respective diplomatic agents." This, strictly construed, provides against an earlier commencement of the legal effects of a state of war, but was probably dictated also by a desire to preclude acts of force without notice.

between China and Japan. The dispute between those powers concerned their respective relations to Korea, and from early in June both parties had been pouring troops into that country. On 25 July a Japanese squadron met near Korea with Chinese men-of-war escorting the *Kow-shing*, a transport loaded with a further number of soldiers; and an action commenced, before indeed the Japanese had sighted the *Kow-shing*, but when it must have been obvious to both parties that each was on the spot in order to assist in strengthening its own position in Korea and prevent that of the other from being strengthened. Whichever side fired the first shot, the government under whose instructions it was fired must be considered to have borne with the preparations of its adversary up to the point at which it did not deem it safe to bear with them any longer, and cannot be blamed for trying to stop them. The emperor of Japan formally declared war on 1 August, and on 10 September Count Ito, his minister president of state, wrote officially "let it be known that the commencement of the present war was 25 July."

The war of 1904 between Japan and Russia began in a more regular manner, for the note which Mr Kurino, the Japanese minister, presented at St Petersburg on 6 February expressly declared the termination of the negotiations and the right reserved by his government to take independent action, while he at the same time announced his intention to take his departure with the staff of his legation. This can hardly be regarded otherwise than as a declaration of war, especially since on 28 January Mr Kurino had said to Count Lamsdorff that "further prolongation of the present condition is not only undesirable but rather dangerous," and on 31 January Count Lamsdorff told Mr Kurino that "he fully appreciated the gravity of the present situation." Indeed the Japanese note bore a close resemblance to that which the Spanish government communicated to General Woodford, the United States minister at Madrid, on 21 April 1898. This declared that relations between the two governments were broken off and that no further American communication would be received, and was answered by the General's demanding his passports the same day, while the Spanish minister at Washington had demanded his the day before. Captures of Spanish vessels were made by the United States navy at least as early as the 22nd, and on the 25th Congress, consulted by President McKinley, determined by a joint resolution that there had been war from the 21st inclusive. That was a legitimate interpretation of the situation created by the Spanish note, and not a retrospective dating of the war to the first acts of force or in order to cover them, as has been represented. If we cannot be content to agree with Grotius that declarations of war are not tied to form, it will be difficult to know where to stop, short of requiring a special messenger to be sent with them.

It remains to say that a declaration of war may be conditional, presenting an ultimatum to be accepted within a given time, otherwise war then to begin. This is very common, and an instance familiar to our British readers is that of the ultimatum delivered on behalf of President Kruger to the British agent at Pretoria on 9 October 1899, by which it was declared that the absence of an affirmative answer to the four terms therein laid down, by 5 p.m. on the 11th, would be regarded as a formal declaration of war. It has never been controverted that a state of war is entered on at the expiry of the delay mentioned for that purpose in a conditional declaration without satisfaction of its demands.

Armed Interventions.

What has been said about the commencement of war will not in general apply to those armed contests which arise out of the intervention of a state in the internal dissensions of another state. Such interventions are usually undertaken by stronger powers in the affairs of weaker ones, or by a coalition in the affairs of a single power, and are therefore usually successful for the time although the resentment they cause may aid in producing a reaction later. Consequently, if the party intervened against is not in possession of the government, it will probably be put down without a state of war having existed between the two powers, although the laws of war ought to be and probably will have been observed in the fighting. There will have been no declaration of war, nor any occasion for one. If on the other hand the party intervened against is in possession of the government, as Napoleon was in possession of that of France in 1815 and the constitutionalists of that of Spain in 1823, there will still be no declaration of war, because the interveners, not recognising the actual government as legitimate, will not admit that their quarrel with it is a quarrel with the state which it claims to represent. Here also, therefore, there will not be a state of war with the usual abrogation or suspension of treaties as its effect, and yet the struggle may be such that at its close some new arrangements between the *de facto* belligerents may be desirable. Thus in 1815 the allies did not declare war, and they allowed the representatives of Louis XVIII to sign on behalf of France their manifesto of 13 March against Napoleon and on 9 June the final act of the Congress of Vienna, while *de facto* hostilities were onward between them and the actual government of that country[1]. The struggle was closed by the treaty of 20 November 1815, which was not nominally one of peace, but in Art. 10 of which "the hostilities" are mentioned; and that treaty was described as one of peace in the protocol and declaration of Aix-la-Chapelle, 15 November 1818. Similarly the French invasion of Spain in 1823 produced no technical state of war, and was followed by a convention, 5 January 1824, about the maritime prizes taken.

The Commencement of War as against Neutrals.

The existence of a state of war as between the belligerents imposes the duties of neutrality on third powers and their subjects, and gives them what are called the rights of neutrality, but which are in truth only the limitations of its duties, for no new right accrues to a neutral as such. But although the duties arise from the facts it would be unjust to impose them without notification of the facts or something equivalent to it. If there has been a declaration of war, whether expressly to the enemy or by a manifesto, it is in practice communicated to third powers, although the publicity of a manifesto might make it as

[1] The only prize case appearing in the English reports as arising out of the short war of Waterloo is that of the French frigate *l'Étoile*, which with her consort commenced the action in which she was taken: 2 Dodson 106.

suitable for the purpose of notice against neutrals as against the enemy. If the declaration of war has been conditional, the fact that the time fixed by it has expired without the ultimatum being complied with will not be of so public a nature as to amount to notice to third powers, and it must be communicated to them. And in any case the communication to a third power will bind its subjects, it being the duty of every government to give the publicity necessary for the protection of its subjects to all international events of which it is apprised. If as between the belligerents the state of war is dated from the first act of force which either side chooses to regard as war, that antedating can have no effect as against third powers or their subjects. But it will not follow that if there has been no declaration of war, or if there has been a failure in the duty of communicating such a declaration, third powers and their subjects can escape the duties of neutrality during the whole of the contest. If they know the existence of the war, or if it is so notorious that they must be held to have known it, they will be bound by those duties. This is taught by all writers, and was applied by the Italian prize court, 8 December 1896, to justify the capture of the Dutch ship *Doelwyk*, carrying contraband during a *de facto* war between Italy and Abyssinia which had not been declared[1]. In the case of a civil war, which commences without declaration, and indeed is not a contest involving a state of war between two powers, duties identical with those of neutrality arise for all powers which are not parties to the contest, and are recognised by them as incumbent on them and their subjects by the fact of their recognising the belligerency of the parties. If either party uses modes of warlike force which affect third parties, as the blockade of ports not within its *de facto* authority and therefore not capable of being closed by a domestic measure, the powers which allow such modes of force to be applied against them or their subjects thereby recognise the war and their duties as neutrals in consequence of it[2].

[1] See an article on the case, by Brusa, in 4 *Revue Générale* 157–175.
[2] See *Part I—Peace*, pp. 52–4.

CHAPTER II.

LEGAL RELATIONS AS AFFECTED BY WAR.

War as a Relation between States: its Effect on Treaties.

THE outbreak of war removes the controversy out of which it arose from the domain of law. It will be settled at the peace on such terms as the superiority of force decides; and if it turned on the disputed interpretation of a treaty, and such interpretation is not declared at the peace for the future, the treaty will be regarded as annulled. There cannot be a contract unless the minds of the parties are agreed, and the war will have shown that their minds are not agreed in the treaty in question.

Further, war interposes a practical obstacle to dealing on the footing of law even with obligations which have not been in dispute, and it may result in such a change of the relative strength of the parties and in the surrounding circumstances that the parties, or at least the stronger of them, will not desire that those obligations should continue. It is therefore the general rule that war abrogates the treaties existing between the belligerents, and that their revival, if desired, must be expressly provided for in the treaty of peace.

To this rule however there are certain exceptions. First, all conventional obligations as to what is to be done in a state of war must continue in force, or they would have no operation at all. Such is the Anglo-French convention providing for a continuance of the postal service between the two countries in the case of a war between them, and such are the St Petersburg declaration against the use of explosive bullets, and all other conventions relating to the laws of war. Another instance is the provision in very numerous treaties for the treatment which their respective subjects and their property are to receive from one another in case of war between them.

Secondly, transitory or dispositive treaties[1], including all those which are intended to establish a permanent condition of things, form another exception. Not only treaties of cession, boundary, recognition of independence or of a dynasty, and such like fall under this head, but also those stipulations which confer rights intended for use in daily life and having no conceivable connection with the causes of war or peace. An example is the clause in the treaty of 1795 between Great Britain and the United States giving to their respective subjects and citizens the right to hold and transmit land then held by them in the other country, notwithstanding their or their heirs or assigns being aliens[2]. The treaty of 1760 between France and Sardinia, now applying to Italy, relative to the execution in either country of judgments rendered by the courts of law of the other country, and the conventions of 12 June 1902 and 17 July 1905 between numerous states, unhappily not including the *penitus toto divisos orbe Britannos*, on important parts of private international law, furnish other examples. All these are delimitations of rights as real and implying permanence as plainly as delimitations of boundaries. During a war the rights may be dormant for want of the opportunity to enforce them, just as boundaries may be transgressed by arms; but the peace, when concluded, is a peace with and on behalf of each belligerent state with all its known equipment of territory and permanent rights, and needs no expression to that effect[3].

[1] See these explained in the volume on *Peace*, pp. 60–62.

[2] That this clause was not abrogated by the war of 1812, notwithstanding that it was not expressly revived at the peace in 1815, was recognised in the United States by the case of the *Society for the Propagation of the Gospel v. Town of Newhaven*, 8 Wheaton 464, Scott 428, and in England by that of *Sutton v. Sutton*, 1 Russell and Mylne 663.

[3] By the treaty of 1783 Great Britain agreed that the inhabitants of the United States should have liberty to fish in the waters of Newfoundland and all other parts of H. B. M.'s dominions in America. The peace of 1815 after the war of 1812 was silent as to this, and the United States thereupon contended and Great Britain denied that the liberty continued.

A third exception is that of treaties establishing arrangements to which third powers are parties, such as guarantees and postal and other unions. These cannot be abrogated by the war, because it cannot affect the rights of third parties. There may during the war be practical difficulties in the way of carrying out their provisions, but at least a belligerent ought not actively to violate them unless they are of a non-political nature and his necessity is great. Guarantees are political, and the plea that he is at war with another party to them will not avail a power which actively violates them to the detriment of the state guaranteed. But although treaties making political arrangements are not destroyed by the mere fact of a war in which all the parties to them are not engaged, it may happen that one of the belligerents is so weakened by the war or by the terms of peace that he can no longer fulfil a guarantee or some other political stipulation to which he has agreed, or that to do so would be a greater burden than in his reduced condition he can be expected to bear. Then he will be freed, not by any rule of law but by the force of circumstances of which those with whom he has contracted must take account.

Outside the exceptions which have been discussed, treaties between belligerents do not survive the outbreak of the war. At the peace there is no presumption that the parties will take the same view as before the war of their interests, political, commercial or other. It is for them to define on what terms

The former did not deny the general rule that treaties are abrogated by war, and the latter did not deny that engagements "in the nature of perpetual obligation" are an exception to that rule. But the former argued that the liberty in question was an integral part of the partition made in 1783 between the two powers, and the latter that it was of such a nature that it could only rest on "conventional stipulation." See Wheaton's *Elements*, part 2, c. 4, § 8, and part 3, c. 2, § 9, with Lawrence's notes, and Hall, § 27. By a convention in 1818 the United States expressly renounced all claim to the liberty except so far as given by that convention, and the incident may suggest an exception to the exception now under consideration, namely that the stipulation of a servitude to be enjoyed in the territory or territorial waters of the other belligerent is not one that can revive after a peace which does not mention it. Wheaton does not admit this character of stipulations of servitude, being evidently under the influence of his country's view in the diplomatic discussion here referred to.

they intend to close their interlude of savage life and to reenter the domain of law. Those terms are at their disposal or at that of the stronger, and if the price exacted for peace is heavy, it ought not to be spoken of as a fine or penalty. Indignation at what was regarded as an unjust pretension, or resentment at what is regarded as a too obstinate resistance, may have contributed to fix it, but law has had no concern in fixing it. It is the last act of the lawless period, and both opinion and practice allow the victor to take advantage of that period by insisting on terms having no relation to the cause or occasion of the war. The terms may be just, more often the consciousness of their injustice is obscured in the victor's mind by his excited feelings, but in any case the genius of law does not inhabit a temple shared by the god of battles, and only returns when he has withdrawn from it[1].

General View of the Relation of Individuals to War.

We have now to consider the relations of each belligerent state to individual subjects of the other, and of the subjects of the respective belligerent states to one another. A good method will be to place in contrast the ideas and practice current about the matter at the close of the middle ages and now, and then to speak of the gradual passage from the one to the other.

At the close of the middle ages the whole matter was governed with unflinching consistency, at least in theory, by the principle of the solidarity between a prince and his subjects

[1] On the subject of this section there is a difference of statement, probably more than of opinion, since those who prefer to say that treaties are not abrogated but suspended by war between the parties seem to build mainly on what those who make abrogation the rule have to treat as exceptions. Also the exception of transitory or dispositive treaties admits, as we have seen, of differences of opinion whether particular cases fall within it. Those who have to draw up treaties of peace ought never to omit the distinct expression of what is intended as to the old stipulations between the parties, and they seldom make such an omission. They will perhaps be less likely to make it if they are under the impression that it would lead to the loss of possibly valuable treaties. Hall's § 125, pp. 399–405 of the 4th edition, is worth reading, but, as might be expected from the nature of the subject, hardly leads to more definite conclusions than those here given.

and between a city and its citizens. The *diffidatio* which introduced the state of war and made prince or city the enemy of prince or city had for its necessary consequence that each prince or city was the enemy of the subjects or citizens of the other, and that the subjects or citizens of each were individually the enemies of those of the other. Peaceful relations were not modified but destroyed, and legal relations during the war there were none, in whatever degree Christianity or chivalry might mitigate practice. Hence the proclamation which accompanied a *diffidatio* did not merely require the subjects to whom it was addressed to capture the property of the other prince and the persons and property of his subjects, as in the case of general reprisals. It went on to require them to break off all commerce, that is all peaceful dealing with the enemies, and to attack them indiscriminately—*courir sus aux ennemis*—a famous formula which meant to kill them, take them captive and pillage them. If any authority were wanted for what lies on the surface of the history of those times, it may be found in the statement of Grotius that "a war declared against him who has the supreme authority in a population is considered to be declared against all his subjects and those who may join themselves to him as allies" (3. 3. 9).

In contrast with what has been described, modern ideas and practice do not present the same simplicity and consistency. They cannot be stated without distinguishing between what may be called the military and the civil aspects of war, the former comprising what is observed or deemed proper in the application of force by sea or land, the latter what is observed or deemed to be legal in courts of justice.

It is recognised on the military side of war that the true principle is that laid down by Montesquieu, namely that "nations ought to do one another in peace the most good, and in war the least evil, that is possible without injuring their true interests." In accordance with that principle, no exercise of force is now placed for its legal justification on the ground that the individual against whom it is directed or who suffers by it is an enemy. It is not deemed lawful to affect an individual except so far as doing so may be a necessary or at least an important means of breaking down the resistance of the enemy state. To that extent he may be considered as identified with his state for the purpose of the war. The case which presents the strongest appearance to the contrary is that of the capture and condemnation of the property of the enemy's subjects at sea where no directly military reason, such as breach of a blockade or carrying contraband of war, is involved; but even that practice is not now upheld by any one except on the ground of the contribution which it may make to depriving the enemy state of the means of carrying on the war. That this is the accepted view of the relation of individuals to war in its military aspect may be shown by the following quotation from Lueder, who of all modern authorities was one of the least disposed to limit military exigencies.

"The commencement," he says, "of war and the entry of the law of war on the scene introduce for the subjects of the belligerent states the condition of war (*kriegsstand*), that is the special relation which in consequence of the outbreak of war arises between them and the opposite party. All the subjects of the states which are at war are under that condition, though not in the same degree, notwithstanding that the rule holds that peaceable private persons belonging to the belligerent states are not mutually enemies. For even those who take no part in the operations of war have to bear, in the measure of what has been above established in general and in the following pages will be carried out in detail, certain burdens, restrictions, sacrifices, disadvantages, in one word duties towards the enemy state, which war naturally brings with it." Holtzendorff's *Handbuch des Völkerrechts*, vol. 4, § 90, p. 371.

On the civil side of war opinion has not moved so far from the mediæval point of view. Of the questions which arise in this department there may be at once dismissed as obsolete that of making prisoners of innocuous persons happening to be in the territory of the enemy state. The others may be arranged in two classes, labelled for convenience as those of Confiscation and Non-Intercourse. The first class concerns the right of a state to confiscate for its own profit all property and rights of the subjects of its enemy state which it finds within its territory or within its power. In the ancient law of war this right was unquestioned and very frequently exercised, founded as it was on the solidarity of individuals with their prince, by virtue of which they were themselves enemies of his enemy. It cannot be and has not been alleged that any necessity, direct or indirect, brings it within the principle which identifies subjects with their state for the purpose of war, and the confiscation of the property or rights of individuals on land in the enemy's territory is now entirely obsolete. Only ships and cargoes which enter the harbours of an enemy state after the commencement of war are considered to be in the same legal situation as if they were still on the high seas, and are liable to seizure and condemnation in the absence of immunities expressly granted.

The questions which have been classed as those of non-intercourse concern the legal relations of individuals belonging respectively to the different belligerent states. Can they contract with one another during the war? And does the outbreak of war rescind contracts then subsisting between them, or merely suspend the remedy on such contracts, or has it no effect at all on them? Here we have to do with the enemy relation in which, as the extreme outcome of the principle of solidarity, mediæval dogma placed the subjects of warring princes towards one another; and it might be expected that here we should find, *a fortiori*, whatever mitigation modern ideas have introduced into the relation between individuals and the enemy state. But it is here that the ancient dogmas most stubbornly maintain their ground, a circumstance for which three causes may be assigned. First, while the propriety of any given military action is discussed before the bar of public opinion, and the wisdom of exercising a right of confiscation is judged by the sovereign who is to profit by it, the rules of non-intercourse have to be judged by courts, which proceed on grounds not of propriety or of wisdom but of law, and incline towards precedent and not towards innovation. Secondly, since there are dealings between individuals on the opposite sides which it would not be reasonable to allow in war, it might well be thought better to let the matter stand on the footing of a prohibition of intercourse tempered by licenses than to introduce a general freedom of intercourse subject to exceptions sometimes disputable. Thirdly, since there is no bar but that of public opinion before which the propriety of military procedure can be brought, it is difficult to maintain a distinction with regard to it between opinion and law. There is little meaning in saying of a particular measure of war that it is condemned by the general conscience of mankind, but that it is not yet contrary to international law. If it is so widely condemned it will not be commonly practised, while, if it is occasionally practised in spite of the general condemnation, the many writers who magnify military necessity will refer the permission which they accord to it rather than to occasional necessity than to law. But the distinction between opinion and law is always present to courts of justice, and tends to hold them back from admitting a change in the law.

After the foregoing general contrast between the ancient and the modern, the latter of which will have in the sequel to be drawn out in detail, we must say what can be said in general terms as to the manner in which the passage from the one to the other was made. There was the progressive influence of Christianity and humanity, and a great effect was produced by Grotius who, while adopting as the strict theory of war what he found in the *jus naturale* and the current *jus gentium*, insisted on the duty of tempering it in practice by the charity which the divine law enjoined. In aid of that charity came the habit, and indeed the necessity, of regularising war which the institution of great standing armies and fleets brought with it. In Vattel the new practice begins to undermine the theory. He writes in 1758 that although the old formula of *courir sus* was still a part of declarations of war, usage had come to interpret it as obliging indeed all subjects to seize the persons and property of enemies when falling into their hands, but not as inviting them to undertake any offensive expedition without commission or particular order (l. 3, § 227). The declaration of war of 2 January 1762 by Great Britain against Spain is based on the view so expressed. It omits the formula of *courir sus*, and calls on the various commanders and officers therein enumerated, "and all other officers and soldiers under them by sea and land, to do and execute all acts of hostility in the prosecution of this war against the king of Spain, his vassals and subjects, willing and requiring all our subjects to take notice of the same, whom we henceforth strictly forbid to hold any correspondence or communication with the said king of Spain or his subjects": Twiss—*War*, § 45. Thus non-intercourse was maintained for the civil aspect of war while an advance was made in regularising war on its military side.

Not long afterwards Rousseau essayed to put the ideas which were gaining ground into a philosophical form. "War," he wrote (*Contrat Social*, liv. 1, ch. 4), "is not a relation of man to man but of state to state, in which individuals are enemies only accidentally, not as men nor even as citizens but as soldiers, not as members of their country but as its defenders. In fact a state can only have other states for enemies and not men, seeing that no true relation can be established between things of different natures." This doctrine Rousseau, with his usual levity, declared to be "conformable to the maxims established in all times and to the constant practice of civilised peoples." We have criticised it as follows. "If no true relation can be established between states and men, it must be impossible for men not only to be the enemies but also to be the citizens or members of a state, which in the same passage they are described as being. And if it is only as soldiers that men are enemies even accidentally, every measure employed in war with reference to the civil population, including the most moderate requisitions, contributions and interferences with their liberty, must be unlawful[1]." But in a revolutionary age the very extravagance of Rousseau's language helped to set it up as a standard for those who desired to limit the overthrow by war of all peaceful relations. It was employed with little or no variation by Portalis, in his discourse on the opening of the French prize court in 1801, and is often quoted with rather unreflecting approval, mainly for the sake of its denial of war as a relation of individual to individual, which element of it may be pronounced philosophically sound notwithstanding the hesitation of courts of law. The other element, that war is a relation of state to state in which individuals are involved only as taking an active part in the defence of their country, does not practically delude any one into denying the identification even of civilians with their state so far as necessary for the purposes of war. Nor is such identification unreasonable, for the acts which lead to war are and must be those of individuals. The state is an abstraction, a mere legal entity, incapable of acting otherwise than by officials representing all its members. And those members are not entitled by any principle of natural law or

[1] *Chapters on the Principles of International Law*, p. 259.

of justice to form an association in which their liability for the mischief they may do by their representatives is limited. Often indeed the action of the ministers who nominally direct the powers of the state is forced on them by the pressure of the opinion of the mass of their fellow subjects.

The conclusion of the matter is that the relation of enemies ought to be held to exist (1) between two states at war with one another; (2) between each of those states and those subjects of the other whom for the purpose of the war it may be necessary to affect by acts of force, and so far only as it is necessary so to affect them; but not (3) between individuals. In the further discussion of the subject the terms "enemy subjects" and "enemy property" will be employed for shortness, and in accordance with their common use, in the sense of "subjects of the enemy state" and "the property of the enemy state or of its subjects," without intending to attribute an enemy character to individuals except within the limits thus laid down as theoretically proper.

Enemy Subjects, and their Property and Rights, within the Territory of a State.

Coming now to the details concerning the legal relations between belligerent states and subjects, so far as concerns their civil as contrasted with their military aspect[1], we first have to deal with enemy subjects and property happening to be within the territory of a state at the outbreak of war, or to come within it during the war, incorporeal rights to be sued for in the jurisdiction or falling under the sovereign power of the territory being included as property within it. One class of property, in this case an incorporeal right, shall be mentioned at the outset, since it no longer gives rise to any question. Neither the principal nor the interest of a state debt can be confiscated or sequestrated because the individuals to whom it is due are enemy subjects. A state contracting a loan is understood "to contract that it will hold itself indebted to the lender and will pay interest on the sum borrowed under all circumstances": Hall, § 144. No attempt to the contrary of

[1] See above, p. 33.

this implied undertaking has been made, either in the case of war or in that of reprisals, since Frederick the Great withheld the payment to British subjects of the interest on the Silesian loan, by way of reprisal for the capture of Prussian vessels under rules of maritime law which he disputed. The affair was compromised, but that did not prevent an adverse opinion on Frederick's conduct from being so generally declared, both at the time and since, that it is universally taken to have settled the question. The reason commonly given is that the debts of a state are debts of honour, to which it may be added, as cause rather than as reason, that if the rule were otherwise states would have to contract their loans at much more onerous rates of interest.

Another class of property, namely enemy ships in the harbours of the territory, may also be singled out for immediate consideration, not as being equally free from question, but because its nature connects it with the military aspect of war, as affecting property at sea, rather than with the civil view as to enemy property within the territory. All ships and cargoes in the harbours of the territory at the outbreak of war, belonging either to the enemy state or to enemy subjects, were seized under the old law for the profit of the state, in England by the name "droits of admiralty"; and this claim was enforced by the British government as late as the outbreak of war with Denmark in 1807. Indeed it was not unusual to lay an embargo on ships belonging to subjects of a power with which war was imminent, in order to detain them within reach of seizure. But since the middle of the nineteenth century it has been the constant practice in declarations of war to name a time within which enemy ships then in harbour may load and depart; and it is usual to add that enemy ships which have sailed from a foreign port before the date of the declaration may enter and discharge their cargoes, and then depart with freedom from molestation on their voyage to any port not blockaded[1]. This,

[1] In 1854 Great Britain and France granted six weeks for Russian ships in their harbours to load and depart, and allowed Russian ships that had sailed from a foreign port before the declaration of war to enter their harbours and discharge, departing forthwith and proceeding to a non-blockaded port.

In 1904 Japan gave Russian ships seven days in which to load and combined with the growing tendency of opinion to favour private enemy property even at sea, may be considered to make it certain that at least ships and cargoes in harbour at the outbreak of war and not belonging to the enemy state will not again be confiscated. Whether or not, having regard to the recent date of the new practice, the law can as yet be considered to have been altered, so as no longer to permit such confiscation, is a question more of language than of substance, on which writers must be expected to express themselves differently. To us, the point as regards wars other than those growing out of reprisals or pacific blockade—as to which see above, p. 10—seems to be one of those on which opinion and practice are sufficiently settled to render it unmeaning to assert a law contrary to them. But the immunity from confiscation will not prevent an embargo being laid for special military reasons, as in 1870 Prussia detained neutral as well as French ships for a time at Kiel, in order to conceal her operations for blocking the harbour. Ships belonging to the enemy state in the harbours of the territory at the outbreak of war, and all enemy ships, public or private, entering the harbours of the territory during the war without express immunity, remain subject to seizure and appropriation. A few instances, now more than a century old, in which enemy ships, even of war, were allowed to leave ports which they had entered in distress may be seen in Hall, § 145, but must, as he rightly considers, be referred to humanity and not to law.

On all other points relating to enemy subjects and property within the territory the first relaxation of the ancient law, which made prisoners of the subjects and confiscated the property, seems to have taken place in favour of merchants. By s. 41 of Magna Carta (1215) King John provided that "if in time of war merchants of the country at war with us shall be found in our country at the outbreak of the war, they shall be attached without damage to their bodies or their goods, until it is known to us or to our chief justice how merchants of our country who are then found in the country at war with us are treated; and if ours are safe there the others shall be safe in our country." When Louis IX arrested the English merchants

depart, and Russia gave Japanese ships two days from the local publication of the decree.

and their goods in France at the outbreak of war with England in 1242, Matthew Paris describes his conduct as an outrage on the ancient dignity of France, and Henry III retaliated. By the Statute of Staples in 1354, 27 Ed. III, it was provided that foreign merchants, on the breaking out of war with their country, should have forty days in which to depart with their goods, and forty more if prevented by accident from availing themselves of the first grace, with liberty to sell their goods. An ordinance of Charles V of France gave foreign merchants, trading in France at the time of a declaration of war, liberty to depart freely with their effects. And by a treaty of 1483 between Louis XI and the Hanse Towns merchants of the latter were allowed to remain in France for a year after a war should break out, with protection for their persons and goods[1]. Later, treaties became common by which not only the merchants but all the subjects of the contracting states were allowed to withdraw themselves and their property from the respective countries in the event of war between them. Bynkershoek, who thought that the law remained unaltered in the absence of treaty, was able to give a list of such[2]; and Hall has added a list of such, concluded since the middle of the eighteenth century, in which the time allowed for withdrawal and arrangement of affairs varies from six months to a year. But the modern practice goes further. A right of residence during good behaviour, with safety to their effects, was allowed to French and Spanish subjects respectively by the British declarations of war in 1756 and 1762, and Hall has given a list of treaties, beginning with that of 1795 between Great Britain and the United States, in which that right is stipulated[3]. Of course no treaty can bind a government to allow foreigners to remain in the country during war if it believes that such a course would be dangerous to the state, either from reasonable suspicion entertained of individuals or from the special circumstances of the case as affecting classes of persons. No general stipulations would be interpreted as contemplating such a case, and no special stipula-

[1] These examples are quoted by Twiss—*War*, §§ 49, 50.

[2] *Quæstiones Juris Publici*, l. 1, c. 3. He says that *utilitas fere jus belli quod ad commercia subegit.*

[3] Hall, § 126; Twiss—*War*, § 47.

tions restricting the power of a government in such a case can be imagined. The French government in 1870 was therefore within its right in expelling Germans from the department of the Seine and requiring them either to leave France or to retire to the south of the Loire, whatever may be thought of the real necessity for any such measure.

Permission to enemy subjects to remain in the country, even if in the express words of a treaty it should happen to stand alone, must in common sense carry with it permission to enjoy their property while so remaining. And if enemy subjects being in the country may enjoy their property, it would be inequitable to confiscate that of those who are not in it and therefore as individuals cause no danger. This has been admitted by the conclusion of many treaties in which it is expressly stipulated that the debts, shares in public funds or in companies, and monies in banks of the respective subjects shall not be sequestered or confiscated in case of war[1]. The system of the treaties may therefore be deemed to amount to a general agreement, on the part of governments, that modern international law forbids making prisoners the persons or confiscating the property of enemy subjects in the territory at the outbreak of war, or, saving the right of expulsion in case of apprehended danger to the state, refusing them the right of continued residence during good behaviour. When in 1803 Napoleon ordered the arrest of all British subjects in France and the Italian Republic, he did not claim to do so on the general ground of their enemy character, but put the measure as one of retorsion for the capture of French merchantships before declaration of war, an excuse which was not justified in view of the then customary character of that practice. The latest measures of interference with enemy property on land, as such, that have been resorted to by governments appear to be the laws as to debts due to British subjects passed by certain of the

[1] Among these may be mentioned the treaties of the United States with Great Britain, 1795, 6 De Martens, R., 358; France, 1800, 7 De M., R., 484; and Peru, 16 De Martens, N. R., i. 132; those of France with Honduras, 1856, ib. ii. 150, and New Granada, 1857, ib. ii. 164; and that of the Zollverein with Mexico, 1855, ib. ii. 260.

American colonies after their declaration of independence[1], and the Danish ordinance confiscating debts due to British subjects on the outbreak of war in 1807. Since the Confederate States of America never became a recognised member of the family of nations, the act of their congress in 1861, confiscating all property except public stocks and securities held within their limits by alien enemies, including persons domiciled in the enemy's country, need scarcely be admitted as another instance.

But the courts of law have not been unanimous in their judgments on the subject. The confiscating law of North Carolina and the sequestrating law of Virginia were held in 1796, by the Supreme Court of the United States, to have been within the rightful powers of those states, but to have been annulled by the stipulation in the treaty of peace of 1783, that creditors on either side should meet with no lawful impediment to the recovery of the full value of their *bona fide* debts[2]. On the other hand the court of King's Bench in 1817, under the guidance of Lord Ellenborough, exacted payment over again from a Danish debtor to his British creditor of a debt which he had paid to the Danish government under its ordinance of 1807, describing the latter as a measure "not conformable to the usage of nations, and which therefore they [the parties] could not expect, nor are they or we bound to regard[3]." In appreciating this judgment it must be remembered that, since the date of the American laws, a quarter of a century filled with numerous European wars had put the court on firmer ground for declaring the usage of nations in the matter. In the mean time the Supreme Court of the United States, under the guidance of Chief Justice Marshall, had held that the outbreak of war with Great Britain in 1812 did not of itself vest in the United States government the property in timber

[1] It was only North Carolina that went to the full extent of confiscation on the ground of enemy property. Georgia made an exception for debts due to persons residing in Great Britain, which may indicate that the action taken against the loyalists in the state was grounded on their conduct being considered rebellious; and in Virginia the debts were only sequestered.

[2] *Hamilton v. Eaton,* 2 Martin's North Carolina Reports 83, Scott 481; *Ware v. Hylton,* 3 Dall. 199, Scott 485.

[3] *Wolff v. Oxholm,* 6 M. and S. 92, Scott 496.

on land belonging to British owners, although it would have been competent to congress to enact its confiscation[1]. Lastly Dr Lushington in 1854, after stating that during the American war, but not since, there were instances in which enemy property on land was seized and condemned, not by the court of admiralty but by those of common law, added that no doubt the search for or seizure of such property "would be competent to the authority of the crown if it thought fit[2]." Our own conclusion is that the time is now fully ripe when a British court should not lag behind the position taken by governments, but should boldly follow Lord Ellenborough[3].

The Doctrine of Non-Intercourse during War.

The doctrine of non-intercourse, stated broadly, is that the right of action by enemy subjects on existing contracts is suspended, that commercial intercourse with enemy subjects is prohibited, and that as a consequence no new contracts can lawfully be made between the subjects of mutually enemy states except in the cases, such as that of ransom bills[4], known as

[1] *Brown v. United States*, 8 Cranch 110, Scott 486.

[2] In the *Johanna Emilie*, Spinks 14, Scott 498. And see what was said by Gibbs, C. J., in *Antoine v. Morshead*, below, p. 47.

[3] If the matter came before a British court on a seizure by the crown, since the crown cannot take property within the realm from its owner by an act of state not grounded in law, the question would be whether the existence of a state of war amounted to a license to the crown to seize and appropriate, or, which is the same thing, had already devested the enemy owner of the property, subject to the condition that only the crown could take advantage of such devesting. The question of international law would therefore arise as well on a British attempt to confiscate as on one by the enemy government, and the opinions of Lord Ellenborough and Dr Lushington would conflict on it. With regard to the case before Chief Justice Marshall, he evidently considered that under the constitution congress held the position in the matter which in England is held by the crown, and consequently that the United States being a party to the suit through the act of some official was not conclusive as to the line taken by his government, although congress had by international law a license to direct seizure and appropriation.

[4] Abroad the enemy captor is allowed to sue on a ransom bill, while in England it is enforced through an action brought by the hostage for the recovery of his freedom, as was decided in *Anthon v. Fisher*, Douglas 650,

commercia belli. This is not incompatible with immunity for enemy subjects from the confiscation of their property and rights, indeed the doctrine that the enemy subject's right of action on contracts existing before the war is not abrogated but only suspended can only take effect so far as his rights under such contracts have not been confiscated, and therefore in the doctrine of non-intercourse as here stated we are dealing with a stage in which the ancient principles have already been modified, at least in practice. But since the disuse of confiscation has been accompanied by a growing disuse of the attribution of the enemy character to individuals, which attribution was equally the historical base of the doctrine of non-intercourse, we shall not be surprised to find that doubt about the latter rule has also begun to creep in. That it has not done so with more strength seems to have been due to the circumstance that the question as to the rights involved is usually one for courts of law, the conservative tendency of which has been pointed out[1].

There are in fact two contrasted opinions. One is that the non-intercourse doctrine is now obsolete, that there is no general objection to contracting with enemy subjects, and that the remedies of such subjects on their contracts are not suspended, except when and so far as a government may deem itself obliged by the circumstances of the war expressly to prohibit intercourse with them[2]. This opinion of course leaves it open to the courts of law to pronounce a contract illegal which in their judgment amounts to a participation by a subject in a war against his country, as the Prussian criminal court in 1871 held the participation of the Berlin banker Güterbock in the French war loan known as the Morgan loan to be not only illegal but treasonable. And on the same principle a court may refuse to entertain an action on a contract made for the purposes of a war against the country, notwithstanding that such contract

note, to be necessary on account of the stringency of the rule against suit by an enemy subject. But this is matter of form. The contract, all the same, is one made during the war with an enemy subject, and enforced as arising from the necessities of war.

[1] Above, p. 35.

[2] In this sense Heffter, § 123; Lueder, in Holtzendorff's *Handbuch des Völkerrechts*, vol. 4, p. 358; Rivier, *Principes du Droit des Gens*, t. 2, p. 231.

was legal when and where made[1]. But the opinion that there is no general objection to contracting with enemy subjects, if adopted by the British courts, would leave their government less able than some may be to protect itself by special prohibitions, for the British crown has no power to issue such, so that the assistance of Parliament would be necessary where the contract did not amount to a participation in the war but was objected to on the ground of expediency.

The other opinion, which is that of the courts in England and the United States, is that the doctrine of non-intercourse as stated at the opening of this section continues in force, and that it is relaxations of it which require to be expressly made by governments[2]. For such relaxations the British crown is not so helpless as it is for prohibitions, since it can grant licenses for oversea trade in time of war, which operate as instructions to its cruisers not to interfere with the trade so licensed. Such instructions directly bind the prize jurisdiction, and the British courts of general jurisdiction recognise contracts made in the course of the licensed trade as lawful[3]. As historical examples of licenses it may be mentioned that during the Crimean war both Great Britain and France, the former by an order in council of 15 April 1854, permitted their subjects to trade with non-blockaded Russian ports, if in neutral vessels and not in articles of contraband, and that Russia, by a declaration of 9 April 1854, allowed goods belonging to British and French subjects to be imported in neutral vessels; also that during their war with China in 1860 both Great Britain and France expressly permitted their subjects to continue their trade with that empire. The opinion now under consideration is main-

1 Contracts made in the Confederate States for the purposes of their war against the United States were held not to be enforceable either in the courts of the latter or in those of the states where they were made after their reconquest. *Ware v. Jones*, 61 Alabama 288, Scott 517, and the other cases quoted in it or in Scott.

2 In this sense, Geffcken, notes to Heffter, § 123; Calvo, §§ 1682, 1708; and the well known words of Bynkershoek, *Quæstiones Juris Publici*, l. 1, c. 3—*quamvis nulla specialis sit commerciorum prohibitio, ipso tamen jure belli commercia esse vetita ipsæ declarationes bellorum satis declarant.*

3 E.g., for insurance; *Flindt v. Scott*, 5 Taunton 674, Scott 526.

tained in practice in France[1], but we must proceed to notice more particularly the decisions of the courts in England and the United States.

The doctrine that an enemy subject's right of action is suspended on those contracts made before the war which the war does not dissolve, but revives at the peace, may be seen in *Exp. Boussmaker*, 13 Ves. 71, Scott 494, where Lord Chancellor Erskine allowed the claim of an enemy creditor in a bankruptcy to be entered, in order that the fund might not be divided among the other creditors, but reserved the dividend.

The doctrine as to new contracts with enemy subjects was thus expressed by Lord Stowell in *The Hoop*, 1 C. Rob. 196, Scott 521: "In my opinion there exists a general rule in the maritime jurisprudence of this country, by which all trading with the public enemy unless with the permission of the sovereign is interdicted." But Chief Justice Gibbs, in *Antoine v. Morshead*, 6 Taunton 332, Scott 573, expressed himself as follows: "A contract made with an alien enemy in time of war, of such a nature that it endangers the security or is against the policy of this country, is void. Such are policies of insurance to protect an enemy's trade." This might be read as an adoption of the former of the two opinions above contrasted, reserving to the court the liberty of treating a contract with an enemy subject as illegal from the circumstances, as was done by the Berlin court in Güterbock's case. But the judgment as a whole will not bear that interpretation. A bill of exchange had been drawn by one of the British subjects detained as prisoners in France by Napoleon, for money which he required for his subsistence, and was sued on after the peace by the French indorsee. The plaintiff succeeded, evidently because the case fell within the principle of the *commercia belli.* "How," said Gibbs, C. J., "was the payee to avail himself of the bill except

[1] *Le principe absolu*—that of this second opinion—*pour tous les contrats, tels que associations, assurances, négociations d'effets de commerce, même pour la correspondance directe, postale ou télégraphique, sous la sanction de la saisie des objets des conventions, a été édicté dans une circulaire du ministre de la marine de France en* 1870; Despagnet, § 517 C. To the special permissions mentioned in the text, France and Russia during the Crimean war added one for their respective subjects to communicate with one another by telegraph: Calvo, § 1685.

by negotiating it, and to whom could he negotiate it except to the inhabitants of that country in which he resided?" At the same time he intimated that the king might have laid hands on the debt and sued on the indorsement during the war, and that the indorsee could only sue because of the peace. He also laid stress on the fact that the drawer and drawee were both British subjects, and slurred over the fact that the indorsing was a contract. His dictum therefore does not indicate that he really differed from the general understanding, namely that what was laid down by Lord Stowell for the maritime jurisprudence of England is true of English law generally[1]. And the contract in *Antoine v. Morshead*, coming as it fairly did within the exception of *commercia belli*, was not in our opinion one on which the king could have sued or on which the remedy was suspended.

The doctrine that when a contract made previous to the war with one who becomes an enemy subject requires to be further acted on, not merely the remedy on it is suspended but it is dissolved, because "it is unlawful to have communication or trade with an enemy," was laid down in the state of New York and applied to commercial partnerships by Chancellor Kent, in *Griswold v. Waddington*, 16 Johnson 438, Scott 504[2]. It was applied by the Supreme Court of the United States, a minority dissenting, to policies of life insurance; and the insured was held entitled to sue after the peace for the equitable value of his policy, "as of the day when the first default occurred in the payment of the premium by which the policy became forfeited," with interest "from the close of the war": *New York Life Insurance Company v. Stathem*, 93 U. S. 24, Scott 512. Its application to the relation of landlord and tenant was refused in the state of Massachusetts, and the landlord was allowed to sue after the close of the war for the unpaid rent: *Kershaw v. Kelsey*, 100 Mass. 561, Scott 535.

[1] In *Potts v. Bell*, 8 T. R. 548, Scott 525, Lord Kenyon said that "it was a principle of the common law that trading with an enemy without the king's license was illegal in British subjects."

[2] In *Matthews v. Mc Stea*, 91 U. S. 7, Scott 508, it was held that a partnership was not dissolved by the outbreak of the civil war, an act of congress and a proclamation by the president under it having fixed a later date for the cessation of commercial intercourse.

It has been held in the United States that a statute limiting the time within which an action can be brought does not run while the right of action was suspended by war: *Hanger v. Abbott*, 6 Wallace 532, Scott 500. And this seems reasonable, but a contrary opinion has been expressed by English writers of high authority[1].

It has also been held in the United States that no interest can be recovered after the peace for the time during which the debtor was prevented from paying the principal by the legal doctrine that all commercial communication with enemy subjects is forbidden: *Hoare v. Allen*, 2 Dallas 102, Scott 498; *Foxcroft v. Nagle*, 2 Dallas 182, Scott 500. But this rule does not apply when the creditor resides or has an agent in the country of the debtor, for then the debtor might have paid the interest, and it would not have been his offence if it had been sent to the enemy country; *Conn v. Penn*, 1 Peter C. C. 496; *Denniston v. Imbrie*, 3 Washington C. C. 396. But the agent must have been appointed before the war: *U. S. v. Grossmayer*, 9 Wallace 72. See also *Small's Administrator v. Lumpkin's Executor*, 28 Grattan 832, Scott 538.

The shares and debentures of companies incorporated under British law which are held by enemy subjects at the outbreak of a war will not cease to exist, but must continue as properties, whatever be decided as to the ownership of those properties. There is therefore no alternative but either to confiscate them for the benefit of the British government, which in many cases would be contrary to treaty[2] and in all cases is now out of the question, or to regard the enemy shareholders and debentureholders as continuing to be such. To strike out the enemy subjects from the lists of persons interested, without more, would practically be to confiscate their properties for the benefit of the other shareholders, a proceeding which would be grotesque in its injustice, and which would fall within the spirit if not within the letter of treaties prohibiting confisca-

[1] Anson on *Contracts*, 10th edition, p. 120; Lindley on *Companies*, 6th edition, v. 1, p. 53, note; Pollock on *Contracts*, 6th edition, p. 92, quoting from *De Wahl v. Braune*, 1 H. and N. 178 and 25 L. J., N. S., Ex. 343, a passage only occurring in the latter report.

[2] See above, p. 42.

tion. But the dividends on the shares and the interest on the debentures, so far as not represented by coupons payable to bearer and of which therefore the ownership would not be apparent to the companies, cannot be paid to the enemy subjects during the war. After its close they will be entitled to claim the back dividends and interest, but not to interest on debentures after their maturity, subject, in the case of shareholders, to their paying any calls made in the meantime[1]. And the prohibition of commercial intercourse with enemy subjects will during the war prevent the shareholders from exercising voting powers, while the enemy directors, who cannot continue to fill their places while their duties would be in suspense, must be regarded as deprived of that character from the outbreak. Lastly, we shall see that for purposes of maritime capture the enemy character of property is not decided in England by the nationality of the owner, but by his domicile in a peculiar sense, differing considerably from ordinary domicile, which is known as trade domicile in war, but is equally applicable to persons not engaged in trade. The analogy, as well as reasons of convenience, suggests that in all this paragraph enemy subjects or directors should be understood as those persons, whatever their nationality, who have such a domicile in the enemy's country and no others[2].

Other parts also of the doctrines for which English or United States authority has been quoted above may require or bear the construction that the enemy character referred to in them depends only on what we may call war domicile. "In the case of *Clarke v. Morey*, 1813, 10 Johnson 69, it was held by Kent, C. J., that aliens residing in the United States at the time of war breaking out between their own country and the United States, or who come to reside in the United States after

[1] Compare the reservation of the dividend in *exp. Boussmaker*, above, p. 47.

[2] The conclusions in this paragraph agree with those of Mr Chadwick, in an article on *Foreign Investments in Time of War*, which appeared in 20 *Law Quarterly Review* 167–185, and has since been separately published. Only he draws a distinction for what he calls "private companies," which appear to me too indefinite a class to make it wise to attempt treating them in a different manner from other incorporated companies.

the breaking out of war under an express or implied permission, may sue and be sued as in time of peace; that it is not necessary for this purpose that such aliens should have letters of safe conduct or actual license to reside in the United States, but that license and protection will be implied from their being suffered to remain without being ordered out of the United States by the executive. See *Seymour v. Bailey*, 1872, 66 Ill. 288, where authorities are collected." Scott 545, note.

"The Supreme Court of the United States in the case of *McVeigh v. United States*, 11 Wall. 259, after citing *Albrecht v. Sussman*, 2 V. and B. 324, Bacon's Abridgment and Story's Equity Pl., § 53, for authority, says; 'Whatever may be the extent of the disability of an alien enemy to sue in the courts of the hostile country, it is clear that he is liable to be sued'": Wagner, J., delivering the opinion of the court in *De Jarnett v. De Giversville*, 56 Missouri 440, Scott 545. "It was likewise held in *McVeigh v. United States* that the right to be sued involved the right to appear in the suit, and inasmuch as the court refused McVeigh's appearance by counsel the judgment of the lower court was reversed": Scott 545, note.

CHAPTER III.

THE LAWS OF WAR IN GENERAL.

A WAR between civilised states is begun because one at least of the parties makes some demand with which the other does not comply, or some complaint of which the other gives no explanation regarded by the first as satisfactory. International law says its last word on that point when it pronounces the demand or the complaint to be legitimate or illegitimate, and, if possible, offers arbitration. If the parties are not content with this, the want of organisation in the world of states compels the law which was concerned with their dispute to stand aside while they fight the quarrel out, in obedience not to the natural law of philosophers, which is a rule prescribing conduct, but to that of the natural historian, which is a record of the habits of the species, good or bad. So far as the in this sense natural procedure of the human species is mitigated in the behaviour of the parties, that is due to the scope which they may allow to the better qualities of our mixed humanity, and to the influence of certain rules which the consent of nations has made a part of international law. These rules are always restrictive, never permissive in any other sense than that of the absence of prohibition, for law can give no positive sanction to any act of force of which it cannot secure the employment on the side of justice alone, even if the particular act be not one which the law would prohibit both to the just and to the unjust if it could. Whenever therefore in speaking of the laws of war it is said that a belligerent may do this or that, it is always only the absence of prohibition that must be understood.

This being so, the object on the part of each belligerent is to break down the resistance of the other to the terms which he requires for peace. These are not necessarily limited to the concession of the demand or the satisfaction of the complaint out of which the war arose. They may include a demand for indemnity, for new arrangements promising greater security in future, or for new arrangements more pleasing to the stronger party for any other reason; and these may go so far as to include the cession of territory. That is to say, the natural man is likely so to expand the original cause of quarrel, and often the just man may do so, for indemnity, security, and the revision of territorial and other arrangements are all of them objects which may in given cases be legitimate. Even the extinction of the weaker state by conquest may be legitimate, if it is a state of which the habitual conduct and known aims make it certain that peaceful relations with it cannot safely exist. But it is only in very simple or flagrant cases that law can be in a position to appreciate the merits of the further objects developed in the course of a war, and even then it has no means of making its voice heard except by the intervention of some third power, which is as likely to be stimulated by interest as by justice. It has therefore nothing more to do than to accept the parties as they again present themselves to it, in the condition and with the relations which they have determined for themselves in concluding peace.

The means which may be employed in war are limited, first, by certain prohibitions, such as those of poison and treachery, which, although they are not recognised by all savages, have been handed down immemorially among all peoples having any degree of civilisation. Secondly, by the principles which are expressed as follows in the preamble to the Declaration of St Petersburg, 1868:

Considering that the progress of civilisation should have the effect of alleviating as much as possible the calamities of war;

That the only legitimate object which states should endeavour to accomplish during war is to weaken the military forces of the enemy;

That for this purpose it is sufficient to disable the greatest possible number of men;

That this object would be exceeded by the employment of arms which uselessly aggravate the sufferings of disabled men, or render their death inevitable;

That the employment of such arms would therefore be contrary to the laws of humanity.

The only application of these principles which is made by the Declaration is that

The contracting parties engage mutually to renounce in case of war among themselves the employment by their military or naval troops of any projectile of a weight less than 400 grammes [about 13½ ounces] which is either explosive or charged with fulminating or inflammable substances.

The limitation of weight corresponds to the penultimate clause of the preamble, an explosive cannon ball not falling within it because it may disable many men by its fragments, but an explosive rifle ball falling within it because it would aggravate the sufferings and cause the useless death of the one man whom it can disable. But that clause may be capable of other applications, and although the Declaration limits its obligation to the case of war between the contracting parties, it can scarcely be doubted that not to employ arms inflicting useless suffering on men who are not disabled is a duty in all wars, even against savages. And the same must be said of observing the immemorial prohibitions previously mentioned. All these precepts concern acts which would degrade the doer, whoever was his opponent.

The same however cannot be said of the wider principle expressed by the second clause of the St Petersburg preamble. Since in a war between civilised states the object is to break down the resistance of the enemy government, measures not aimed at the military forces of that government or the organisation and wealth which support them would exceed the object and be inhuman. And the advance of public opinion has even condemned all action in war the connection of which with the weakening of the enemy's military forces is not proximate. Slaughter of non-combatants or carrying them off as prisoners, and the devastation of territory not necessary for covering the retreat of an army or for any other directly military purpose, but intended to create general terror or distress, may indeed help to break down resistance but are universally condemned.

Here we encounter the principle which we have already pointed out as now governing war in its military aspect, namely that an individual is not an enemy, or therefore to be affected, further than it may be necessary, in the strict sense or practically, for the purpose of the war to identify him with his state. But often the inroads or other outrages committed by savages or half civilised tribes can only be repressed by punitive expeditions, in which the whole population must suffer for want of a government sufficiently marked off from it. All civilised states which are in contact with the outer world are, to their great regret, familiar with such expeditions in their frontier wars, and the principle that to weaken the military forces of the enemy is the only legitimate mode of action can have no application to them. But no humane officer will burn a village if he has any means of striking a sufficient blow that will be felt only by the fighting men.

After the immemorial prohibitions and the principles which in the St Petersburg preamble have received the highest expression yet officially given to them, we come in the third place to those rules as to particular matters which up to the present have been fortunate enough to command general assent. The first occasion on which any of these were embodied in a conventional form aspiring to be general was that of the Declaration of Paris in 1856, which related only to maritime war. Then, in 1863, came the *Instructions for the Government of Armies of the United States in the Field*, prepared by Dr Francis Lieber, revised by a board of officers, and issued by authority for use during the great civil war: they immediately acquired a high scientific reputation, as well for their excellence as from the novelty of such a comprehensive codification of the laws of land war. In 1864 there followed the *Convention of Geneva for ameliorating the condition of the Wounded in Armies in the Field*; and at a further conference held at Geneva in 1868 *Additional Articles*, chiefly relating to maritime war, were agreed on, but were not ratified by the powers represented.

In 1874 the laws of land war as a whole were for the first time submitted to an official conference, which sat at Brussels and drew up a code largely based on the work of Dr Lieber; but this again was not adopted by the powers in any binding form. And in 1880 the Institute of International Law adopted a *Manual of the Laws of War on Land*, in which some improvement on the Brussels code was attempted[1]. But the crowning work is the *Regulations respecting the Laws and Customs of War on Land*, annexed to the convention on the subject which was concluded at the Hague Conference in 1899, and to which nearly all the states in the world have become parties by signing and ratifying it or by adhering to it[2]. Art. 1 of that convention binds the parties to "issue instructions to their armed land forces in conformity with the Regulations" so annexed, and the British government complied with this obligation by issuing from the War Office, 28 November 1903, *The Laws and Customs of War on Land, as defined by the Hague Convention of* 1899*; edited, with Supplementary Matter and Notes, by Professor Holland.* The Regulations adopt the Geneva Convention of 1864 but not the Additional Articles of 1868, and "the prohibitions provided by special conventions," therefore the operative part of the Declaration of St Petersburg but not its preamble; and thus amount to a code of the laws of land war so far as yet officially sanctioned. Besides these, the Hague Conference produced three declarations on special points, to which most of the states in the world but not Great Britain are parties, and a *Convention for the adaptation to Maritime Warfare of the Principles of the Geneva Convention of* 1864.

It is important to note the precise authority and range of

[1] The documents thus far mentioned may be consulted in a number of publications, but with the single exception of the St Petersburg declaration, not there included, perhaps most conveniently in the appendixes to the 2nd volume of Lorimer's *Institutes of the Law of Nations*, which brings all the others together: the *United States (Lieber's) Instructions*, p. 303; the *Code of the Brussels Conference* with the report on it by the British delegate, Sir A. Horsford, p. 337; the *Manual of the Institute* (which is in 5 *Annuaire* 157), p. 403; the *Geneva Convention*, 1864, p. 436; the *Additional Articles of* 1868, p. 438; and the *Declaration of Paris*, p. 445. We gladly take the opportunity of directing the attention of our readers to the work of so deep a thinker as the late Professor Lorimer. The Paris and St Petersburg declarations, the Geneva convention, and the Hague documents of 1899 are also given in the Appendixes to Dr Oppenheim's *International Law*, vol. 2.

[2] *Parliamentary Papers; Miscellaneous, no.* 1 (1899)—*c.* 9534.

the Hague Regulations as intended by their framers and now a matter of international compact. In the preamble to the convention to which they are annexed the High Contracting Parties say that the provisions which they have adopted, "the wording of which has been inspired by the desire to diminish the evils of war as far as military necessities permit, are intended to serve as a general rule of conduct for belligerents in their relations with each other and with populations." Therefore military necessity has been taken into account in framing the Regulations, and has not been left outside them, to control and limit their application in the circumstances which they embrace. The preamble then proceeds as follows:

It has not however been possible as yet to agree on provisions embracing all the circumstances which occur in practice. On the other hand it could not be intended by the High Contracting Parties that the cases not provided for should, for want of a written provision, be left to the arbitrary judgment of military commanders. Until a more complete code of the laws of war is issued the High Contracting Parties think it right to declare that, in cases not included in the Regulations adopted by them, populations and belligerents remain under the protection and empire of the principles of international law, as they result from the usages established between civilised nations, from the laws of humanity, and the requirements of the public conscience. They declare that it is in this sense that especially Articles 1 and 2 of the Regulations adopted must be understood.

The authority of the Hague Regulations is therefore supreme to the extent of their range, and their range, wherever it may be found defective, is to be supplemented by approved usage and humanity. Two articles of the convention are as follows:

"ART. 2. The provisions contained in the Regulations mentioned in Art. 1 [those annexed] are only binding on the contracting powers in case of war between two or more of them. Those provisions shall cease to be binding from the time when, in a war between contracting powers, a non-contracting power joins one of the belligerents.

ART. 5. In the event of one of the High Contracting Parties denouncing the present convention, such denunciation shall not take effect until a year after a notification of it shall have been made in writing to the government of the Netherlands, and immediately communicated by that government to all the other contracting powers."

These articles show an intention to place the obligation of the Regulations on a contractual footing; an intention very suitable to the first step in a codification on so large a scale. All the same, the general adoption of the Regulations even on that footing is a testimony rendered by the society of states to their practical and not excessive character, which, if they should not be denounced by any state, must before long cause them to rank as a whole among the laws of that society, as much of them already ranks through the effect of custom and approval. So far as they embody the dictates of humanity, interpreted with due regard to the difficulties which have been already noticed as occurring in dealings with uncivilised tribes, their obligation already extends beyond the wars of the society of states. In the mean time the possession of such an official document is a fact of so great value, both for the theoretical discussion of the laws of land war and for the inculcation of them on governments and commanders charged with the direction of war, that it seems better to keep it prominently before students and the public by taking the Hague Regulations as our text, in their own order, than to seek any other arrangement for their matter on the chance of its being scientifically better. We shall refer to them in the following chapters as Hague (or H) I, II, &c., and to the unratified articles of the Brussels conference, which it will often be interesting to compare in order to mark the advance of 1899 over 1874, as Brussels (or B) I, II, &c.

One point remains to be mentioned. It has been said by a very able writer that the contractual laws of war consented to by a state do not bind the insurgents in case of a civil war arising in that state, because, not being a distinct international person, they cannot have become parties to its treaties[1]. With this opinion we cannot agree. The question can only arise with regard to insurgents treated as belligerents, and certainly no body of men would be invested with that honourable character, either by the government against which they rose or by third parties, if it was considered that they revolted not only against measures internal to their state, but against the ties binding their state to the world in matters so vitally

[1] Pillet, *Lois Actuelles de la Guerre*, p. 31.

affecting civilisation as the laws of war. And when to this consideration is added the difficulty of determining which of those laws, notwithstanding the contractual form which may have been given to them, may not justifiably be deemed to rest on a broader foundation, we must hold that belligerent insurgents cannot stand on a different footing from their state as to any part of the laws of war[1].

[1] Pillet illustrates his doctrine by a reference to the Declaration of Paris, the part of which prohibiting the capture of neutral property under the enemy flag he considers to be law independently of any convention, and therefore to be such as he admits would bind insurgents. But his own country has been in its history far from taking that view of the rule in question. Compare what we have said as to the obligation of international law on new states, in our volume on *Peace*, p. 49.

CHAPTER IV.

THE LAWS OF WAR ON LAND, BEING THE HAGUE REGULATIONS WITH A COMMENTARY.

[The Hague Regulations are distinguished in this chapter by italics.]

Section I—On Belligerents.

Chapter I—On the Qualification of Belligerents..

ART. I. *The laws, rights and duties of war apply not only to armies but also to militia and volunteer corps fulfilling the following conditions:*

After the old formula of *courir sus* had ceased in practice to launch all the subjects of a prince into hostilities against his enemies, it became the military fashion to regard professional soldiers as alone entitled to fight, any other persons who presumed to contend with them doing so at the peril of their lives without any protection from the usages of war. Thus "in 1742 the Austrians excluded the Bavarian militia from belligerent rights," and "it became the habit to refuse the privileges of soldiers not only to all who acted without express orders from their government, but even to those who took up arms in obedience to express orders when these were not addressed to individuals as part of the regular forces of the state[1]." In the capitulations of Quebec in 1759 and Canada in 1760 the militia were not left to the mercy of the English general only because

[1] Hall, §§ 179 and 178, quoting in support of the latter statement the proclamations of the Austrians with regard to Provence in 1747 and to Genoa in 1748, and those of the French with regard to Hanover in 1761 and Newfoundland in 1762.

it was "customary for the inhabitants of the colonies of both crowns to serve as militia[1]." And as late as 1870, notwithstanding that public opinion had been slowly gaining ground in favour of irregulars, the Prussian commander-in-chief required that "every prisoner, in order to be treated as a prisoner of war, shall prove that he is a French soldier by showing that he has been called out and borne on the lists of a military organised corps, by an order emanating from the legal authority and addressed to him personally[2]." This bad custom, which gave an unfair advantage to the nations most lavishly providing themselves during peace with the standing means of war, was condemned by B IX, reproduced as above by H I.

1. *To be commanded by a person responsible for his subordinates*[3];

The Russian draft of B IX added to this the condition that the person commanding should be subject to orders from headquarters, but that addition was not maintained in the text adopted for B IX, and therefore must not be understood here. Probably the responsibility intended is nothing more than a capacity of exercising effective control.

2. *To have a fixed distinctive emblem recognisable at a distance*;

The Prussians in 1870 and the French law of 20 August 1870 for the National Guard required the distinctive character to be recognisable at the distance of rifleshot, but this, if it ever could have been a requirement internationally valid, would certainly not be so now that the range of rifleshot has become so great.

3. *To carry arms openly; and*

4. *To conduct their operations in accordance with the laws and customs of war.*

This must mean "generally to conduct" &c. A few breaches of the laws and customs of war by individuals would not disqualify a corps.

In countries where militia or volunteer corps constitute the army or form part of it, they are included under the denomination army.

[1] Hall, § 179. [2] Hall, § 178.

[3] This continues H I as above, p. 60.

ART. II. *The population of a territory which has not been occupied who, on the enemy's approach, spontaneously take up arms to resist the invading troops without having time to organise themselves in accordance with Art. I, shall be regarded as belligerent if they respect the laws and customs of war.*

H II reproduces B X. At Brussels the weaker states opposed B IX and X as unduly restricting the right of patriotic resistance to invasion, which was important to them in proportion to their inferiority in standing military preparation. This opposition was renewed at the Hague to H I and II, and with a view to its satisfaction the passage in the preamble which has been quoted on p. 57 was inserted on the proposition of the Russian delegate M. de Martens, and was accepted by the delegates of the states in question and by the British delegate who had sympathised with them, with the exception of Switzerland, which has not signed the Hague convention respecting the Laws and Customs of War on Land[1]. Those who study closely the passage in the preamble will perceive that, since it applies only to cases not included in the Regulations, it does not profess to relax those Regulations as operative in the cases which they include; and they may wonder how it produced the assuaging effect which it is recorded to have produced. The answer must be that, in large diplomatic gatherings as well as in the British parliament, words are sometimes adopted from an appreciation more of their spirit than of their meaning. Only, while an act of parliament is construed in accordance with the meaning of its words, by judges who can have no cognisance of the spirit which animated the members of the legislature, the methods of diplomacy are looser, and the preamble to the convention may be considered as deprecating a literal interpretation of H I and H II[2].

ART. III. *The armed forces of the belligerent parties may consist of combatants and non-combatants. In case of capture by the enemy both have a right to be treated as prisoners of war.*

[1] Sweden and Norway (now to be read disjunctively) and Turkey signed the convention but have not ratified their signatures.

[2] The incident is recorded in the report of the British military delegate, Sir John Ardagh, in the Bluebook "*Miscellaneous, no.* 1, 1889"—c. 9534—pp. 160, 161.

The persons who form part of the armed forces though non-combatants are such as chaplains, quartermasters, persons in the commissariat, and doctors and persons in the sanitary service except so far as protected by the Geneva convention. They are contrasted with the "individuals who follow an army without directly belonging to it," who are dealt with in H XIII.

Chapter II—On Prisoners of War.

ART. IV. *Prisoners of war are in the power of the hostile government, but not in that of the individuals or corps who captured them.*

They must be humanely treated.

All their personal belongings, except arms, horses and military papers, remain their property.

ART. V. *Prisoners of war may be interned in a town, fortress, camp or any other locality, and bound not to go beyond certain fixed limits; but they can only be confined as an indispensable measure of safety.*

ART. VI. *The state may utilise the labour of prisoners of war according to their rank and aptitude. Their tasks shall not be excessive, and shall have nothing to do with the military operations.*

Prisoners may be authorised to work for the public service, for private persons, or on their own account.

Work done for the state shall be paid for according to the tariffs in force for soldiers of the national army employed on similar tasks.

When the work is for other branches of the public service or for private persons, the conditions shall be settled in agreement with the military authorities.

The wages of the prisoners shall go towards improving their position, and the balance shall be paid them at the time of their release, after deducting the cost of their maintenance.

The first clause of H VI is an advance on B XXV, which said that the work required from prisoners should have no direct connection with the operations on the theatre of war.

For instance, they are not now to be used in constructing fortifications even before the theatre of war has reached them.

ART. VII. *The government into whose hands prisoners of war have fallen is bound to maintain them.*

Failing a special agreement between the belligerents, prisoners of war shall be treated, as regards food, quarters, and clothing, on the same footing as the troops of the government which has captured them.

ART. VIII. *Prisoners of war shall be subject to the laws, regulations, and orders in force in the army of the state into whose hands they have fallen.*

Any act of insubordination warrants the adoption, as regards them, of such measures of severity as may be necessary.

Escaped prisoners, recaptured before they have succeeded in rejoining their army, or before quitting the territory occupied by the army that captured them, are liable to disciplinary punishment.

Prisoners who after succeeding in escaping are again taken prisoners are not liable to any punishment for the previous flight.

H VIII omits from B XXVIII the express permission to use arms against a prisoner attempting to escape, after summoning him, but to fire on him would certainly remain allowable. The disciplinary punishment mentioned is not understood to include death, but plots, rebellion or riot would bring a prisoner under the former part of the article, and the penalty of death might be incurred for them.

ART. IX. *Every prisoner of war, if questioned, is bound to declare his true name and rank, and if he disregards this rule he is liable to a curtailment of the advantages accorded to the prisoners of war of his class.*

ART. X. *Prisoners of war may be set at liberty on parole if the laws of their country authorise it, and in such a case they are bound on their personal honour scrupulously to fulfil, both as regards their own government and the government by whom they were made prisoners, the engagements they have contracted.*

In such cases their own government shall not require of nor accept from them any service incompatible with the parole given.

"In the British army only commissioned officers are allowed to give their parole for themselves or their men": Holland, *Laws and Customs of War on Land*, p. 14. "And even officers, so long as a superior is within reach, can only give their word with his permission. Finally, the government of the state to which the prisoners belong may refuse to confirm the agreement, when made; and if this is done they are bound to return to captivity, and their government is equally bound to permit, or if necessary to enable, them to do so." Hall, § 133.

The terms of the parole are a matter of contract, as will be seen to result from H XI. The usual terms are that the prisoner, unless exchanged, will not serve during the existing war against the captor or his allies engaged in the same war; and this is understood to refer only to active service in the field, and not to debar the paroled prisoners from performing military or administrative duties of any kind at places not within the seat of actual hostilities. The parole is in any case terminated by the conclusion of peace, and if it was given for a specified period, during which peace is concluded and war again breaks out, its obligation will not revive.

Art. XI. *A prisoner of war cannot be forced to accept his liberty on parole; similarly the hostile government is not obliged to assent to the prisoner's request to be set at liberty on parole.*

Art. XII. *Any prisoner of war, who is liberated on parole and recaptured, bearing arms against the government to whom he had pledged his honour, or against the allies of that government, forfeits his right to be treated as a prisoner of war, and can be brought before the courts.*

These are the military courts.

Art. XIII. *Individuals who follow an army without directly belonging to it, such as newspaper correspondents and reporters, sutlers and contractors, who fall into the enemy's hands, and whom the latter thinks fit to detain, have a right to be treated as prisoners of war, provided they can produce a certificate from the military authorities of the army they were accompanying.*

Foreign officers acting as *attachés* or as correspondents are bound by the neutrality of their own state to take no part in directing the movements of the army which they follow.

ART. XIV. *A bureau for information relative to prisoners of war is instituted, on the commencement of hostilities, in each of the belligerent states and, if the case happens, in the neutral countries on whose territory belligerents have been received. This bureau, being charged with answering all inquiries about prisoners of war, is furnished by the various services concerned with all the necessary information to enable it to keep an individual return for each prisoner of war. It is kept informed of internments and changes, as well as of admissions into hospital and deaths.*

It is also the duty of the information bureau to receive and collect all objects of personal use, valuables, letters, &c., found on the battlefields or left by prisoners who have died in hospitals or ambulances, and to transmit them to those interested.

ART. XV. *Relief societies for prisoners of war, which are regularly constituted in accordance with the law of their country with the object of serving as intermediaries for charity, shall receive from the belligerents for themselves and their duly accredited agents every facility, within the bounds of military requirements and administrative regulations, for the effective accomplishment of their humane task. Delegates of these societies may be admitted to distribute relief at places of internment, as also at the halting places of repatriated prisoners, if furnished with a personal permit by the military authorities, and on giving an engagement in writing to comply with all regulations for order and police prescribed by such authorities.*

ART. XVI. *The information bureau shall have the privilege of free postage. Letters, money orders and valuables, as well as postal parcels destined for prisoners of war or dispatched by them, shall be free of all postal rates, alike in the countries of origin and destination and in those passed through.*

Gifts and relief in kind for prisoners of war shall be admitted free of all duties of entry and others, as well as of payments for carriage by the government railways.

ART. XVII. *Officers taken prisoners may receive, in proper cases, the full pay allowed them in this position by their country's regulations, the amount to be repaid by their government.*

ART. XVIII. *Prisoners of war shall enjoy every latitude in the exercise of their religion, including attendance at their own church services, provided only they comply with the regulations for order and police issued by the military authorities.*

ART. XIX. *The wills of prisoners of war are received or drawn up on the same conditions as for soldiers of the national army.*

The same rules shall be observed regarding certificates of death, as well as for the burial of prisoners of war, due regard being paid to their grade and rank.

ART. XX. *After the conclusion of peace the repatriation of the prisoners of war shall take place with the least possible delay.*

It is generally admitted that prisoners of war may be detained after the conclusion of peace until they have paid the debts incurred by them during their captivity, and while they are serving out sentences of imprisonment pronounced against them for common law crimes. Whether they may be detained during terms of imprisonment imposed on them for disciplinary offences is a moot point. In principle such imprisonment is merely a modification of the captivity, therefore an incident of the war, and cannot continue after the peace has put an end to the exercise of warlike force and therefore to the captivity itself. The case is different from that of the condemnation by a court of admiralty, after the peace, of an enemy ship the title to which was complete by capture during the war, since there is then no new or continuing exercise of warlike force, merely the existing title is declared. On the other hand it is argued that disciplinary punishments imposed when the war was plainly nearing its end would not be deterrent if the peace terminated them, and it would be difficult at that stage of the war to keep the prisoners in order. In 1871 the Prussian government acted on this practical view, and France remonstrated but did not retaliate. Calvo (§ 2957) defends the French view, but Lueder is inclined to justify Prussia without controverting the principle[1]. At the Hague in 1899 the draft of H XX proposed by the Belgian delegate M. Beernaert contained a clause prohibiting the detention of a prisoner for condemnations pronounced or facts occurred since his capture, except common law crimes or offences; but the clause was struck out on the German technical delegate's objecting to it. Japan in 1905, after her war with Russia, released the prisoners who were serving disciplinary imprisonments[2]; and this appears to be the proper course to follow.

Chapter III—On the Sick and Wounded.

ART. XXI. *The obligations of belligerents with regard to the sick and wounded are governed by the Geneva Convention of 22 August* 1864, *subject to any modifications which may be introduced into it.*

The maxim *hostes dum vulnerati fratres* is old, and in support of it many particular conventions were concluded, but the condition of the wounded was still so terrible that, when a picture of it was given by the Swiss philanthropist M. Dunant in his book *Un Souvenir de Solferino*, a movement of humanity was aroused which led to a conference invited by Switzerland, and to the first general convention on the subject as its result. Since by H XXI that convention is incorporated with the Hague laws of land war, we will give its text. On reading it many will be surprised to find in it no mention of philanthropic agencies emanating from neutral states, it being a familiar fact that Red Cross societies have been formed throughout the civilised world and pursue their work of mercy under its protection on the theatre of every war. The explanation is that, even in the interest of humanity, it is impossible to recognise any other authority on the field of battle or within the area of contest than that of the belligerents. The forces of mercy must therefore place themselves under the command and responsibility of one or the other flag, and then the Geneva convention applies to them irrespective of their origin, which

[1] In 4 *Holtzendorff's Handbuch*, pp. 806, 807.
[2] Oppenheim's *International Law*, vol. 2, p. 289.

may lie either in the public provision made by the belligerent state or in the voluntary action of individuals or societies, and in the latter case, whether those individuals or societies belong to the belligerent or to a neutral state.

After reciting that the parties are "equally animated by the desire to mitigate as far as depends on them the evils inseparable from war, to suppress useless severities, and to ameliorate the condition of soldiers wounded on the field of battle," the Geneva Convention proceeds thus.

ART. 1. *Ambulances and military hospitals shall be acknowledged to be neutral, and, as such, shall be protected and respected by belligerents so long as any sick or wounded may be therein.*

Such neutrality shall cease if the ambulances or hospitals shall be held by a military force.

The neutrality is not forfeited by the presence of a few guards who offer no resistance on the approach of the enemy, and it has been usual to allow such guards to return to their army, but as they are not mentioned in Art. 2 it does not seem that the convention prevents their being made prisoners.

ART. 2. *Persons employed in hospitals and ambulances, comprising the staff for superintendence, medical service, administration and the transport of wounded, as well as chaplains, shall participate in the benefit of neutrality while so employed, and so long as there remain any wounded to bring in or to succour.*

These persons may bear arms for self-defence, but they must not spy, and the hospital or ambulance must not be used to cover spies or to quarter troops. The chaplains meant are those in the service of the sick and wounded, not army chaplains, as to whom see H III with the comment on p. 63. No chaplains must excite the fanaticism of the troops, or stimulate them by referring to religious differences between the belligerents. "While so employed" covers marching.

ART. 3. *The persons designated in the preceding Article may continue to fulfil their duties in the hospital or ambulance which they serve, even after its occupation by the enemy, or may withdraw in order to rejoin the corps to which they belong.*

In such circumstances, when those persons shall cease from

their functions, they shall be delivered by the occupying army to the outposts of the enemy.

The precise time at which the *personnel* must be allowed to withdraw cannot avoid being in some degree dependent on military necessity, and they must continue to perform their functions until they withdraw. No. 1 of the unratified *Additional Articles* of 1868 provided for these points, which perhaps are clear enough without it.

ART. 4. *As the equipment of military hospitals remains subject to the laws of war, persons attached to such hospitals cannot in withdrawing carry away any articles but such as are their private property.*

Under the same circumstances an ambulance shall, on the contrary, retain its equipment.

The distinction intended between hospitals and ambulances is explained by No. 3 of the unratified *Additional Articles*, which runs that "in the conditions provided for by Arts. 1 and 4 of the convention, the denomination of ambulances applies to field hospitals and other temporary establishments, which follow the troops on the field of battle to receive there the sick and wounded." So it is the base hospitals that are contrasted with ambulances.

ART. 5. *Inhabitants of the country who may bring help to the wounded shall be respected and shall remain free. The generals of the belligerent power shall make it their care to inform the inhabitants of the appeal addressed to their humanity, and of the neutrality which will be the consequence of it.*

Any wounded man entertained and taken care of in a house shall be considered as a protection thereto. Any inhabitant who shall have entertained wounded men in his house shall be exempted from the quartering of troops, as well as from a part of the contributions of war which shall be imposed.

The last paragraph of this article goes too far. In the interest of the others who have to bear the burdens of war, the exemption of any one from them ought not to be disproportionate to the service which he has rendered to the wounded. Therefore No. 4 of the unratified *Additional Articles* runs that "in accordance with the spirit of Art. 5 of the convention, and under the reserves mentioned in the protocol of 1864, it is explained that, as regards the division of the charge relative to the lodgment of troops and the contributions of war, account will only be taken in an equitable degree of the charitable zeal exhibited by the inhabitants."

ART. 6. *Wounded or sick soldiers shall be entertained and taken care of, to whatever nation they may belong.*

Commanders-in-chief shall have the power to deliver immediately to the outposts of the enemy soldiers who have been wounded in an engagement, when circumstances permit this to be done, and with the consent of both parties.

Those who are recognised after their wounds are healed as incapable of serving, shall be sent back to their country.

The others may also be sent back, on condition of not again bearing arms during the continuance of the war.

Removals (évacuations), together with the persons under whose directions they take place, shall be protected by an absolute neutrality.

No. 5 of the unratified *Additional Articles* would have given an imperative character to the penultimate paragraph of Art. 6, "with the reservation of officers the detention of whom may be important to the success of the war." This would not be consistent with the caution usually thought necessary as to liberation on parole, and might be dangerous.

ART. 7. *A distinctive and uniform flag shall be adopted for hospitals, ambulances and removals. It must, on every occasion, be accompanied by the national flag. An arm-badge (brassard) shall also be allowed for individuals neutralised, but the delivery thereof shall be left to military authority.*

The flag and the arm-badge shall bear a red cross on a white ground.

Notwithstanding the last paragraph Turkey has been allowed to adopt a red crescent as her symbol, and Persia a red sun, and Siam has reserved the right to adopt a Buddhistic symbol. The national flag is not that of the possibly neutral society, but that of the belligerent under whom it is acting.

ART. 8. *The details of execution of the present convention shall be regulated by the commanders-in-chief of belligerent armies, according to the instructions of their respective governments and in conformity with the general principles laid down in this convention.*

We now return to the Hague code.

Section II—On Hostilities.

Chapter I—On the Means of Injuring the Enemy, Sieges and Bombardments.

ART. XXII. *The right of belligerents to adopt means of injuring the enemy is not unlimited.*

ART. XXIII. *Besides the prohibitions provided by special conventions, it is especially prohibited:*

(a) To employ poison or poisoned arms;

(b) To kill or wound treacherously individuals belonging to the hostile nation or army;

(c) To kill or wound an enemy who, having laid down arms, or having no longer means of defence, has surrendered at discretion;

(d) To declare that no quarter will be given;

(e) To employ arms, projectiles, or material of a nature to cause superfluous injury;

(f) To make improper use of a flag of truce, the national flag, or military ensigns and the enemy's uniform, as well as the distinctive badges of the Geneva Convention.

(g) To destroy or seize the enemy's property, unless such destruction or seizure be imperatively demanded by the necessities of war.

ART. XXIV. *Ruses of war and the employment of methods necessary to obtain information about the enemy and the country are considered allowable.*

The special conventions referred to in H XXIII are the Declaration of St Petersburg (above, pp. 53, 54), the three Hague declarations on special points (above, p. 56), and any others which may have been or may be concluded, whether generally or between particular powers. The prohibition in (*e*) expresses the principle on which the Declaration of St Petersburg is based, without giving it the extreme extension which we have noticed as being given to it in the preamble to that declaration. The prohibitions in (*a*) and (*b*), subject as to (*b*) to what will be said about treachery, and that in (*f*) of any improper use of a flag of truce, belong to the immemorial ones noticed above, p. 53. H XXIV is contrasted with H XXIII (*f*) in a manner which makes this an appropriate place for discussing the nature of the faith which is to be observed with an enemy.

The duty of truth is relative, as we may see from the familiar instance of a wayfarer who deceives a highwayman into the belief that help is at hand, that being conduct of which no sane moralist disapproves. When we seek to generalise the conditions on which the duty depends, it would be going much too far to say that we are released from it by every failure in duty towards us. Thus, in bargaining, the certainty that the other party is trying to deceive us will not justify us in deceiving him. We must be exposed to the peril of serious damage, and that from a party whom or the cause which he maintains we regard as being in the wrong, and who has no reason to think that he is dealing with us otherwise than at arm's length. In the case of bargaining these conditions would be wanting. To break off the bargain might defeat an expectation of profit but, leaving us where we were, would not cause damage; and by continuing to bargain we continue normal relations with the party who has deceived us, and thereby prevent him from perceiving that he is dealing with us at arm's length. But war is an arm's length dealing from the first, and one in which the enemy is regarded as being in the wrong, while the damage to which we are exposed is incalculable. Therefore no duty is violated by ruses, even to the extent of spreading false reports; and even using the enemy's national flag, military ensigns and uniform, being in substance spreading a false report by acts instead of words, is allowed up to the last moment before fighting, when the true colours must be resumed. An attack or any employment of force can only be made under the external symbols of the proper nationality, or war would lose the characters on which such humanity as is possible in it depends;

and the "improper use" of the enemy's symbols which is mentioned in H XXIII (*f*) must be understood in the sense of this established usage, and not more widely.

But conventions entered into for the conduct to be observed during war would be meaningless if war released the parties from the duty of observing them. Take for instance the convention which exists between Great Britain and France for the continuance of the postal service between them in the case of war, or the Geneva Convention, or indeed the Hague laws of war themselves. And when usage tacitly attaches a certain meaning to acts done during war, as the offer of truce or surrender is attached to hoisting the white flag, it has always been felt that there is a real convention which cannot be broken without bad faith. Another example of conventions arising from usage is that the word of a commander given to a commander, and intended to be acted on without time for enquiry, must be truthful. Thus even French writers, military as Marbot and jurists as Pillet, severely condemn the false statement that an armistice had been concluded, by which Murat and Lannes obtained from the Prince of Auersperg the abandonment of the bridge of Spitz a few days before the battle of Austerlitz[1]. The same principles apply to certain cases concerning individuals. The giving and receiving quarter is a tacit convention or at least a convention the terms of which are not fully expressed, and if one who has yielded himself a prisoner should shoot his captor after he had passed on, or should shoot any other soldier of the enemy, he would be guilty of bad faith and would justly have forfeited his life.

When it is prohibited in (*b*) to kill or wound individuals treacherously, cases such as those last mentioned are included, but the notion of treachery is wider than what without straining language can be described as breach of convention, and will certainly now cover acts which have not been always condemned. To appreciate it we must take account of the modern notion of war as the prosecution of a public quarrel *militari manu*, in

[1] Pillet, *Lois actuelles de la Guerre*, p. 94, quoting Marbot's *Mémoires*, t. 1, p. 240, and pointing out by numerous instances the defective ethics which allowed Greeks, Romans and Carthaginians to violate outrageously in spirit promises which they kept in the letter.

which individuals are not to be affected except so far as the military proceedings, with their necessary adjuncts and consequences, may touch them[1]. It follows from this that killing individuals, outside the cases of fighting or military punishment to which they have made themselves liable, is killing persons who have had no reason to put themselves on their guard, and is therefore treacherous killing. Not only is it unlawful to employ murderers, but to set a price on the head of an individual, to offer a reward for bringing in an individual "dead or alive," or to outlaw him is unlawful as tending to murder and encouraging it[2].

H XXIII (*d*) denounces an ancient practice of declaring that no quarter will be given, especially used for terrifying besieged places into surrender, and, read in the spirit rather than in the letter, consecrates the modern practice of giving quarter whenever practicable. The admitted case in which it is not practicable is that which occurs during the continuance of fighting, when the achievement of victory would be hindered and even endangered by stopping to give quarter instead of cutting down the enemy and rushing on, not to mention that during the fighting it is often impracticable so to secure prisoners as to prevent their return to the combat. Hence it is especially difficult to avoid ruthless slaughter in the storm of a place or of a position, but the rule formerly dictated by military pride, that those are not entitled to quarter who insult a superior force by defending a place after a breach has been made and the counterscarp blown in, or who defend an ill fortified place at all against a superior force, is entirely obsolete and condemned[3]. Another case, rather asserted than

[1] See above, p. 33, for the complete disuse of the enemy character of individuals as the justification of any proceeding on the military, contrasted with the civil, side of war.

[2] So Lueder in 4 *Holtzendorff's Handbuch* 392, quoting Neumann and Bluntschli; the latter in *Le Droit International Codifié*, § 562.

[3] Hall is unable to find any instance of the indiscriminate slaughter of a garrison later than the massacre of the garrison and people of Ismail by the Russians in 1790, but quotes the Duke of Wellington (*Despatches, 2nd Series*, i. 93) as saying that "it has always been understood that the defenders of a fortress stormed have no right to quarter," although he never acted in conformity with that rule: § 129.

admitted, is that which occurs "when from special circumstances it is impossible for a force to be encumbered with prisoners without danger to itself." On this we agree with Hall's remark that "prisoners who cannot safely be kept can be liberated," and, remembering that they are or may be disarmed, we can scarcely treat as more than theoretical the danger that they may be rescued and re-armed by a relieving force[1].

The missiles "of a nature to cause superfluous injury," prohibited by H XXIII (*e*), are understood to include glass, nails, and bits of iron of irregular shape. Many writers include red-hot shot in the prohibition, which may be admitted when they would be directed only against men, but their utility in causing the destruction of things cannot always be foregone, even when the fate of men may be involved with that of the things. Red-hot shot saved Gibraltar in the great siege by setting the Spanish rafts on fire.

H XXIII (*g*) refers to pillage as distinguished from requisitions, and to devastation not directly necessary for a military purpose, as to which see above, p. 54. Before quitting the Means of Injuring the Enemy, we must notice that it is considered unlawful to incite the enemy's troops to treason or desertion, a rule which was probably introduced for the mutual convenience of commanders and by a kind of chivalry between them, and which should carry with it the unlawfulness of enrolling deserters as recruits; also the allied rule that communications intended for the enemy can only be made to the highest officer in rank who is within reach. But it is not considered unlawful to stir up insurrection in the enemy's country. The projects of France in 1859 and of Prussia in 1866 to enrol Hungarian legions seem to lie on the very border between incitement to desertion and incitement to insurrection.

ART. XXV. *The attack or bombardment of towns, villages, habitations or buildings which are not defended is prohibited.*

It must not be forgotten that the Hague code deals only with war between civilised states, and therefore that this article cannot be quoted against the attack or bombardment of a town not having a government sufficient to be the proper object of

[1] See Hall, § 129.

hostilities. Such an operation may be an example of the punitive expeditions which are necessary as pointed out on p. 55.

Another limitation of the Hague code being to land war, the article now before us has no direct application even between civilised states to the bombardment of undefended coast towns from the sea; but since that is an operation not included in the ordinary scope of naval war, the present is a good occasion for considering the principle which underlies the article, with a view to seeing whether it may not throw light on a subject which has not been free from controversy. The principle of H XXV is that a land force can occupy an undefended place and, if it must afterwards evacuate it, can destroy before doing so all that its military value to the enemy exposes to lawful destruction; therefore bombarding the place without or before occupying it would be wantonly to endanger both the lives of the population and the property not lawfully subject to destruction. The same reason will apply to the dealings of a fleet with an undefended coast town, unless it cannot spare the force or the time required for landing and occupying it, including reembarkation if necessary: in that case only can the question of its right to bombard it arise. Now suppose that in such a case the town contains government stores or factories, or important government offices from which orders relating to the war are issued. These are things exposed to lawful destruction, and cannot claim to be spared because in the circumstances they can be destroyed only by fire from the sea, but the enemy is bound to take care that he does no avoidable damage to life or to innocuous property. This is the justification of the bombardment of the large government stores at Odessa by the British during the Crimean War, and of the opinion which has been given by a large number of international lawyers of all countries that the government offices at the Hague, which is virtually a coast town, might be bombarded[1].

But suppose that the undefended coast town contains no such public invitations to attack as have been under our consi-

[1] It was not the town of Alexandria, which is open, but the forts outside it erected or strengthened by Arabi Pasha, that were bombarded by the British fleet in 1882.

deration, but that it abounds in private wealth. This, as at Liverpool, may be of such nature and amount that its destruction would be a serious, but by no means a decisive, blow to the resources of the country available for continuing the war; or, as at Brighton, its loss might fall only on the luxury of a certain number of individuals. In either case the destruction is not imperatively demanded, and therefore as an act of land war would be prohibited by H XXIII (*g*); and there can be no reason for passing a different judgment if the engine of destruction should be a fleet. And where actual bombardment would be unlawful, it must be equally unlawful to use a threat of it as a means of exacting a money ransom, whether called a contribution or by any other name.

ART. XXVI. *The commander of an attacking force before commencing a bombardment, except in the case of an assault, should do all he can to warn the authorities.*

B XVI was to a similar effect, only that "except in the case of surprise" stood in it where H XXVI, following Art. 33 of the *Manual* of the Institute of International Law, has "except in the case of an assault," and Lueder, notwithstanding the *Manual*, expressly allowed bombardment without notice as a means of hampering the defence by causing surprise and confusion[1]. It may be hoped that such harsh doctrine will not in future be met with.

ART. XXVII. *In sieges and bombardments all necessary steps should be taken to spare as far as possible edifices devoted to religion, art, science or charity, hospitals, and places where the sick and wounded are collected, provided they are not used at the same time for military purposes.*

The besieged ought to indicate these buildings or places by some particular and visible signs, which should previously be notified to the besiegers.

Thus firing on the houses of a fortified town is not forbidden, but when it can be avoided it is cruel, it is generally useless, and it ought to be forbidden unless there is reason to suspect

[1] 4 *Holtzendorff's Handbuch*, § 109.

that the houses are occupied by troops of the garrison or are used as magazines.

ART. XXVIII. *The pillage of a town or place, even when taken by assault, is prohibited.*

In connection with the laws of war in the case of sieges it must be mentioned that the besieged cannot claim free exit for the useless mouths in the place, and that neutral diplomats in the place must submit to the restraints on their correspondence with their governments which military necessity may reasonably be thought to require[1]. It is even possible that some restraint might be imposed from military necessity on their right of quitting the place at critical moments.

Chapter II—On Spies.

ART. XXIX. *An individual can only be considered a spy if, acting clandestinely, or on false pretences, he obtains or seeks to obtain information in the zone of operations of a belligerent, with the intention of communicating it to the hostile party.*

Thus, soldiers not in disguise who have penetrated into the zone of operations of a hostile army to obtain information are not considered spies. Similarly, the following are not considered spies: soldiers or civilians, carrying out their mission openly, charged with the delivery of despatches destined either for their own army or for that of the enemy. To this class belong likewise individuals sent in balloons to deliver despatches, and generally to maintain communication between the various parts of an army or a territory.

"In the zone of operations of a belligerent" has been substituted for "in the localities occupied by a belligerent," which stood in B XIX, because an army in the field is entitled to protect itself from spying even in places only visited by its scouts. Where the danger to the spy is great enough for him to resort to clandestinity or false pretences, the danger to the army spied on must be great enough to justify the severity necessary for its protection.

[1] See our volume on *Peace*, p. 265.

The article leaves open the case of persons sent in balloons in order to gain information. In the war of 1870 the Germans claimed to treat these as spies, and actually imprisoned them in fortresses; but there is no justification for this, ballooning for information being free from clandestinity and false pretences, although it is a participation in the war, and therefore civilians as well as soldiers may be made prisoners of war for it.

At Brussels an article of the Russian draft, to the effect that "any inhabitant of the country occupied by the enemy who communicates information to the opposing force is likewise to be handed over to justice," was omitted in conformity with the unanimous opinion of the committee.

Guides are not spies. If they are captured and are soldiers they become prisoners of war. If they are civilians, an invading army might find it necessary to detain them; but subjects of the country who are caught guiding an invading army without being compelled to do so are liable to punishment for treason.

It needs only to be added that spying in war is not less honourable than fighting, and the punishment of it is to be regarded as having no other motive or justification than that of deterring others.

ART. XXX. *A spy taken in the act cannot be punished without previous trial.*

The trial will be by court martial, and, subject to the Hague code, by the military law of the capturing army. The punishment is death.

ART. XXXI. *A spy who, after rejoining the army to which he belongs, is subsequently captured by the enemy, is treated as a prisoner of war, and incurs no responsibility for his previous acts of espionage.*

The offence of spying being thus cleared in the case of a soldier by its successful completion, there can be no reason for a different rule in the case of a civilian who is afterwards exposed to capture, but at Brussels there was a discussion on the point.

Chapter III—On Flags of Truce.

ART. XXXII. *An individual is considered as bearing a flag of truce who is authorised by one of the belligerents to enter into communication with the other, and who carries a white flag. He has a right to inviolability, as well as the trumpeter, bugler or drummer, the flag-bearer and the interpreter, who may accompany him.*

ART. XXXIII. *The chief to whom a flag of truce is sent is not obliged to receive it in all circumstances.*

He can take all steps necessary to prevent the envoy taking advantage of his mission to obtain information.

In case of abuse, he has the right to detain the envoy temporarily.

A permission to declare that flags of truce will not be received during a certain time was omitted at the Hague from B XLIV, the permission not to receive the flag of truce being regarded as sufficient.

ART. XXXIV. *The envoy loses his rights of inviolability if it is proved beyond doubt that he has taken advantage of his privileged position to provoke or commit an act of treachery.*

Chapter IV—On Capitulations.

ART. XXXV. *Capitulations agreed on between the contracting parties must be in accordance with the rules of military honour.*

When once settled, they must be scrupulously observed by both parties.

"A subordinate commander cannot without reference to superior authority grant terms under which the enemy gains any advantage more solid than permission to surrender with forms of honour"; and any political terms "cannot be consented to even by an officer commanding in chief without the possession of special powers." Capitulations therefore which transcend these limits require to be ratified by the commander-in-chief or the state of the officer granting them, and, if and when such ratification is received, the commander who accepted the terms is entitled to reconsider the situation and refuse the surrender.

The article and these maxims apply equally to the capitulations of fortresses and of field forces, and no less to those of naval forces[1].

Chapter V—On Armistices.

ART. XXXVI. *An armistice suspends military operations by mutual agreement between the belligerent parties. If its duration is not fixed, the belligerent parties can resume operations at any time, provided always the enemy is warned within the time agreed on by the terms of the armistice.*

ART. XXXVII. *An armistice may be general or local. The first suspends all military operations of the belligerent states; the second, only those between certain fractions of the belligerent armies and in a fixed radius.*

It seems superfluous to say that no general can conclude an armistice for forces not under his command, but even within that limit the superior commander or the authorities of the state may refuse to ratify an armistice. There is no difference between truces, suspensions of arms and armistices.

The principle which governs the suspension of military operations by an armistice is that nothing may be done by either party which the other party would have been in a position to hinder. It has been contended that the principle ought to be that during the armistice the state of things shall remain unchanged, which would give to a besieged fortress a right to be revictualled to the extent of the provisions consumed, but it is certain that the besiegers will not allow such a right unless stipulated. See Hall, § 192.

ART. XXXVIII. *An armistice must be notified officially and in good time to the competent authorities and the troops. Hostilities are suspended immediately after the notification, or at a fixed date.*

ART. XXXIX. *It is for the contracting parties to settle, in the clauses of the armistice, what may be the relations on the theatre of war with and between the populations.*

[1] See Hall, § 194, from which the quotations are made.

This does not refer to the powers of contracting and suing as settled for each country by the view which its courts take of the legal doctrine of non-intercourse, but to the intercourse in fact which the military authorities will permit.

ART. XL. *Any serious violation of the armistice by one of the parties gives the other party the right to denounce it, and even, in case of urgency, to recommence hostilities at once.*

ART. XLI. *A violation of the terms of the armistice by private individuals acting on their own initiative only confers the right of demanding the punishment of the offenders, and, if necessary, indemnity for the losses sustained.*

Section III—On Military Authority over Hostile Territory.

ART. XLII. *Territory is considered occupied when it is actually placed under the authority of the hostile army.*

The occupation applies only to the territory where such authority is established and can be exercised.

What an invader may do in the territory which he has invaded depends in part on whether his presence in the district in question, combined with his means of influence in that district, amounts to an occupation of it, for with regard to the territory which he occupies and its population he has special rights and duties. H XLII, which reproduces B I, lays down the principle that occupation in this military sense must be real, a character which it shares with the occupation necessary to confer the ownership of a *res nullius*, although these two senses of the word are distinct and there can be no reasoning from one to the other. It will be a great mitigation of the sufferings of invaded countries if the principle should finally prevail over the practice of presumptive occupation, which Hall sums up as follows from the wars of Napoleon and that of 1870. According to the view embodied in that practice, he says, occupation "is complete throughout the whole of a district forming an administrative unit so soon as notice of it has been given by placard or otherwise at any spot within the district, unless military resistance on the part of duly organised national troops still continues. When occupation is once established it does not cease by the absence of the invading force, so that flying columns on simply passing through a place can render the inhabitants liable to penalties for disobedience to orders issued subsequently when no means of enforcing them exists, or for resistance offered at any later time to bodies of men in themselves insufficient to subdue such resistance. Although also occupation comes to an end if the invader is expelled by the regular army of the country, it is not extinguished by a temporary dispossession effected by a popular movement, even if the national government has been reinstated." And he adds that "the administrative unit adopted by the Germans in 1870, as that the whole of which was affected by notice of occupation given at any spot within it, was the French canton," of which "the average size is about 72 square miles." Excessive however as are such claims, it must be admitted that difficulty will sometimes arise in deciding on the reality of occupation on the flanks or in the rear of an invading army. In trying to express more precisely the spirit of B I or H XLII we can scarcely do better than again quote Hall, who says that the just requirements of an invader "might probably be satisfied, and at the same time sufficient freedom of action might be secured to the invaded nation, by considering that a territory is occupied as soon as local resistance to the actual presence of an enemy has ceased, and continues to be occupied so long as the enemy's army is on the spot; or so long as it covers it, unless the operations of the national or an allied army, or local insurrection, have re-established the public exercise of the legitimate sovereign authority[1]."

ART. XLIII. *The authority of legal power having passed de facto into the hands of the occupant, the latter shall take all steps in his power to re-establish and insure, as far as possible, public order and safety, while respecting, unless absolutely prevented, the laws in force in the country.*

The word "safety," used in the official English translation, does not adequately render the *vie publique* of the original, which describes the social and commercial life of the country.

[1] These quotations are from § 161.

Down to the middle of the eighteenth century the authority of an invader was not distinguished from conquest. The doctrine had not been established that the sovereignty over a territory and its population is not transferred till the end of a war, when it may pass by cession in the treaty of peace, or by conquest if all contest ceases and the war comes to an end without such a treaty, as happens when one of the belligerent states is extinguished. The documents drawn up by local authorities in the ordinary course of administration were expressed in the name of one prince or another, as the tide of invasion and recovery swayed to and fro over the locality[1]. Frederick the Great taught that the business of an invader in winter quarters was to raise recruits from the country by compulsion, and that was his practice as well as that of other commanders in the war of the Austrian Succession and in the Seven Years war[2]. But now that the distinction between conquest and military occupation is firmly drawn, the source of an invader's authority cannot be looked for in a transfer of that of the territorial sovereign. It is a new authority, based on the necessities of war and on the duty which the invader owes to the population of the occupied districts. In B II this was intimated by saying "the authority of legal power *being suspended* and having passed *de facto* into the hands of the occupant." And in H XLIII the suspension, not the

[1] See this illustrated in detail by Lameire, *Théorie et pratique de la conquête dans l'ancien droit*, 1902; *Les occupations militaires en Italie pendant les guerres de Louis XIV*, 1903; *Les occupations militaires en Espagne pendant les guerres de l'ancien droit*, 1905.

[2] "It was sometimes necessary to stipulate on the conclusion of peace for the restitution of men taken in this manner. See for example Art. 8 of the peace of Hubertsburg, *De Martens, Rec.* i. 140." Hall, § 154. The modern doctrine appears in Vattel, liv. 3, § 197, in a hesitating form, since he says that the acquisition by the invader is not complete, his property does not become stable and perfect, but by the treaty of peace or the extinction of the invaded state. It appears fully in the decision of Lord Stowell that the inhabitants of a part of a friendly country (Spain) which the common enemy has occupied are not enemies as owners of ships; *The Santa Anna*, Edwards 180; and in the official French *Manuel de droit international pour les officiers de l'armée de terre*, which says, p. 93, that "*l'occupation est simplement un état de fait qui produit les conséquences d'un cas de force majeure; l'occupant n'est pas substitué en droit au gouvernement légal.*"

transfer, of the power previously legal must equally be understood; what it is intended to express as having passed to the occupant is the fact of having legal authority, not the preexisting authority with its nature and limits.

H XLIII indicates that the law to be enforced by the occupant consists, first, of the territorial law in general, as that which stands to the public order and social and commercial life of the district in a relation of mutual adaptation, so that any needless displacement of it would defeat the object which the invader is enjoined to have in view, and, secondly, of such variations of the territorial law as may be required by real necessity and are not expressly prohibited by any of the further rules which will come before us. Such variations will naturally be greatest in what concerns the relation of the communities and individuals within the district to the invading army and its followers, it being necessary for the protection of the latter, and for the unhindered prosecution of the war by them, that acts committed to their detriment shall not only lose what justification the territorial law might give them as committed against enemies, but shall be repressed more severely than the territorial law would repress acts committed against fellow subjects. Indeed the entire relation between the invaders and the invaded, so far as it may fall within the criminal department whether by the intrinsic nature of the acts done or in consequence of the regulations made by the invaders, may be considered as taken out of the territorial law and referred to what is called martial law. The committee of the Brussels Conference which drew up B III, substantially equivalent to the latter part of H XLIII, explained it as meaning that political and administrative laws should be subject to suspension, modification or replacement in case of necessity, but that civil and penal laws should not be touched. In this they had in view the penal laws relating to offences committed by one member of the population against another, they certainly did not intend that the territorial penal law should not be modified or extended by martial law. On the other hand the right of an occupant as to political laws should perhaps have been more guardedly stated. It will often be necessary to suspend them, but not to modify or replace them. The political rights of an occupied population are indestructible as long as its national character is not affected, and so in 1871 the inhabitants of Alsace-Lorraine were allowed by the Germans to take part in the election of the French national assembly their cession by which was already a foregone conclusion[1].

To the extent to which the legal power of the occupant is admitted he can make law for the duration of his occupation. Like any other legislator he is morally subject to the duty of giving sufficient notice of his enactments or regulations, not indeed so as to be debarred from carrying out his will without notice, when required by military necessity and so far as practical carrying out his will can be distinguished from punishment, but always remembering that to punish for breach of a regulation a person who was justifiably ignorant of it would be outrageous. But the law made by the occupant within his admitted power, whether morally justifiable or not, will bind any member of the occupied population as against any other member of it, and will bind as between them all and their national government, so far as it produces an effect during the occupation. When the occupation comes to an end and the authority of the national government is restored, either by the progress of operations during the war or by the conclusion of a peace, no redress can be had for what has been actually carried out but nothing further can follow from the occupant's legislation. A prisoner detained under it must be released, and no civil right conferred by it can be further enforced. The enemy's law depends on him for enforcement as well as for enactment. The invaded state is not subject to the indignity of being obliged to execute his commands[2]. This however, if the occupation has been prolonged,

[1] The following, taken from the *considérants* of a French court, is a better general statement than that of the Brussels committee. *"Il est de principe que l'occupation du territoire par l'ennemi n'entraîne pas la suspension du droit politique ou privé du pays occupé; que les lois civiles et pénales conservent au contraire tout leur empire, à moins qu'elles n'aient été l'objet d'abrogations expresses et spéciales commandées par les exigences de la guerre. Telle est l'opinion des auteurs les plus accrédités qui ont écrit sur le droit international."* Nancy, 27 August 1872; Dalloz, 1872, II, p. 185; 1 Clunet 126.

[2] The cases decided in the United States as to the effect after the conclusion of peace of measures taken during the war by their officers, at

may be subject to an exception which will be best understood from an example. The French island of Guadeloupe in the West Indies was occupied by the British in 1810, and was restored to France only by the treaty of Stockholm in 1814, Great Britain having ceded her rights in it to Sweden in 1813. The French court decided that certain benevolent institutions (*bureaux de bienfaisance*), founded by the inhabitants with the aid of the British Government, retained the character of public establishments. "Progress," the court said, "being the supreme law of societies, a conqueror who is *de facto* sovereign fills the place of the legitimate sovereign, and is bound to satisfy in his stead the needs of the country which he occupies; and the measures which he takes with that view have the same force and stability as if they had been taken by the legitimate authority itself....The inhabitants, in order to found benevolent institutions with the aid of public authority, were not bound to wait indefinitely for the chances of war or a peace to replace them under their legitimate government[1]."

It remains to explain more fully the martial law which has been spoken of as governing the relations between the invaders and the invaded, and so entering as an element into the law administered by an occupant. It must be distinguished both in its purpose and in its rules from the martial law or "state of siege" to which governments often have recourse in times of internal disturbance: the internal measures which pass under that name can be discussed only in connection with the constitutional laws of the respective countries in which they are taken. It must also be distinguished from the military laws issued by governments for the discipline and conduct of their armies. So far as these deal with the conduct of the respective armies towards the populations of the countries invaded by them, they cover the same ground as the martial law of international jurists and ought to be in accordance with

places which they acquired by the peace, do not touch what is here said. Naturally such measures would continue to produce their effect until the acquiring sovereignty made other regulations for the places in question. See *Cross v. Harrison*, 1853, 16 How. 164, Scott 658.

[1] *Beauvarlet c. Bureau de bienfaisance de la Pointe-à-Pître*, Guadeloupe, 31 August 1869, comfirmed by *Cassation Req.* 6 January 1873; Dalloz, 1873, I, p. 115; 1 Clunet 243.

whatever has been agreed on as internationally binding, but, being the regulations of particular states, they have no international force. The martial law of international jurists consists of the regulations which by convention or approved custom are agreed on as internationally binding for the relations between invaders and invaded, and, as such, is not peculiar to the cases in which invasion has ripened into occupation. It comes into play from the first moment of an invasion, but during an occupation its rules are increased in stringency in proportion to the greater security which the invader claims to enjoy in the midst of a population which he benefits by maintaining social order among them. Its courts of justice are courts martial, to be held with as great security for full enquiry and fair dealing as circumstances permit, but so that drumhead courts martial are not necessarily excluded. Its code is draconic, and in the case of occupation is thus described by Hall. "All acts of disobedience or hostility are regarded as punishable, and by specific rules the penalty of death is incurred by persons giving information to the enemy or serving as guides to the troops of their own country, by those who while serving as guides to the troops of the invader intentionally mislead them, and by those who destroy telegraphs, roads, canals or bridges, or who set fire to stores or soldiers' quarters. If the inhabitants of the occupied territory rise in insurrection, whether in small bodies or *en masse*, they cannot claim combatant privileges until they have displaced the occupation, and all persons found with arms in their hands can in strict law be killed, or if captured be executed by sentence of court martial. Sometimes the inhabitants of towns or districts in which acts of the foregoing nature have been done, or where they are supposed to have originated, are rendered collectively responsible and are punished by fines or by their houses being burned[1]." Even so humane a writer as Hall felt himself unable to rule out any of these claims as never being admissible, although he observes that "in very many cases, probably indeed in the larger number, the severity of the measures adopted by an occupying army is entirely disproportioned to the danger or the inconvenience of the acts which it is intended to prevent; and when others than the perpetrators

[1] § 156.

are punished, the outrage which is done to every feeling of justice and humanity can only be forgiven where military necessity is not a mere phrase of convenience but an imperative reality[1]."

Probably however the above list of lawful severities is capable of some revision. That the inhabitant of an occupied district should incur death for giving information to the enemy, or for serving as a guide to the troops of his own country, is a relic of the time when occupation meant conquest, transferring the allegiance of the occupied population. There is no other foundation for the epithet of "war-treason" (*kriegsverrath*) which German writers apply to every act of one of that population directed against the occupying army, for the duty owed in return for the maintenance of order will not extend so far. No act of that kind can be regarded as treasonable without violating the modern view of the nature of military occupation, and to introduce the notion of moral fault into an invader's view of what is detrimental to him serves only to inflame his passions, and to make it less likely that he will observe the true limit of necessity in his repression of what is detrimental to him. And in the cases of giving information and serving as guide to one's own people, the attempt at sanguinary repression would have the additional demerit of inutility, since it could not succeed except among a people more abject than it would be possible to discover[2]. And when the inhabitants of an occupied district rise in insurrection, and satisfy the conditions of loyal fighting laid down by H I, it is difficult to refuse the privileges of combatants to a body of them operating on a scale which may fairly be considered as war. If they are to have those privileges when "they have displaced the occupation," they cannot reasonably be refused them when taking the necessary means of displacing it; and that H I applies in occupied territory may be inferred from the restriction of H II to unoccupied territory.

[1] Ib.

[2] The question of "war-treason" is well discussed by Pillet, *Le Droit de la Guerre*, 2me *partie*, pp. 239, 240. Of giving information and serving as guide to one's own people, he says: *nous ne prétendons pas que ces faits ne puissent être punis dans l'intérêt de la discipline, mais nous soutenons qu'il est injuste et barbare de leur appliquer les peines de la trahison.*

ART. XLIV. *Any compulsion of the population of occupied territory to take part in military operations against its own country is prohibited.*

This article condemns the forced enrolments which, as has been mentioned, used to be made in occupied territory as a consequence of the transfer of sovereignty formerly considered to have taken place. But since it is based on a principle of humanity it applies or ought to apply to all services which it might be desired to exact from enemy subjects, and this as well before as after occupation has been established. One of the most important of those services is that of acting as guides to the invading or occupying forces, and the military importance of such enforced action is so great that there can be no doubt of its falling within the principle. Nevertheless that very importance causes it to be the universal practice to exact the services of guides: the German General Staff, while echoing the sentiment of its inhumanity, treats it in its work of 1902 as indispensable[1], and the Japanese followed it in their war against China. Even the Hague code, when read in connection with the Brussels project, is perhaps not quite so much opposed to the practice as at first sight it would seem to be. B XIV was to the same effect as H XXIV (above, p. 72), except that it contained the reservation "subject to the provisions of Art. XXXVI," which was reproduced by H XLIV. This expressly limited the lawfulness of means employed to obtain information about the country by the obligation not to compel the inhabitants to take part in the invader's military operations, and the omission from H XXIV of the reservation contained in B XIV can only indicate that the delegates at the Hague hesitated to apply their own principle to the case of compulsory guidance. If the inhabitants act voluntarily as guides to the enemy, they of course render themselves liable to the penalties of treason from their own government when restored in the locality; and

[1] *Les lois de la guerre continentale (publication de la section historique du grand état-major allemand,* 1902), *traduites et annotées par* Paul Carpentier, p. 110. The Manchurians were not enemies of the Japanese in their war with Russia. For the practice of the Japanese in their Chinese war see *La Guerre Sino-Japonaise au point de vue du Droit International,* by Nagao Ariga, p. 160.

the invader ought therefore to furnish requisitions in writing to the guides whom he decides to employ.

ART. XLV. *Any pressure on the population of occupied territory to swear allegiance to the hostile power is prohibited.*

Here we have the express condemnation of another of the practices which resulted from the old theory of occupation. The principle extends to prohibit every thing which would assert or imply a change made by the invader in the legitimate sovereignty. His duty is neither to innovate in the political life of the occupied districts nor needlessly to break the continuity of their legal life. Hence, so far as the courts of justice are allowed to continue administering the territorial law, they must be allowed to give their sentences in the name of the legitimate sovereign. With the modifications of the territorial law which the invader may introduce, they have nothing to do: those belong to his martial law, and he must enforce them. But if during the occupation the form of the national government should be changed by a revolution in the part of the territory which remains free from invasion, it is no part of the invader's duty to allow that change to take effect in the occupied districts. What their future political life will be must depend on the result of the war, and a political change which may affect that result cannot be indifferent to the invader. Thus the Germans in 1870 were within their right when, after the fall of the French empire, they refused to allow the courts of the occupied departments to give their sentences in the name of the republic.

ART. XLVI. *The honour and rights of the family, the lives of individuals and private property, as well as religious convictions and public worship, must be respected.*

Private property cannot be confiscated.

This article applies both to the regulations which the invader may make by his prerogative of martial law and to the behaviour of his troops. By the prohibition of confiscation it is only meant that private property cannot by any regulation of the invader be taken from its owner for no other reason than that he is an enemy, not that it cannot be taken for military necessity or by way of punishment for disobedience to a regulation or a requisition. Speaking of the punishment which an enemy may inflict for such causes a learned writer has said that it ought to be in proportion to the importance of the cause, and never to be inspired by the spirit of vengeance, intimidation or cruelty[1]. We however would rather say that, whatever may be thought of the right of a legitimate sovereign to inflict punishment as an expression of the vengeance of the community against outraged morality, an enemy occupant cannot justify punishment except for the purpose of intimidation, that is, to prevent others from doing the like. But the caution against cruelty and in favour of proportion is just.

For the rest, it is only movable property that an enemy as occupant can possibly confiscate. Immovable property (land) must necessarily remain subject to the laws of the sovereign who is restored or introduced at the peace.

ART. XLVII. *Pillage is formally prohibited.*

Pillage, as an untechnical term, means indiscriminate plundering, such as under the old rule of *courir sus* was habitually practised against the enemy. As a term of modern law it may be defined as the unauthorised taking away of property, public or private, so that in order to appreciate the prohibition contained in this article we must know what taking away is authorised. With regard to public property we shall find in H LVI the line of demarcation between what may and may not be appropriated by an invader. Private property may only be appropriated by way of requisition, with which we shall meet in H LII, or in pursuance of a regulation made by the occupant, of which we have spoken under H LI, or when it consists of arms or munitions of war, which even though not being used are always seizable, subject to what is said about them when private properties in H LIII, and to the recognition in H IV that the arms, horses and military papers belonging to prisoners are seizable. And it will be pillage if even what may be taken is taken in a way not authorised by the military authority, or if

[1] Bonfils, *Manuel de Droit International Public*, 4th edn., by Fauchille, p. 647.

the individual captor appropriates to himself what by the regulations of his state or army he ought to give account of.

The abolition of the old indiscriminate plundering is one of the greatest advances towards humanity that have been realised in the practice of war. Hall well points out that it was made "partly for the selfish advantage of belligerents, who saw that the efficiency of their soldiers was diminished by the looseness of discipline inseparable from marauding habits, and who found when war became systematic that their own operations were embarrassed in countries of which the resources were destroyed[1]." He also shows that one of the most important steps towards it was made by Gustavus Adolphus. "It would seem," he says, "that as a general rule pillage was only permitted in the Swedish army after a battle or the capture of a town; the Swedish soldiers however were at that time far better organised and disciplined than those of any other country, and the habits of the Imperialists were very different[1]."

ART. XLVIII. *If in the territory occupied the occupant collects the taxes, dues and tolls imposed for the benefit of the state, he shall do so as far as possible in accordance with the rules in existence and the assessment in force, and will in consequence be bound to defray the expenses of the administration of the occupied territory on the same scale as that to which the legitimate government was bound*—(*sic*, but as there would seldom be a law binding the legitimate government to any scale of expense, the scale existing at the date of the invasion would probably be understood as meant).

The wording of this article was slightly altered from that of B V in order not to seem to give the occupant a right to collect the taxes. But although framed hypothetically H XLVIII, by its separate mention of the taxes and of the consequence attached to their collection, still distinguishes between money exacted by the occupant under that name and the contributions of which we shall presently read. The origin of the distinction, which is generally maintained by writers on international law, no doubt lay in the old theory of occupation being conquest, so that the occupant, as the new sovereign, was entitled to the taxes due by

[1] § 139.

the laws which he found established. This ground will not hold now, nor is there any other solid legal ground. If the proceeds of the taxes are already in a public treasury seized by the occupant, he takes them just as he takes the balance of the money in the treasury. If they are not, and he is not a new sovereign, will his physical power over the persons of the debtors entitle him to exact the payment to him of sums due to his enemy state, and to give them a discharge valid as against that state? There does not seem to be any juridical reason for so holding, and, if there were, the doctrine would be applicable to other debts due to the legitimate sovereign as well as to the taxes. But it is certainly equitable that if the usual administration is carried on it should be paid for by the usual taxes, and that the legitimate sovereign, on recovering his power over the district, should hold the inhabitants discharged by what they have paid to the occupant as such taxes.

ART. XLIX. *If besides the taxes mentioned in the preceding article the occupant levies other money contributions in the occupied territory, this can only be for military necessities or the administration of such territory.*

B XLI ran that "the enemy in levying contributions, whether as equivalents for taxes or for payments which should be made in kind or as fines, will proceed as far as possible according to the rules" etc. (see H LI). The "payments which should be made in kind" are those which H XLIX contemplates as being levied for military necessities, and that H XLIX was not intended to prohibit fines is shown by H L regulating them. B XLI is not therefore, at variance with H XLIX in respect of the objects for which it contemplates the levy of money contributions, but the later article marks a step in advance in expressly limiting them to those objects. The invader must not exact them in order further to eke out the cost of the war.

ART. L. *No collective penalty, pecuniary or other, can be inflicted on a population on account of the acts of individuals for which it cannot be regarded as collectively responsible.*

This provision, which was not contained in the Brussels code, completes H XLIX by showing that no extraordinary contributions or requisitions can be excepted from it unless they are penalties in the strict sense, imposed by the occupant with the purpose of repression, in retribution for acts done, and limited in their incidence by the responsibility for those acts which can be justly imputed. For example, no penalty, whether in money or in services, can be imposed on a district which it is claimed has been constructively occupied by virtue of a notice posted at some point of it, if such notice could not come to the knowledge of the district as a whole before the act which it is desired to punish was committed. Nor can a penalty be imposed on a district more extensive than can justly be supposed to share the responsibility for the act which it is desired to punish.

It must be observed that H XLIX and H L have nothing to do with a payment in the nature of ransom, which an invader may make the condition of sparing to a place not yet occupied the mischief that would result from a lawful operation of war.

ART. LI. *No contribution shall be collected except under a written order and on the responsibility of the commander-in-chief.*

The levy shall only take place, as far as possible, in accordance with the rules in existence and the assessment in force for taxes.

For every contribution a receipt shall be given to the payer.

B XLI allowed contributions to be levied also by the civil authority established by the occupant.

ART. LII. *Neither requisitions in kind nor services can be demanded from communes or inhabitants except for the necessities of the army of occupation. They must be in proportion to the resources of the district, and of such a nature as not to imply for the population the obligation to take part in the operations of the war against their country.*

These requisitions and services shall only be demanded on the authority of the commander in the locality occupied.

What is furnished in kind shall as far as possible be paid for in ready money; if not, the fact of furnishing shall be recorded by receipts.

The money, things and services which invaders take from the inhabitants of the enemy territory are now classified as contributions when they are money, requisitions when they are things or services, though formerly that distinction of terms was not strictly observed. Contributions have been dealt with in the articles H XLVIII to H LI, and the code now proceeds to deal with requisitions. Since military necessities (H XLIX) or, which is the same thing, the necessities of the army of occupation (H LII), are referred to in giving the measure of both, there is a connection between them, and as we have reached a point at which both have been brought before us some general observations may now be made on the connected matters. The first such observation is that the character of the laws of war, as being always restrictive and never giving a positive sanction to violence[1], is plainly indicated in the articles in question. No right to levy contributions or make requisitions is declared, but H XLVIII and H XLIX are hypothetical on the payment of the money being imposed, and H XL, H LI and H LII are expressly provisions of restraint.

If we ask what at different times it has not been prohibited to take from the inhabitants of the enemy territory, the answer for the oldest time is—every thing. Neither in antiquity nor under the doctrine of *courir sus* had the inhabitants of the enemy territory any rights against the invader. He took without scruple whatever the pillage by his troops had left, so far as he desired to take it. But when the view prevailed that occupation was conquest, as soon as his inroad became an occupation he was placed in a new relation to the inhabitants of the occupied territory. They would no longer be properly regarded as his enemies but as his subjects, and the worst government that ever existed with the pretension of being civilised never dreamed of leaving the property, money and persons of its subjects, not chargeable with active opposition to it, to the arbitrary will of its military commanders. The question then for the invading sovereign should have been how much of the burden of the war, as between his old subjects and his new, he could justly throw on the latter. But there is no trace that

[1] See above, p. 52.

that question was ever put. With a thoughtless want of logic the burden of war which it was customary for the people of occupied districts to bear as enemies was still imposed on them as subjects; they only acquired a better title than the occupant's mercy to keep what was left to them after all requisitions and contributions were satisfied. Afterwards military occupation came to be distinguished from conquest, and about the same time Rousseau proclaimed that war is a relation of state to state, in which citizens who are neither soldiers nor defenders of their country are not implicated[1]. But again the passive citizen was not allowed to profit by the new doctrine, though this time there was not a thoughtless want of logic. The requisitions and contributions were still exacted from him though he was neither a soldier nor a defender of his country, and pens were, and are still, employed to reconcile his fate with the proclamation of Rousseau. Lastly there has come the modern doctrine that between the passive citizen and the enemy state war introduces a relation by virtue of which the former may be made to suffer what for the purpose of the war it is "necessary" or "natural" for the latter to inflict[2]. Combine with this the fact that most nations do not consider themselves rich enough to conduct a campaign on enemy's territory without availing themselves of the resources of that territory, and the exaction of requisitions and contributions is justified in the measure in which the invader's own resources are deemed by him to be insufficient. In sum, requisitions and contributions have continued to be exacted, by force of tradition and circumstance, through a series of successive theoretical views none of which has been capable of fixing a limit to them.

When the Duke of Wellington carried the Peninsular War from Spain into France his army paid for what it took, and found its reward in the abundance of supplies offered to it. But this was a procedure of which history furnishes few examples. The Prussians paid their way in the kingdom of Saxony in 1866, it being their desire to preserve the friendship of the Saxon population as a portion of the intended North German confederation. And in 1871 Germany repaid, out of the war

[1] See above, p. 37. [2] See above, pp. 33, 34.

indemnity received from France, the exactions which she had imposed on the territory ceded to her. But it results from the historical sketch which we have given that no obligation on the part of an invader to pay the amounts represented by the receipts which he gives for requisitions and contributions is acknowledged by public opinion and practice, that is, by what is called public law. It is sometimes suggested—for it can scarcely be put more strongly—that, if the invader does not pay those amounts, an ultimate liability for them rests on the territorial government[1]. But since that government does not regard itself as having provoked the war by wrongful conduct, it will not acknowledge itself to be more responsible for the calamities which its subjects have suffered by the invasion than for those which they may suffer from tempest or earthquake, and it has not been usual for it to assume such responsibility. It was a novel instance of generosity when, in 1871, the French legislature, expressly repudiating liability, voted a large sum of money, but not equal to the amount of the German exactions, for the relief of those who had suffered from them. In short, as between the invading government and the individuals from whom it takes requisitions and contributions, all question about them is concluded by the taking them; as between the invading and the territorial governments, the latter as representing the grievances of its subjects, it is concluded by the peace; and as between the mass of the nation represented by the territorial government and the suffering individuals, no juridical question arises, there arises only the political claim that losses incurred for a cause in which the whole people were embarked together should be borne with some approach to equality. In these circumstances the Hague laws of war adopt a line which does not commit them to any conclusion. By saying that requisitions shall be paid for in ready money as far as possible, they must mean that this shall be done by the invading army, since it is with its conduct that the whole of Section III is concerned: but they leave it open to

[1] The German general staff says in the work above quoted that "in order to secure to the owners of these things [private property taken] an indemnity from their own government, equity commands the delivery to them of receipts for the requisitions carried into effect." Carpentier's translation, p. 131.

the invading government to plead that it is not rich enough to invade a neighbour at its own cost. And so far as the requisitions are not paid for in ready money, it is not demanded that the receipts shall express a liability, but only that they shall record the fact of the requisitions having been furnished—*les prestations en nature seront constatées par des reçus*—leaving the person who gets the record to make such use of it as he can.

Coming now to the limits which the best modern opinion seeks to place on the exactions of an invader, we observe that H LII restricts requisitions to "the necessities of the army of occupation," which in conformity with present understanding are described by Hall as consisting "of articles needed by the army for consumption or temporary use, such as food for men and animals and clothes, wagons, horses, railway material, boats and other means of transport, and of the compulsory labour, whether gratuitous or otherwise, of workmen to make roads, to drive carts, and for such other services." The German general staff describes digging ditches, and work on streets, bridges, railways and buildings as lawful objects of compulsory labour. Indeed, even in times when the civil population was treated with less humanity than now, the practical difficulty of carrying articles requisitioned in kind out of the country in general limited demands of that class to the consumption or immediate use of the army[1]. The restriction which places modern opinion in the sharpest contrast to what was common as late as the early part of the nineteenth century is that by which H XLIX, as we have seen, limits contributions, so far as not expended on the administration of the occupied territory, to an equivalent for requisitions. Where the things or services which an army wants in kind for its use are to be found or obtained in the territory,

[1] Not always. Under the decrees of the *Comité de Salut Public* and the instructions of the "representatives of the people" who accompanied the French revolutionary armies, whatever was thought likely to be of future use was to be sent to the rear, and an instance is mentioned in which wines, taken from the persons who for their real or presumed political opinions were classed as enemies of the republic, were ordered to be sold on the spot. Basdevant, *La révolution française et le droit de la guerre continentale*, pp. 140, 144, quoted by Nys, 8 *Revue de Droit International et de Législation comparée*, 2e *série*, p. 307.

it may be better both for itself and for the population that it shall levy the amount of their price and buy them or pay for them than that it should take them without payment from their owners or from those who can render them. The burden is then more equally distributed, and the things and services themselves may be more easily obtained in the requisite quantities. It was not intended by H XLIX to permit the levy of money to be spent in the invader's own country in supplying the necessities of his army. The provision made at home must be borne by him out of his general resources, except so far as he may be able to recover its cost from the enemy as a war indemnity at the peace. The exactions which he makes as an occupant are not to be the means, as they were often made to be, of increasing his general ability to carry on the war. The line thus drawn, it is true, is not to be deduced from the principle that the passive citizen may be made to suffer only what it is "necessary" or "natural" for the enemy of his state to do in order to break down the resistance of his state, even when it is guarded by the qualification, necessary or natural in the course of military operations. But it is a practical alleviation of the application of that principle, and it can only be made a tangible line by insisting, first, on the limitation of requisitions to the consumption or immediate use of the occupying army, and secondly, on a limitation of contributions which makes them a substitute for requisitions so limited.

H LII further lays down that requisitions, and by consequence the contributions which may be substituted for them, even when imposed for the necessities of the army of occupation, shall not be in cruel disproportion to the resources of the district, and that no services shall be required which would amount to *taking part in* the operations of the war. The last clause is worded similarly to H XLIV (above, p. 91), and less strictly than that (H VI; above, p. 63) which provides that the tasks of prisoners shall *have nothing to do with* the operations of the war (*n'auront aucun rapport avec*). Work on roads, bridges and railways, which has very much to do with the military operations, is constantly requisitioned. But there must be a limit, and we suppose that to require an enemy civilian to assist in placing a gun in position would be forbidden by H LII. Even service as a guide is requisitioned, as we have mentioned under H XLIV, although that case is a particularly cruel one.

Among or analogous to the services which may be requisitioned from the population of an occupied district is that of serving as hostages, "to ensure prompt payment of contributions or compliance with requisitions," "as a guarantee against insurrection," or "as a protection against special dangers which it is supposed cannot otherwise be met." In 1870 the Germans placed on the railway engines notable inhabitants of districts in which the lines had been frequently damaged, a proceeding which "was universally and justly reprobated on the ground that it violated the principle which denies to a belligerent any further power than that of keeping his hostage in confinement." And it may be also condemned as inflicting, if any harm happened to the hostage, an individual penalty for facts with which he was not individually connected. It would not be more unjust if civilians of the enemy state were placed in the front of battle in order to induce the enemy's troops to withhold their fire. Where the seizure of hostages is lawful, "under a usage which has long become obligatory it is forbidden to take their lives, except during an attempt to escape, and they must be treated in all respects as prisoners of war[1]."

ART. LIII. *An army of occupation can only seize cash, funds and realisable securities belonging strictly to the state, but can seize depôts of arms, means of transport, stores, supplies, and generally all movable property of the state of a nature to be used in the operations of the war.*

Railway plant, land telegraphs, telephones, steamers and other ships apart from cases governed by maritime law, as well as depôts of arms and generally all kinds of munitions of war, even though belonging to companies or to private persons, are likewise means of a nature to be used in the operations of the war; but they must be restored and the indemnities for them regulated at the peace.

ART. LIV. *Railway plant coming from neutral states, whether the property of those states or of companies or private persons, shall be sent back to them as soon as possible.*

[1] The passages in this paragraph in quotation marks are from Hall, §§ 135, 156.

The opening provision of H LIII is so worded as to exempt from seizure both, first, cash, funds and realisable securities of which the state is only custodian, such as savings bank funds, and secondly, debts due to the state not falling under the description of realisable securities. The first exemption speaks for itself. In the second exemption the original French is *valeurs exigibles*, which Professor Holland translates "realisable securities," and which has been translated officially into German as *eintreibbare forderungen*. Professor Holland describes it as purposely ambiguous, and there are grave differences of opinion as to what the rule on the matter ought to be. There is no doubt that if the occupation should be ripened into conquest, all the debts due to the extinguished state will belong by the laws of state succession to the conqueror and may be sued for by him[1]. There is also no doubt that documents payable to bearer may be seized by an occupant as part of the state treasure, so that he thereby becomes not only their actual but their lawful bearer, and can sue on them as soon as due, whether or not his occupation of the place where they were seized has continued in the mean time or not. But the occupant who is not a conqueror does not represent the person of the enemy state, and therefore, as it seems to us, can supply nothing which remains to be done by the enemy state in order to complete the right to judgment on a debt. If he has seized a document payable to order, he cannot endorse it: if the debt is claimed by any other kind of title, he may have seized the evidence necessary for proving it but he cannot put himself forward as plaintiff, or use his physical power in the locality to enforce payment. This however is not the modern German view. By an ordinance of 26 November 1870 the Germans required persons who owed payments for timber from the state forests, in what they had established as "the general government of Alsace," to make those payments to their cashiers in the district[2]. And this is approved by no less an authority than Rivier, on the ground

[1] See our *International Law—Peace*, pp. 68, 74.

[2] All payments to the French treasury had already been forbidden by an ordinance of 29 August 1870, rightly, since such payments would have strengthened the enemy. But that the debtors were restrained from paying their creditors did not make them liable to pay anyone else.

that the absence of the relation of debtor and creditor between the person owing and the occupant furnishes an argument valid only from the point of view of private law, it being sufficient from the point of view of public law to say that the occupant exercises the rights of the supreme power in the state, and may therefore compel the payment of matured debts. In those words, if we may venture to say so, there is a confusion between the strongest power in the district, which is certainly that of the occupant, and the supreme, which implies or ought to imply supreme legitimate, power in the state, which is not that of an occupant. It can scarcely be doubted that by *valeurs exigibles* the authors of the Hague code intended matured debts, but it may still be contended that their silence as to any other condition than maturity does not prove that, in denying to an occupant the right to exact debts not matured, they intended to allow him to exact money due to the enemy state from any persons whom he can physically coerce, or on the ground that the consideration for the debt, as timber from a forest, is connected with the occupied district[1].

The second paragraph of H LIII concerns two classes of things belonging to companies or private persons. One class, composed of railway plant, land telegraphs, telephones and ships, consists of things liable indeed to be much deteriorated by

[1] See Rivier, 2 *Principes du Droit des Gens* 307, 308. He quotes Löning, 5 *Revue de Droit International et de Législation comparée* 105, 106, who makes the same distinction between the principles of private and public law, and expressly disallows the exaction of payments in advance of maturity. Löning adds: *toutefois la poursuite de ces créances* (those which he allows to be got in) *ne peut avoir lieu que dans les limites du territoire occupé. Là où s'arrête l'occupation, expire le droit de l'occupant.* What then is to be the force of receipts given by the occupant, if the legitimate government sues for the debts outside the occupied territory, in its capital or in a neutral country? To the rules of jurisdiction on which the force of foreign proceedings, or of receipts given in order to avoid foreign proceedings, is founded, must there be added a jurisdiction of a military occupant? Since public law cannot help reacting on private law, it ought not to leave the principles of private law out of account. What we conceive to be the true rule is maintained by Heffter, § 134, and Calvo, § 1977. Pillet allows an occupant to enforce payment of the interest on a debt due to the enemy state, but not that of the principal: *Le Droit de la Guerre*, 2me p^ie^, p. 215.

rough usage, but which, unlike most things requisitioned, would in general remain in some condition at the end of the war, and which during the war the occupying force would need to keep under its control, as well to prevent their use by the enemy as for its own use from time to time. For these the obvious rule is that they shall be restored at the peace so far as they then exist, and the article adds that the indemnities for them shall be regulated at the peace, a formula which, one step in advance of that employed about receipts in the case of ordinary requisitions, seems to admit that there is a liability somewhere but does not fix it on either side. As to this class, H LIII repeats B VI with the addition of telephones. The other class of things consists of depôts of arms and generally all kinds of munitions of war, as to which there is the same necessity for preventing their use by the enemy, but which would not in general continue to exist and have any substantive value after their use by the occupant. B VI enumerated these among means of a nature to be used in the operations of the war, thereby allowing their seizure by the occupant, but did not include them among the things to be restored and the indemnities for them regulated at the peace. The growing respect for private property caused them to be so included in the *Manual* of the Institute of International Law, Art. 55, and they are now so included by H LIII.

A proposal was made at the Hague by the Danish delegate to describe the shore ends of cables as included in land telegraphs—*y compris les câbles d'atterrissage.* But it was not approved by the naval authorities who assisted at the conference, and as Lord Lansdowne, Secretary of State for War, remarked, "the dominant military power on land would under any circumstances have adequate control over the landingplaces of cables in an occupied territory, whether the words are inserted or not[1]."

ART. LV. *The occupying state shall be regarded as only administrator and usufructuary of the public buildings, immovables, forests and agricultural undertakings belonging to the enemy state and situated in the occupied country. It must protect*

[1] *Parliamentary Papers; Miscellaneous, no.* 1 (1899); pp. 83, 178.

the capital of those properties and administer it according to the rules of usufruct (life tenancy).

Immovable property, which comprises the real property and leaseholds for years of English law, whether belonging to the state or to private persons, cannot be appropriated by an occupant. If it belongs to private owners, they or their agents remain on the spot for its management, subject to such interference with it as military necessity may require; but if it belongs to the state the duty of its management is almost necessarily thrown on the invader, and he is entitled to the profits, as well for his remuneration and an inducement to good management as because, so far as they are in tangible shape, he can seize them like any other corporeal movable property of the enemy state. Perhaps too the confusion of occupation with conquest has left some trace on the relation of the occupant to public immovables, and caused him to be regarded as their temporary owner. But, whatever the explanation, there is no doubt that the occupant is entitled to get in the rents and dues of public immovables maturing during the occupation, and that his receipt for them will be a good discharge as against the enemy state, whatever opinion may be held on the general question of an occupant's right to enforce payment to him of debts due to that state. If the sovereign of the invaded state owns immovables in his private capacity, there is the same necessity for their management by the occupant, who cannot be expected to discriminate between the agents of the sovereign in his private and in his political capacity, but it may be presumed that the respect now paid to private property would cause him to account for the proceeds at the peace.

In the case of forests, the right of a usufructuary is to cut the trees which regularly come to cutting during his tenancy; and this right the occupant has, subject to the condition that those who buy the timber from him must remove it during the continuance of the occupation, for the restored government would not be bound to allow its removal. And if the occupant sells timber which has not regularly come to cutting, the courts of the legitimate government will give no effect to any claims founded on such an illegal transaction[1]. In the case of public

[1] *Guérin's case*, court of Nancy, 27 August 1872, Dalloz, 1872,

buildings, their furniture is considered as belonging to them, so that it must not be carried off, independently of the protection given to objects of art by H LVI.

ART. LVI. *The property of communes, and that of institutions dedicated to religious worship, charity, education, art or science, even when belonging to the state, shall be treated in the same manner as private property.*

All seizure of and destruction or intentional damage done to such institutions, historical monuments, or works of art or science, is prohibited and should be made the subject of prosecution.

All local bodies must be considered as included under communes.

Ships engaged on voyages of discovery have usually been treated as neutral, and a collection of Italian paintings and prints, taken by a British vessel on its passage from Italy to the United States in 1812, was restored to the Academy of Arts at Philadelphia; but the principle was first recognised as obligatory by B VIII, which H LVI repeats.

Section IV—On the Internment of Belligerents and the Care of the Wounded in Neutral Countries.

ART. LVII. *A neutral state which receives in its territory troops belonging to the belligerent armies shall intern them, as far as possible, at a distance from the theatre of war.*

It may keep them in camps, and even confine them in fortresses or localities assigned for the purpose.

It shall decide whether the officers may be left at liberty, on giving their parole that they will not leave the neutral territory without authorisation.

"Each belligerent will be responsible for the expenses caused by the internment of its own troops, in the absence of any treaty provision to the contrary." Holland, *Laws and Customs of War on Land*, p. 48.

II. p. 185, and 1 Clunet 126; *Mohr et Haas c. Hatzfeld*, Nancy, 3 August 1872, and Court of Cassation, 16 April 1873, Dalloz, 1872, II. p. 229, and 1 Clunet 181.

ART. LVIII. *Failing a special convention, the neutral state shall supply the interned with the food, clothing and relief required by humanity.*

At the conclusion of peace, the expenses caused by the internment shall be made good.

ART. LIX. *A neutral state may authorise the passage through its territory of wounded or sick belonging to the belligerent armies, on condition that the trains bringing them shall carry neither combatants nor war material. In such a case, the neutral state is bound to adopt such measures of safety and control as may be necessary for the purpose.*

Wounded and sick brought under these conditions into neutral territory by one of the belligerents, and belonging to the hostile party, must be guarded by the neutral state so as to insure their not taking part again in the operations of the war. The same duty shall devolve on the neutral state with regard to wounded or sick of the other army who may be committed to its care.

The subcommission at the Hague adopted unanimously the commentary that "this article has no other bearing (*portée*) than to establish that considerations of humanity and hygiene may determine a neutral state to allow wounded or sick soldiers to pass across its territory without failing in the duties of neutrality." Blue book, as quoted above, p. 153.

ART. LX. *The Geneva Convention applies to sick and wounded interned in neutral territory.*

CHAPTER V.

THE HAGUE REGULATIONS CONSIDERED GENERALLY.

The Three Hague Declarations and other cases not provided for in the Hague Regulations.

WE have seen (p. 57) that the Hague Regulations, by the terms of the convention about them, are to be supplemented in cases for which they do not provide by "the usages established between civilised nations, the laws of humanity, and the requirements of the public conscience." These words look both backward and forward; backward to the usages which help to determine the laws of war in their actual shape, and forward to the growth, more than possible, of what the public conscience, interpreting the laws of humanity, may require in the future. Taking first the sanction which they give to the past, it must be said that any thing which has been done in civilised warfare, and is still defended in spite of adverse criticisms, is not to be considered unlawful merely because no clause of the Hague text can be quoted in its favour. Any proposition opposed to it which has been put forward, if it had been deemed at the Hague to be already law or to be proper for enactment, would have been included in the text, of which as of all laws of war the restriction of violence is the main purpose, so that disallowance cannot be inferred from its silence. Those who would disallow what has been done and justified within the recognised pale of civilisation may continue their efforts, indeed by the reference to humanity and the public conscience they are encouraged to continue them, but they must not give out their proposition as one of the laws of war until they have procured its admission to a revised code or have silenced its opponents.

A remarkable example is furnished by the three declarations made at the Hague Conference in 1899, the first agreeing to prohibit for a term of five years the launching of projectiles and explosives from balloons or by other new methods of a similar nature; the second agreeing to abstain from the use of bullets which expand or flatten easily in the human body, such as bullets with a hard envelop not entirely covering the cone or pierced with incisions; the third agreeing to abstain from the use of projectiles the only object of which is the diffusion of asphyxiating or deleterious gases. The first is now at an end by effluxion of time, but during its continuance it had the adhesion of all the parties to the Hague Regulations except Great Britain and Turkey; to the second there are the same exceptions and that of the United States; to the third, the same exceptions as to the second with the addition of Portugal; and it must be noted that all three were signed at the Hague by the Turkish delegates, though their signature of none of them has been ratified by the Porte. The expansive bullets called Dum-Dum from the place of their manufacture in India were not considered by the British authorities to fall within the principle of the explosive bullets condemned by the Declaration of St Petersburg, because it was thought that the impact of an ordinary bullet did not give a shock sufficient to stop the onrush of certain assailants, so that the suffering caused to such assailants by the expansion of the bullet in the body was not useless. However that may be, the intention of using the Dum-Dum bullets in ordinary war was always disclaimed, and they were not employed in the South African war. It is possible that all three declarations may become laws of war in the near future, but at present they are not so.

Another example is furnished by the proposition sometimes laid down that barbarous forces—that is, either savage tribes and barbarous races with their native organisation or troops composed of individuals of such tribes or races—must not be employed against a civilised people. In the eighteenth century Red Indians were incited by white powers to act as tribes in alliance with them in their American wars, but the condemnation of any such proceeding is now absolutely universal. On the other hand, there can be no objection to the employment, as soldiers in organised military bodies under civilised command, of any individuals who in fact obey that command and observe the laws of war. It would therefore be frivolous to condemn the employment of British Indian or French Algerian organised bodies, even in war outside the limits of India or Algeria; *a fortiori* if they were defending the respective territory against invasion. In the South African war Kafirs were not used on either side as fighting troops, but they were used by the British in the transport service, to which it does not seem that any reasonable censure can apply.

A further matter as to which the Hague Regulations are silent is that of the fate of the population of a district the devastation of which, so far as the property in it is concerned, is permitted by H XXIII (*g*) as being imperatively demanded by the necessity of the war. Their removal into what are known as concentration camps, where they are maintained but restrained from communication with the enemy, presents itself as an inevitable corollary and has passed into practice. The patriotic conduct of the population, or the mere effect of their situation in the theatre of war, in furnishing the troops on their side with information, refuge, and starting points for fresh operations, may be the cause which makes the devastation necessary. People so placed are made, will they nill they, instruments of war, and must submit to a position as analogous to that of prisoners of war as their position before their removal was analogous to that of the fighting force.

Lastly, it may be worth while to enquire how the civil officials of the territorial or legitimate government are affected by the district in which they serve passing into the occupation of an enemy. It will generally be the better course for the population whose interest they ought to consult that they should continue to carry on the ordinary administration under the invader, but he has no right to force them to do so. If they decline to do it, his only right, and it is also his duty, is to replace them by appointees of his own, so far as necessary for maintaining order and the continuance of the daily life of the district: other purposes, as those of the superior judicial offices, can bide their time.

The Laws of War in relation to Reprisals.

The next question is one which concerns every possible body of laws of war, whether enacted by convention or resting on the consent of opinion, as well as the Hague Regulations, namely, does it exclude the breach of any law comprised in that body by way of reprisal or retorsion for a breach by the other side? And if the answer is negative, then is the breach permitted by way of reprisal limited to one of the same law which was broken by the other side? Universal practice and consent have given negative answers to both these questions. To the further question, whether any limit at all can be put to breaches of laws of war by way of reprisal, the following answer with reference to land war was given by the Russian draft which formed the base of the discussions at Brussels.

§ 69. Reprisals are admissible in extreme cases only, due regard being paid as far as shall be possible to the laws of humanity, when it shall have been unquestionably proved that the laws and customs of war have been violated by the enemy, and that they have had recourse to measures condemned by the law of nations.

§ 70. The selection of the means and extent of reprisals should be proportionate to the degree of the infraction of law committed by the enemy. Reprisals that are disproportionately severe are contrary to the rules of international law.

§ 71. Reprisals shall be allowed only on the authority of the commander-in-chief, who shall likewise determine the degree of their severity and their duration.

But the conference felt itself compelled to decline to discuss even these moderate propositions, among the reasons given by General Horsford in his report being that "it seemed to be the general feeling that occasions on which reprisals of a severe character had been executed were of far too recent a date to allow the practice to be discussed calmly[1]." Thus neither the Brussels nor the Hague Regulations contain any thing on the subject, and so far as the latter are concerned reprisal forms one of the cases not included in them which they expressly leave to humanity and conscience: we cannot apply to

[1] See above, p. 56, note 1.

this particular case the reference to "the usages established between civilised nations," because what occurred at Brussels proves that no usages on it are established in the sense of being not merely practised but approved with sufficient definition. But the *Manual* of the Institute of International Law has the following articles, which carry the matter very little further than the Russian propositions at Brussels.

85. Reprisals are forbidden whenever the wrong which has afforded ground of complaint has been repaired.

86. In the grave cases in which reprisals become an imperative necessity, their nature and scope must never exceed the measure of the infraction of the laws of war committed by the enemy.

They can only be made with the authorisation of the commander-in-chief.

They must in all cases be consistent with the rules of humanity and morality.

It will be observed that in the last clause "in all cases" replaced the Russian "as far as shall be possible," and that Art. 85 was new.

It is probably impossible to say more on the subject in general terms, and with regard to its total omission in the official codes we will associate ourselves with what the Russian delegate, General Jomini, said at Brussels. "I regret that the uncertainty of silence is to prevail with respect to one of the most bitter necessities of war. If the practice could be suppressed by this reticence, I could but approve of this course. But if it is still to exist this reticence may, it is to be feared, remove any limits to its exercise. Nevertheless, I believe that the mere mention in the protocol that the committee, after having endeavoured to regulate, to soften and to restrain reprisals, has shrunk from the task before the general repugnance felt with regard to the subject, will have a most serious moral bearing. It will perhaps be the best limitation we have been able to affix to the practice, and especially to the use which may be made of it in future."

The difficulty of obtaining a more precise definition of the right of reprisal in war calls for a jealous examination of the principle on which it rests, in order that no false theoretical view may assist the tendency to excess in practice which results from human nature and is seen in experience. The principle is thus put by Lueder.

> "The right not to observe the laws of war exists in the case of retorsion because, according to known maxims, non-fulfilment by one party deprives that party of the right to claim fulfilment by the other. At least this may be the case in war where, if the violations of the laws of war by the enemy were passed without retaliation, a belligerent would be at a disadvantage and worse off than his enemy who was guilty of the violations, with reference to the end which has to be striven for by all means, namely breaking down the determination of the other side and gaining the victory[1]."

The practical reason for reprisals given in the latter part of this passage is as convincing as any necessity alleged in war can be, but we must record our dissent from the generality of the assertion that a mutual obligation is dissolved by the failure of one party to perform it. If the mutual obligation under which we all lie to obey the law of the land in what concerns one another is intended, it is certain that the lawless behaviour of our neighbour towards us does not authorise us to behave lawlessly towards him, but only to call for redress. If the mutual obligation of contract is intended, it must be said that the laws of war are too deeply rooted in humanity and morality to be discussed on the footing of contract alone, except it may be some parts of no great importance which convention might have settled otherwise than it has. Nor, if the footing of contract be accepted for the discussion, is it true in all cases that a contract is dissolved by the failure of one party to perform it. In many cases the other party continues to be bound, although entitled to damages for the breach. The true basis of the right of reprisal in war seems to be, not the impairment of any obligation, but the redressing, by punishment or the exaction of damages, of a violated obligation. And thus the articles which have been quoted from the *Manual* of the Institute occur in its "Part III—Penal Sanction." If it can get to be generally felt that the illegalities of the enemy do not set a state or its com-

[1] 4 *Holtzendorff's Handbuch* 255.

manders loose from law, but entrust them with a right, not capricious but sacred, to vindicate law by fitting punishment or the exaction of fitting reparation, it may be expected that excessive reprisals, and reprisals falling on innocent parties, will be of less frequent occurrence.

Are the Laws of War liable to be overridden by Necessity?

Another question which concerns every possible body of laws of war as well as the Hague Regulations is whether its observance ceases to be obligatory "when the circumstances are such that the attainment of the object of the war and the escape from extreme danger would be hindered by observing the limitations imposed by the laws of war[1]." An affirmative answer is commonly given in Germany, where a distinction is made between the ordinary rules of war (*kriegsmanier*, *les lois de la guerre*), and what is permitted in virtue of the overmastering necessity referred to (*kriegsraison* or *kriegsräson*, *raison de guerre*), both being included in the law of war (*kriegsrecht*, *le droit de la guerre*); and a maxim is current that *kriegsräson geht vor kriegsrecht* (it should be *vor kriegsmanier*), which we may translate "the reason of war overrides its ordinary rules." Rivier also supports this view, saying *la nécessité de guerre peut excuser des rigueurs que les lois de la guerre condamnent. Elle prime les lois de la guerre*[2].

In what may be regarded as the classical passage on the doctrine, Lueder supports it on two or three grounds, which we will give fully in order to do justice to what we regard as highly pernicious. One is that commanders will act on it, whatever may be laid down. "It ought to happen because it must happen, that is, because the course of no war will in such extreme cases be hindered and allow itself to end in defeat, perhaps in ruin, in order not to violate formal law." This ground reduces law from a controlling to a registering agency[3]. Another ground is that "if the necessity of individuals is

[1] This is Lueder's language, 4 *Holtzendorff's Handbuch* 255. The classical passage referred to covers §§ 65, 66.

[2] *Principes du Droit des Gens*, t. 2, p. 242.

[3] See above, p. 52.

recognised as exempting them from punishment for things never so injurious done by them from that necessity, this must be still more the case in war, since so much more is at stake." This attributes to necessity a legal effect which it may have had in Roman but certainly has not in British law[1]. Again it is said that "*kriegsraison* is related to the law of war as necessity to criminal law, and it might be said with the same right and supported by the same argument that there was no criminal law because its rules have not to be observed in cases of necessity." This reads at first sight like a repetition of the second ground, but is perhaps meant to present necessity from the point of view of a government, which may have to disregard the ordinary criminal law in times of insurrection or great disturbance. And probably the view of *kriegsraison* which is taken by its advocates is best expressed by comparing it to martial law or the state of siege within a state. But such a comparison would encourage in military commanders a tone of moral superiority to the enemy which must be detrimental to moderation, the tone in which we have seen a desperate though hopeless resistance denounced as culpably frivolous, and entitling the stronger party to take any measures.

In any case the struggles of its advocates to make out that their *kriegsraison* is not inconsistent with allowing legal force to the ordinary laws of war prove that the necessity which they invoke is to be distinguished from the ordinary necessity, inherent in all the operations of war, of which account must be taken in drawing up any body of rules for belligerents. Of that necessity the Hague Convention introducing the Regulations notes that account has been taken in them[2]. The term *kriegsmanier*, the custom or we might almost say the etiquette of war, was first used when belligerents were restrained only by the courtesy of commanders and the sense that a more or less orderly behaviour towards the enemy was indispensable to the discipline and effectiveness of their own forces. It has grown to a code in which humanity to the enemy on the one side and the essential needs of war on the other have been considered. And the

[1] Necessity as an excuse in law is discussed in our volume on *International Law—Peace*, pp. 296–299.

[2] See above, p. 57.

question raised under the term *kriegsraison* is not whether that code is defective or misconceived, in any of its clauses, but whether a necessity, not of war but of success, is to be allowed to break it down. It is contended in effect, however innocent may be the intentions of authors, that the true instructions to be given by a state to its generals are: "Succeed—by war according to its laws, if you can—but, at all events and in any way, succeed." Of conduct suitable to such instructions it may be expected that human nature will not fail to produce examples, but the business of doctrinal writers should be to check and not to encourage it. Otherwise, the most elementary restraints on war, which have been handed down from antiquity, are not safe.

The Laws of War in relation to Neutral Persons and Property in Enemy Territory.

A last question remains on the conduct of land war, namely whether the persons and property of the subjects of neutral states, so far as they may be found within enemy territory, are exposed to violence equally with the persons and property of enemy subjects. There is no doubt that as a general rule they are so exposed. Neutral subjects have no claim to be allowed to leave a besieged place, except perhaps diplomats when military necessity does not oppose[1], and neutral residents have to furnish their share to money contributions. With regard to requisitions of things or services, an invader can rarely have much time for drawing distinctions, but if he had the time he would probably choose to take what he wanted from enemy rather than from neutral subjects, without prejudice to his right to take it from the latter in case of need without incurring greater liability than he would incur towards the former. These are the chances which neutral individuals and companies residing or carrying on business in a foreign country must run, for themselves and for all property which they possess in that country in connection with such residence or business, whether the residence amounts to domicile or not. They increase the strength and wealth of that country, and to protect them against the consequences of

[1] See what is said under H XXVIII, above, p. 79.

an invasion of it would be an intolerable task for their own governments. The same reasons do not apply to property which may enter a territory in the course of a business carried on elsewhere, and which in the same course would soon leave it again. Such is the rollingstock of a foreign state or railway company, which cannot avoid crossing and recrossing the frontier from time to time, or a ship which enters a port of the territory in the course of the trade of a merchant in a foreign country, to whom she belongs or by whom she is chartered. In such cases the neutral owner has in some measure entrusted his property to the fortunes of the enemy, though not so far as to identify it with him, and the just course is to allow it to be requisitioned for a real military necessity, compensation being paid. In the case of rollingstock the invader may further plead that it takes the place of a corresponding quantity belonging to the railways of the country, which is probably abroad, or that if those railways are worked by the aid of foreign rollingstock in excess of an equal exchange, then the foreign owners who consent to that mode of working are really carrying on business in the country. In 1870–1871 the Germans detained and used large quantities of Swiss and Austrian rollingstock in France, and were deaf to demands for its return. It must therefore be considered that H LIV does not require so immediate a return of neutral rollingstock as to prevent its being at all used by the invader, but only prohibits its abusive detention, and, by acknowledging a right to its return, requires the invader to pay compensation for its use and deterioration.

The same principles were applied to ships during the war of 1870. The German commander at Rouen desired to sink in the Seine at Duclair certain British vessels trading with France, in order to bar the way to French gunboats. The captains refused to unload them and accept payment of their value, and they were then sunk by force, which was quite fair, if it had not been done by firing on them while some at least of the crew were on board[1]. Compensation for the persons whose property was destroyed was demanded by the British Government, without disputing the right to sink the vessels, and was paid.

[1] The excuse made was that the refusal of the captains to enter into an agreement was an infraction of neutrality!

The invader's right as to neutral property is sometimes spoken of as one of angary, a name given to the right of a prince to impress neutral ships lying in his ports at the outbreak of war. The conditions of modern naval war are such that that right cannot now be often useful, though it was once of considerable importance, but it seems still to exist in case of real necessity, and its exercise would certainly be subject to the duty of compensation. Any right, however, of a sovereign in his own territory could scarcely be made to apply to the claims of an invader except on the exploded notion of occupation being conquest, and it is therefore better to discuss the claims of an invader on their separate merits.

CHAPTER VI.

NAVAL WAR AS BETWEEN BELLIGERENTS.

THE title of the present chapter is intended to exclude those parts of our subject which raise the question of what belligerents assert to be their rights against neutrals as such; for example, blockade, contraband of war, visit and search, and the unneutral employment of neutral territory. So far as neutrals may be affected by the operations of a belligerent based on the rights claimed by him against his enemy—for example, when of a ship and its cargo one is enemy property and the other neutral, or when a belligerent claims to treat a neutral subject as his enemy on account of his conduct—the consideration of the questions raised cannot well be separated from that of the operations themselves.

Private Property at Sea.

In the dark and middle ages war was conducted at sea as well as on land in accordance with the principle of solidarity, which established the relation of enemies between each party and all its subjects or citizens on the one side and the other party and all its subjects or citizens on the other side. To this there was added for naval war the absence of the modern notion of a ship as floating territory[1], with the consequence that not only ships at sea but also their cargoes were regarded as so many valuables which might be picked up in "no-man's-land," the circumstance that to get at the cargoes you must board the ship then appearing to be quite without importance. The legal ideas of the time therefore presented no obstacle to the seizure

[1] See our *International Law—Peace*, pp. 163, 164, 254.

and appropriation by a belligerent of the property of all enemy subjects whether on board enemy or neutral ships, together of course with the ships themselves if enemy ones. And the motives for putting in force all the rights given by the current legal ideas were even stronger at sea than on land, inasmuch as the trade and fisheries of the enemy were desirable objects of conquest. The resulting rules of naval war are formulated in the Consolat del Mar[1], a code of maritime law which enjoyed wide acceptance in the Mediterranean, and in its existing form appears to have been drawn up at Barcelona in the Catalan language at some time in the fourteenth century, but which certainly embodies a much older usage. By chapter 231 of that code the admiral may compel a friend's ship to carry her cargo the property of an enemy to a place of safety (the *infra præsidia* of the Latinists), paying the freight which the ship would have earned by carrying the cargo to its destination; and in case the friend should refuse so to carry it, the admiral may sink the ship if the cargo or the greater part of it is enemy's property, "saving always that he ought to save the lives of those on board of her." On the other hand the admiral is bound to take an enemy's ship carrying friends' property "to the place where he was fitted out," and the merchants—that is, the cargo-owners—must pay him the freight which would have been earned by their property being carried to its destination; but the merchants may require him to let them have the ship "for a suitable price," and if he refuses he will earn no freight and must make full compensation to them. By chapter 245 a friend recapturing a ship which the captor has not brought to a place of safety must receive a suitable salvage reward, "according to the maltreatment which they [the owners] may have undergone and according to the loss which they may have incurred"; but if the ship had been brought to a place of safety, the recaptor will be entitled to her. Here we have all the leading elements of the system, namely enemy property, whether ship or cargo, capturable, while neutral property, whether ship or cargo, is

[1] Often called the Consolato del Mare, its name in the Italian version. It forms vol. 3 of Sir Travers Twiss's *Black Book of the Admiralty,* in which its chapters 231 and 245 are at pp. 539 and 611; and it is also printed in the second volume of the *Collection de Lois Maritimes* by Pardessus.

free—the neutrals purchasing its freedom by having the destination both of their cargo on board an enemy's ship and of their ship carrying enemy's cargo changed for the captor's convenience, they paying or receiving the freight which would have been due for the voyage intended but thwarted, with the saving provision that the neutral cargo-owners may buy an enemy's ship from the captor at a fair price if they like to continue their voyage—the rule that the property of the prize is vested in the captor when, and only when, he has taken her where she can be considered as fully reduced into his possession—and the admiral as the authority on the side of the captor.

The title of admiral was derived from the Saracenic *emir*, and is said to have come into use about the time of the fourth crusade[1]. But whatever may have been his older designation, the officer in question was originally the commander of those fleets of armed merchantmen which used to sail as consorts for their better protection against pirates and enemies, and may often have held no commission except from his employers, although no doubt in many cases the civil authorities of the ports early intervened to arrange such fleets and appoint their leaders. In England the maritime towns were less populous and wealthy than in the Mediterranean, and lay nearer to the central power of a great prince, who, having no special navy of war, was in the habit of assembling the mercantile navies of his subjects, armed as all such then were, for his own public enterprises. We should expect therefore to find the royal authority exerting itself in all maritime matters, and in fact, while in 1300 we meet with Gervase Alard as admiral of the Cinque Ports, on the other hand we meet in 1295 with an admiral "of the Bayonnese fleet of Edward I," in a document of 1296 the office is called Admiratus or Admiralty, and in the same year there is mention of "Amiraux de nostre navire d'Engleterre." But the courts of a martial nature by which these officers maintained discipline and, no doubt, regulated the affairs of the merchants

[1] If so, the statement in Art. 17 of Part C of the *Black Book of the Admiralty*, that "this order was first made at Ipswich in the time of Henry the first by the admirals of the north and west and other lords thereat assisting," must employ the title by anticipation. Twiss's edition, v. 1, pp. 64, 65.

and shipowners arising on their voyages, had not yet become a definite part of the English judicial system. "In a case which came before the Common Pleas in 1297, as to a ship which had been seized at sea and brought into a Norfolk harbour, it was suggested by the defence that the matter was properly triable before the admiral and not in the king's court. The judges however would not listen to the suggestion, saying 'of the power of the admirals of whom you speak we know nothing'." But during the fourteenth century a great change took place. "In 1339 and for many years before claims made against the king of England by foreign sovereigns, in respect of depredations committed by Englishmen at sea, had always been referred to arbitrators or dealt with by the ordinary courts." "In 1357 for the first time we read of the admiral holding a court. In that year the king of Portugal claimed redress from Edward III in respect of some Portuguese goods which had been captured by an English ship on board a Frenchman. The answer given by Edward was that the owners had already taken proceedings for recovery of the goods before the admiral, in which the goods had rightly been decided to be good prize[1]." And about the same time the dignity of admiral was raised by the appointment of one for all the realm, and, probably, the term "high admiral" was introduced. Twiss says: "when this term first came into use is not certain, but the first admiral of all the fleets of ships—south, north and west—was Sir John de Beauchamp, 34 Edward III. His commission will be found in Rymer, *Fœdera*, iii, p. 505[2]." The admiral of France, his lieutenants and his jurisdiction, appear in an ordinance of Charles V, dated 7 December 1373[3].

The system of the Consolat with respect to enemy and neutral property was the common law of the Mediterranean, and in England the Black Book of the Admiralty, by Art. 7 of its Part B which Twiss assigns on internal evidence to a date

[1] The quotations thus far made in this paragraph are from R. G. Marsden, *Six Centuries of the Admiralty Court*, in 67 Nautical Magazine 86–88.

[2] Twiss, *Black Book of the Admiralty*, v. 1, p. 55, note. Local admirals however are still met with later.

[3] Printed by Twiss, op. cit., v. 1, p. 430.

between 1337 and 1351, adopts the rule that enemy property is good prize in neutral ships[1]. But in spite of the assertion commonly made that in this country the system of the Consolat was adopted in its entirety, the rule that neutral property is to be free in enemy ships does not seem to have been approved during the middle ages by English policy. In 1294, during war between England and Spain, the former power forbade the Portuguese to carry Spanish cargoes. In 1338 Edward III requested the king of Castile to prohibit commerce between his subjects and the Flemings, with whom England was at war, but the Castilians declined to comply. And a line of treaties by which England stipulated that neither party was to comfort the enemies of the other, or to suffer that they have aid from his country, begins with one with France in 1303[2], and includes one of some unknown date which appears to have existed with Scotland[3]. The st. 20 Hen. VI [1461–2], c. 1, expressly lays down that the king's subjects taking goods laden in enemy's ships shall have them as their own; and the line of treaties referred to is continued by those of Edward IV with Burgundy, 1467 (no enemies' goods to be admitted by sea)[4], with Brittany, 1468[5] (persons and goods on board enemy ships to be good prize), and with Burgundy again, 1478[6] (mutual agreements not to carry enemies' goods, and to submit to visit for enforcing such agreements, which stipulations were also in the treaty with Brittany). It seems to have been thought that the neutral who entrusted his goods to the ship of an enemy gave aid and comfort to the latter, by the freight which he enabled him to earn, by the useful commodities which he caused to be imported into his country, and perhaps not least by the assistance which the merchants who accompanied their goods were likely to give in the defence of the ship, in times when every one had to be more

[1] The Black Book appears to have been compiled for the use of the Duke of Exeter, Admiral, who died in 1446. Twiss's judgment of the age of Part B is in op. cit., p. xxx.

[2] 2 Rymer, *Fœdera*, 927 (954, edition of 1816).

[3] Sir Ralph Sadler's *Letters and Negotiations in Scotland*, p. 381, quoted in Robinson's *Collectanea Maritima*, p. 58, note.

[4] 11 Rymer, *Fœdera*, 596.

[5] 11 Rymer, *Fœdera*, 622.

[6] 12 Rymer, *Fœdera*, 73.

or less a fighting man. In the face of the facts quoted, coupled with the silence of the Black Book as to any thing more than we have adduced from it, treaties concluded by England with the maritime towns of Biscay and Castile in 1351[1], and the cities of Portugal in 1353[2], stipulating the freedom of neutral goods in enemy ships, are scarcely a sufficient base for the assertion that the English practice on that point then agreed with the Consolat del Mar. It is more likely that the currency of that document embraced the Atlantic as well as the Mediterranean ports of the Spanish peninsula, and that these obtained the adoption of its system in their treaties with England, than that the latter country spontaneously took up for a few years a line to which neither its earlier nor its later manifestations during the middle ages point.

In France the Ordinance of 1533 adopted the rule that neutral goods in enemy ships are good prize, and that of 1543 added to it the rule that a neutral ship carrying enemy goods is good prize, so that the maxim *robe d'ennemi confisque robe d'ami* resulted: whether the enemy property was the ship or the cargo, it infected the other and both were condemned. The ordinance of 1584 maintained this severity, but in 1592 the parliament of Paris decided against the condemnation of neutral ships carrying enemy goods. The smaller northern powers adhered more closely to the principles of the Consolat. In 1438 the senate of Holland decided that neutral property found in the ships of Lubeck and other towns on the Baltic and the Elbe, with which the Hollanders were at war, was not good prize; and this, says Grotius, was thenceforward held to be the law. But Lubeck did not willingly admit it to be the law except when it told in her favour. What Grotius calls *significationes* used to be made by belligerents to neutrals, warning them to break off their trade with their enemies. In 1458 Lubeck refused to obey such a warning from Dantzick, but in 1551 gave one herself to the Hollanders, who were able to refuse obedience without inconsistency[3]. These warnings were of course not limited to the shipment of cargo on board vessels of the enemy. They expressed a natural, though from any legal point of view

[1] 5 Rymer, *Fœdera*, 719. [2] Ib., p. 764.

[3] Grotius, note to l. 3, c. 1, s. 5.

extravagant, desire, entertained by people who knew well that it is not only commerce in things now called contraband which strengthens a nation, to cut off their enemies from all intercourse with the outside world. The same is true of the efforts which we have seen were made by England to isolate her enemies by warnings to neutrals or treaties with them. But as the shipment of cargo on board vessels of the enemy would be included so far as those efforts succeeded, the warnings, and the treaties so far as they were obtained, are important testimonies to the sentiment on that point[1].

Such was the practice on the continental shores of the Atlantic and Baltic at the time when the *Select Pleas of the Court of Admiralty*, published by the Selden Society under the able editorship of Mr Marsden[2], enable us to speak of the English practice with fuller knowledge. The rule that neutral goods become good prize when carried in an enemy ship was applied in 1545, in a case in which there was no question of contraband, the cargo consisting of satins, girdles, hose and wearing apparel[3]. An order in council of 26 July 1557 directed that the maxim *robe d'ennemi confisque robe d'ami* should be applied against Frenchmen in both its branches, because they "put the same in execution against the subjects of this realm." In the same year the council directed that their order just cited should be applied against the Scots, who were also enemies, so as to make a ship taken with goods on board belonging to Scots

[1] The examples of the *significationes* and treaties referred to are too numerous for quotation, but a treaty between the Dutch and Lubeck in 1613 may be mentioned, since it is somewhat alien to the spirit commonly shown in the matter by the Dutch. Neither were to aid the enemies of the other with money, troops, ships or victual, or to permit the subjects of the other's enemies to trade in their country: Grotius, u. s. The first clause is based on the doctrine of contraband, but the second is excessive.

[2] Vol. 1, 1892, and vol. 2, 1897; their principal contents being summarised by Mr Marsden both in the introductions to the volumes and in *Six Centuries of the Admiralty Court*, 67 Nautical Magazine, pp. 85, 169, 241, 337, 387, 445, 605.

[3] *Insano c. Elsdon*, *Select Pleas &c.*, v. 1, pp. 138, 235; v. 2, p. lxvi; 67 N. M. 388. Marsden says of this case that "perhaps the statute of Henry VI was resuscitated as a set-off against the French rule": u. s., p. 389. This assumes that the statute had fallen into disuse, and that independently of it the English rule was different.

good prize. After the death of Queen Mary and the peace with France and Scotland no more is heard of any claim on the part of England to condemn neutral ships for carrying enemy's goods[1], and in the closing wars of the sixteenth century the claim to condemn friends' goods captured on board enemy ships was not pressed against our Dutch and French allies, but goods of Venetian (neutral) owners taken in Portuguese (enemy) ships were condemned "according to the exigency of the law and the laws and statutes of this realm of England[2]." After this time, however, the rules of the English admiralty were those of the Consolat, and it is easy to see how the necessity of conforming to the principles of our Dutch allies must have helped to bring about that result, just as we shall see that the necessity of a concordant practice on the part of allies brought about a further change in English practice at the time of the Crimean war.

The seventeenth century was marked by the efforts of the Dutch, in the interest of their carrying trade, to establish the rule "free ships free goods," that is that enemy goods in neutral ships should be free, to which the rule "enemy ships enemy goods," that is that neutral goods in enemy ships should be confiscable, was regarded as a corollary though seldom mentioned in the official documents embodying the former rule. For this system they obtained the assent of a large number of European powers, including not only France but even England, by treaties which the latter power repeated with France and Holland, though not with Spain, at Utrecht in 1713. Such treaties can only bind as between parties one of whom is a belligerent and the other a neutral, and at the commencement of the Seven Years War in 1756 Great Britain

[1] In 1601 an unsuccessful attempt was made by the captors of the *Henri*, a French (friend's) ship carrying Spanish (enemy's) goods, to have her condemned, carrying enemy's goods being alleged to be "against the exigency of right and against the laws and customs of the realm of France passed and promulgated." So the order in council was not relied on. *Six Centuries &c.* 67 N. M. 453; see, for a reference to the record, 2 *Select Pleas &c.* lxxiv, no. 215.

[2] Case of the *St Mark* and other Portuguese ships captured by the *Refusal* and other ships owned by the Earl of Nottingham (lord high admiral) and other Englishmen, *Six Centuries &c.*, 67 N. M. 453; see, for references to the records, 2 *Select Pleas &c.* lxxv, no. 155.

refused to be bound by them towards the Dutch, whom she charged with a refusal to fulfil their contractual obligations of defensive alliance and guarantee. As between belligerents such treaties are abrogated by the war, and although Great Britain has often after wars renewed her stipulations of Utrecht, the last occasion on which she did so was that of her commercial treaty with France in 1786. Thus in her wars she has been practically free to apply the rules of the Consolat, while France, so far as not bound by treaty, repeated her maxim *robe d'ennemi confisque robe d'ami* by her ordinance of 1681, which was relaxed by those of 1744 and 1778.

The Armed Neutralities in which the Baltic powers confederated themselves in 1780 and 1800 adopted the rule "free ships free goods," and the refusal of England to assent to it became one of the chief sources of the charge so widely made against her on the continent of exercising an unjust domination over the sea. At the outbreak of the Crimean war in 1854 the different principles of England and France as to maritime law made it necessary for them to enter into a compromise enabling them to act as allies on a common system, and the terms arranged were the assent of Great Britain to the rule "free ships free goods" without the corollary "enemy ships enemy goods." At the close of the war this compromise received the concurrence of the other great powers of Europe, since extended to almost all the world, in the Declaration of Paris, 16 April 1856, which begins with a preamble amply justified by the history which we have passed in review.

"Considering," it says, "that maritime law in time of war has long been the subject of deplorable disputes;

"That the uncertainty of the law and of the duties in such a matter gives rise to differences of opinion between neutrals and belligerents which may occasion serious difficulties and even conflicts;

"That it is consequently advantageous to establish a uniform doctrine on such a point;

"[The signatories] have adopted the following solemn declaration:

"1. ....

"2. The neutral flag covers enemy's goods, with the exception of contraband of war.

"3. Neutral goods, with the exception of contraband of war, are not liable to capture under the enemy's flag.

"4. ...."

An agitation was long maintained in England with the view of inducing this country to withdraw from the Declaration of Paris, which it was not within her power to do, that document being really a convention. And had it been possible to do so, the signature of England to the statement in the preamble, that the law was previously uncertain, might have been quoted against any attempt on her part to fall back on the rules of the Consolat as being law in the absence of convention. The United States, which refused to become a party to the Declaration because it did not completely exempt enemy property as such from capture at sea, covered by that refusal the narrower ground of enemy property under a neutral flag; and neither they nor Spain in their war of 1898, nor Japan and Russia in their war of 1904, acted contrary to the Declaration. We may therefore conclude that enemy ships and enemy goods on board them are now, by international law, the only enemy property which, as such, is capturable at sea. That result is the only one conformable to principle, for the assimilation of ships to territory is now sufficiently established to make it no longer possible to ignore the fact that the invasion of a neutral ship, which is not reasonably believed to be offending against any law, is the invasion of a field in which innocent neutral authority is exclusive[1].

In support of the complete exemption of enemy property, as such, from capture at sea a great mass of public opinion is enrolled, and a certain amount of diplomatic success has been obtained. It was adopted by the treaty of 1785 between the United States and Prussia, and again by that of commerce in 1828 between the same powers, and by the treaty of commerce between the United States and Italy in 1871; and in 1823 Russia was willing to adopt it on the proposition of the United States, but only on the condition that all other naval powers should join in it. Italy adopted it for herself by her Marine Code in 1865, and in the war of 1866 Prussia, Austria and Italy acted on it. In 1870 Prussia proclaimed it at the beginning of

[1] The Declaration of Paris mentions contraband and not blockade as an exception to the rules of immunity which it lays down, because it is only in the former that the question turns on the nature of the goods, and can therefore be assimilated to the question of their being enemy or neutral property.

the war, but dropped it when she found that France stood by capture; and the United States continue to carry on a diplomatic propaganda in its favour. On principle we must say that the capture at sea of enemy property as such is a military measure, an operation of war, and that its defence is therefore independent of the mediæval doctrine of the solidarity of sovereigns and states with their subjects, on which the civil courts maintain the doctrines of Non-Intercourse and even perhaps of Confiscation[1]. Its justification must lie in its effect on the fortunes of a war. To appreciate that effect it is not sufficient to consider the damage done to the pecuniary resources of a belligerent power by seizing and appropriating the property of those from whom it can levy taxes and cutting off their opportunities of trade. It must also be remembered that the capture of enemy ships has always carried with it the right to detain their crews as prisoners. Indeed the doctrine of *courir sus aux ennemis* was from the first as much directed against persons as against things. Hence the existing practice deprives the enemy of important resources, both of ships which might be available as transports or for purposes of supply, and of men who might render service on board ships so employed or men in the fighting navy, and indeed would in general be legally compellable to do so. In the war of 1870 Prussia protested against such detention of North German sailors captured in merchant vessels, as having lost its legal base by the abolition of privateering. The connection of ideas is difficult to see, and France maintained her right. This aspect of the case is peculiarly important to England, of which no soldier and only some sailors consider the invasion to be unthinkable, but to the invasion of which the rapid collection of a sufficient number of transports would be indispensable. And the damage arising from the capture of British shipping has never been fatal in the past, would probably be much less in the altered conditions due to the use of steam in navigation, loses through insurance most of its character as a hardship on individuals, and might be still more equitably apportioned among the people if the state accepted the liability for the losses, as was recommended by the Royal Commission on

[1] See above, pp. 34, 35, as to the backwardness of the civil courts.

the Supply of Food and Raw Material in Time of War[1]. There does not then seem any sufficient reason why England should promote the immunity of private property at sea from the burden of military necessity, which lies heavy on private property on land in the shape of requisitions and contributions.

But the subject must not be dismissed without noticing some of the arguments used by advocates of the change. One is that since enemy property is now not capturable, as such, under the neutral flag, while even neutral property under a belligerent flag is still liable to the interruption of its transit by the capture of the ship, the present state of the law would cause the carrying trade to be transferred from England, if a belligerent, to neutral nations. It may be answered that for that purpose it would be necessary to transfer the shipping itself, which French prize law does not allow to be done in time of war, while British prize law is that "the circumstances attending a sale are severely scrutinised, and a transfer is not held to be good if it is subjected to any condition or even tacit understanding by which the vendor keeps an interest in the vessel or its profits, a control over it, a power of revocation, or a right to its restoration at the conclusion of the war[2]." It would therefore be difficult to find on short notice sufficient capital to pay for a safe and wholesale transfer of British shipping, and the delay and expense caused to freighters by ships being brought in for adjudication on the validity of their transfers would seriously diminish the supposed advantage of entrusting their goods to alleged neutral bottoms. Another argument is derived from the danger to the supply of food and raw material to the British Isles through the capture at sea of enemy property as such. The answer is that the abolition of that capture would almost certainly lead to our supplies of food and raw material being attacked through a straining of the laws of blockade and contraband, and that whether neutral powers resisted such

[1] In 1905; Cd. 2643. "We wish to place distinctly on record our opinion that the advantages to be gained from some well considered scheme of the kind [national indemnity against loss from capture by the enemy] seem to us very largely to outweigh any objections which have been stated to us": paragraph 266.

[2] Hall, § 171.

straining would depend chiefly on their political sympathy. Neutrals, however they may complain of unwarrantable interference with their commerce by belligerents, have seldom interfered on that ground as long as they could persuade themselves that the war would be short. Again, some jurists argue that the capture of enemy ships and the detention of enemy sailors, so far as based on the desire of preventing their being used for invasion or for the transport of a force to a seat of war, does not require to be insisted on as a part of the laws of war, because it can always be done when needed for safety by virtue of the necessity which they preach as overriding all laws. Our objection to that view of necessity has been stated[1]. If and so long as cases can be foreseen in which the capture and detention in question will be indispensable, the right should in our opinion be preserved as one of the necessities which ought to be provided for in the expression given to the laws of war, and not accepted as an indulgence setting a belligerent free from law. Still another topic urged is that, if enemy ships must be brought in, they ought to be sequestrated and not condemned as prize. If that rule were laid down the situation of private property would be much better at sea than on land, where receipts binding no one to repayment are all that is given for requisitions and contributions. But if the shipowner or cargo-owner, whose trade brings him into contact with the hard facts of war, will not protect himself by insurance, and his own state will not accept any responsibility for his losses, it is ludicrous to expect that the enemy state will show such care for him.

Droits of admiralty. The rules relating to the capture of private property at sea are equally applied by the states which maintain such capture to the seizure for the state of private property arriving in their ports during a war. In England the case is comprised in the "droits of admiralty" together with property in port at the outbreak of war.

[1] See above, p. 115.

Exceptions to the Capture of Enemy Property at Sea.

Personal Effects. Whether from a feeling of humanity, or because personal effects are not within the justificatory reasons for the existing practice of naval war, although they were included in the original doctrine of *courir sus*, the personal effects of the captain and crew of a captured ship are not condemned as prize. And the same favour is extended, so long as the parcels are really small, to small parcels of merchandise being the "adventures," *pacotilles* in French, which it has been customary to allow captains to make on their own account[1]. Passengers would no doubt enjoy the same immunity for their personal effects, but even supposing them to enjoy an immunity for their adventures, the question of degree arising in the case of an adventure might be less easily decided in their favour than in the case of the captain, since there would be nothing but the degree to distinguish them from merchants.

Coast Fisheries. Immunity from capture on the ground of their being enemies or enemy property, but not from capture and condemnation on the ground of breach of blockade, is enjoyed by the men, boats and tackle employed in coast fisheries, and their cargoes of fresh fish, including fish kept alive by contrivances on their way to market; so long as the men and boats are not engaged in any warlike employment—in which scouting, exchanging signals with the forces on their side, and carrying arms would be included—so long also as in the opinion of the hostile government or its naval commanders concerned they are not likely to be engaged in any warlike employment. If the opinion here referred to is only that of the naval commanders concerned, the prize court before which the captures are brought will have to release them unless the warlike intention of the captured is proved to its satisfaction; but if the captures were

[1] Example. *Les effets, hardes, instruments nautiques et cartes, ainsi que les 2000 noix de coco réclamées par le capitaine Holtz, sont restitués à ce marin dans l'état où ils se trouvent et sans frais, à titre de pacotille personnelle.* Sentence on the *Joan*, in *Jurisprudence du Conseil des Prises pendant la guerre de* 1870–71, Henri Barboux, p. 106. In *The Friendship*, on prayer that the master's adventure might be restored, Lord Stowell said: "I shall leave him to the mercy of the captors. He is a man who has not made an ingenuous disclosure of the facts in his possession": 6 C. Rob. 429.

made in pursuance of a government order, the prize court, in the absence of any thing to the contrary in the constitution of the country, will be bound by such an order as emanating from the authority under which it sits. To this statement, which appears to be sufficient as regards the duties of prize courts and commanders, it must be added that a government is not entitled to issue orders interfering with the coast fisheries of its enemy state, unless as an inseparable part of a military operation, or when it has good reason to expect that that state will make a warlike use of the men or boats. The history of the immunity and the authorities on it were so fully treated by Mr Justice Gray in delivering the opinion of the majority of the Supreme Court of the United States in the case of *The Paquete Habana and the Lola*, 1899, 175 U.S. 677, that a general reference to that judgment may dispense with a multitude of particular references which would otherwise be necessary[1].

[1] The vessels in question in the case mentioned were Spanish fishing boats, of 25 and 35 tons respectively, captured off the coast of Cuba during the Spanish-American war and released by the court. On two of the points incorporated in the statement in our text, blockade and probability of warlike employment, we may quote the answer which the United States Secretary of State, Mr Day, made on 30 April 1898 to Admiral Sampson, who had recommended that the Spanish fishermen should be detained as prisoners of war. He said: "Spanish fishing vessels attempting to violate blockade are subject, with crew, to capture, and any such vessel or crew considered likely to aid enemy may be detained." Cited by Mr Justice Gray, p. 713, from the *Bureau of Navigation Report of* 1898, appendix, 178. On this it may be remarked that the authority so given by the government, for the case of the admiral's thinking warlike employment probable, was only to detain, and would not have bound the Supreme Court to condemn even if the constitutional relation of that court to the executive government had been the same as that of a British prize court to the crown.—Another point incorporated in the statement in the text is the mention of fresh fish in defining the immunity. This was expressly contained in the French regulations of 1779 and 1780, with the addition "even if not caught by the vessels" which should claim the immunity, so as to cover vessels employed in carrying the fish home: *Paquete &c.*, p. 690. And the British orders in council of 23 May 1806 and 2 May 1810 described the immunity as belonging to "vessels employed in catching and conveying fish fresh to market," where "and" evidently ought to be read "or," the latter order adding, "such vessels not being fitted or provided for the curing of fish:" 5 C. Rob. 408 and Edw. Adm. appendix L. In the cases

The coast fisheries which enjoy the immunity thus described are contrasted with what is called the great fishery, such as that for cod, right or sperm whale, seal or sea calf; indeed England, in the correspondence carried on with the French Government through M. Otto, the French commissioner resident at London for the exchange of prisoners, declared, with regard to the order in council of 16 March 1801, that the concession was never extended to the great fishery or to commerce in oysters or in fish[1]. On the other hand it is not limited to vessels fishing off the coast of their own country, for the Spanish boat *Lola*, which was declared by the Supreme Court of the United States to be entitled to it, had been fishing on the coast of Yucatan. The condition that the fish must be brought to market alive appears to supply the necessary distinction.

The immunity of which we are treating was known in the middle ages: Froissart says that "fishermen on the sea, whatever war there were between France and England, never did harm to one another, so they are friends and help one another at need[2]." Of course it could not then have existed in the precise shape which can now be given to it, the whole subject of naval war was still so confused even in theory—in particular blockade had not emerged as a distinct branch of it—and the times were too disorderly for practice to follow closely such theory as was possible. We can indeed perceive that the practical enjoyment of the immunity mainly depended on edicts and treaties, sometimes limited in their terms[3]. Indeed this is confessed in Art. 49 of the French *Ordonnance* of 1543 and Art. 79 of that of 1584, which Cleiron reproduces as Art. 80 of his *Jurisdiction de la Marine*, namely that "the admiral may in time of war grant fishing truces to the enemy and his subjects, provided the enemy

of the *Paquete Habana* and *Lola* the fish were kept alive by contrivances: p. 718.

[1] *Martens, Recueil,* 2 *Suppl.* 295.

[2] Vol. 3, c. 41, p. 133, of the edition of 1574.

[3] English orders of 1403 and 1406, at which dates there were hostilities between England and France notwithstanding the 28 years' truce of 1396; the order of 1403 with geographical limits. Agreement of 1521 between Francis I and Charles V, then at war with one another, limited in time. French and Dutch edicts in favour of the herring fishery in 1536. Agreement of 1675 between Louis XIV and the States General.

will likewise grant them to Frenchmen." The ordinance of 1681 did not repeat this article, and that of 1692 declared fishing vessels to be good prize, the enemies of France being accused of not observing the agreements. But France expressly restored the indemnity during the War of American Independence, and in the same war England acted in the same sense; and from that time prize courts have not waited for it to be expressly given, but have allowed it whenever it has not been withheld by government orders[1]. It was so withheld by England at the commencement of the War of the French Revolution, and again in 1798 and 1800, on which latter occasions there was serious fear of a French invasion, for which fishermen and their boats might have been very helpful, so that those occasions fall within the true measure of the rule as we have stated it. The danger having disappeared, the orders against French fishermen were revoked in 1801[2].

Another historical fact calls for an accurate appreciation of the rule, which, as we have stated it, is not one for a general immunity of coast fisheries, but for their immunity from capture on the ground of enemy character, and therefore does not entitle them to stand in the way of and prevent or frustrate a military operation, which is what private property on land is not allowed to do. Their want of immunity for breach of blockade, for which we have seen authority from a source generally favourable to them, is a particular instance of that principle. The fact to which we refer is what took place in the sea of Azof during the Crimean war, when the instructions of the British admiral were "to clear the seaboard of all fish stores, all fisheries and mills, on a scale beyond the wants of the neighbouring population, and indeed of all things destined to contribute to the main-

[1] By an order of 11 April 1780 Sir James Marriott, judge of the Court of Admiralty, provided for the consolidation of causes of prize of small fishing boats, but occasion cannot have arisen for putting that order in exercise, or at least condemnation cannot have ensued under it, as England in that war abstained from interfering with the coast fisheries.

[2] In 1800 the British government complained that French fishing boats had been made into fireboats at Flushing, and that the French government had impressed fishermen and their boats, even those whom the British had released on condition of their not serving, and sent them to Brest to serve in the flotilla.

tenance of the enemy's army in the Crimea." Thereupon the British and French ships in cooperation "destroyed large fishing establishments and storehouses of the Russian government, numbers of heavy launches, and enormous quantities of nets and gear, salted fish, corn and other provisions intended for the supply of the Russian army[1]." It may well be believed that private property of fishermen was involved in such an operation, and that it would have been impossible to carry the instructions into effect, purely military as their purport was, consistently with the scrupulous sparing of private property. The French instructions to naval commanders, as well during the wars of 1859 and 1870 as during the Crimean war, forbade them to trouble the coast fisheries or to seize any vessel or boat engaged therein, unless naval or military operations should make it necessary. Those of 1854 required the commanders, in case of operations in the White Sea, to spare the trade in fresh fish, provisions, utensils and fishing tackle between the country people of the Russian coast and the Norwegian fishermen from Finmark, except in case of abuse[2].

We can now deal with the question whether the immunity of coast fisheries is a rule of international law, properly so called. The answer depends in part on the meaning with which the word "law" is used in the question, and in part on the terms in which the immunity is stated. If stated too largely it is either not a rule of law in any sense, or it is one subject to that violation from necessity which, as we so often urge, is to our thinking the negation of legal principle. If stated as we have stated it, it appears to have arrived in the course of centuries at satisfying the conditions which we regard as those of international law in the only true sense, namely that the conscience of our international society demands it and that it is observed. When the Addington ministry in 1801, revoking the order of 1800, declared that "the freedom of fishing was nowise founded upon an agreement but upon a simple concession," which "would be always subordinate to the convenience of the moment," they probably intended to rate the obligatory character of the concession lower than we must rate it after the further practice of

[1] United Service Journal, 1855, part 3, pp. 108–112.

[2] 2 Ortolan, App. Sp. VI.

a century. Nor need we be led to an opposite opinion by what Lord Stowell said: "in former wars it has not been usual to make captures of these small fishing vessels, but this was a rule of comity only and not of legal decision; it has prevailed from views of mutual accommodation between neighbouring countries, and from tenderness to a poor and industrious order of people.... As they are brought before me for my judgment they must be referred to the general principle of this court; they fall under the character and description of ships constantly and exclusively employed in the enemy's trade[1]." The same remark occurs on the effect of practice since continued; we may not feel sure as to the sense which that great judge attached to comity; and we may remember the extreme sensitiveness which he always showed about his position relatively to the government. To condemn as the inevitable result of the government's having allowed the case to come before him was more congenial to his habit of mind than to recognise that the immunity invoked depended for a prize court on the government's not withholding it.

Science, Art &c. Expeditions despatched for purposes of science, religion or humanity enjoy an immunity from interference on the ground of enemy character, so long as they observe all the duties of neutrality and engage in no commerce not necessary for the object of the expedition. When starting for localities where communication with the civilised world may be for long impossible, they have often been furnished by friendly governments with safe-conducts in advance, as in the cases of Bougainville in 1766, La Pérouse in 1785, the expeditions in search of Sir John Franklin, and that of Nordenskiöld in the Vega. The latter examples show that the privilege is not confined to public expeditions, but full information would be required by any government asked for a safe-conduct, and any departure from the particulars so communicated might entail serious consequences by reason of the suspicions excited[2].

Works of art or learning were at one time regarded as proper spoils of the victor, when they were not protected by the mutual

[1] *The Young Jacob and Johanna,* 1 C. Rob. 20.

[2] See particularly 2 Kleen, *Neutralité,* 503–5—who cites the Japanese prize law of 9 Sep. 1894 as enumerating the purposes of religion and humanity along with those of science—and Lawrence, § 205.

courtesy of sovereigns, who were then considered as the owners of what we now say belongs to their state. The Hague Art. LVI at last protects them on land, when belonging to the state or to public institutions; and they had already been pronounced exempt in such cases from maritime capture by two remarkable judgments. One was that of the vice-admiralty court of Nova Scotia restoring paintings and engravings, taken by a British ship in 1813, to the Academy of Arts at Philadelphia; the other was that of the United States court in 1861, restoring cases of books to a university in the insurgent state of North Carolina[1]. Works of art or learning belonging to private individuals enjoy no immunity. The concession is made to the public ends promoted by the body which profits by it.

Licenses. A state may forego its rights by licensing trade with the enemy. The effect when an enemy is interested in such a license is to convert him into a friend to the extent of its conditions, so that he can insure his property and enforce the contract of insurance by suit in the name of an agent, and when his property is at sea it will not be capturable, and will be subject to his right of stoppage *in transitu*[2]. A commander, as such, may regulate trade within the district of which he is in military occupation, but only the supreme power can grant such a license for oversea trade as to exempt it from capture.

The French instructions of 25 July 1870 gave to enemy ships entering French ports in ignorance of the war thirty days for departure. This was held to leave confiscable the enemy's cargoes on board such ships, the only express mention of cargoes in the instructions being of those loaded for France and for French account before the declaration of war[3].

Cartel ships, as those are called which are employed in the exchange of prisoners or on other special services under agreement between the belligerents, are licensed for themselves and any merchandise which they carry by express permission, but

[1] See above, p. 107; *The Marquis de Somarveles,* Stewart Adm. (Nova Scotia) 445, 482; *The Amelia,* 4 Philadelphia 417.

[2] See *Flindt v. Scott* and the cases cited in it: 5 Taunton 674, Scott 526. As to whether a suit can be brought on the insurance in the enemy's name, see the note on ransom bills, below, p. 159.

[3] *La Ghérardine,* Barboux, p. 60.

not for any goods carried in excess of the permission[1]. And if the permission is grossly exceeded, the ship herself will be confiscated[2]. All contracts entered into for equipping and fitting a cartel ship for her service are considered as made between friends, and may be enforced in the courts of either belligerent having jurisdiction in the case[3].

Shipwreck or Peril of the Sea. Enemy ships entering the harbours of a state after the outbreak of war are liable to capture as if they were still at sea, with such exceptions as are often made when declaring war for ships then on their voyage (above, p. 39). Enemy ships wrecked on the coast have not been placed by international consent under any different rule, and their liability to capture is affirmed by French ordinances and practice[4], but the Institute of International Law has recommended that an immunity should be granted to vessels of the mercantile marine compelled by an accident of *force majeure* to take refuge in an enemy port[5]. Humanity seems to dictate this, especially when it is considered that a ship which might have found a refuge in an enemy port may otherwise be lost in trying to reach a home or a neutral one.

Criterions of Enemy Character.

Nationality, Domicile, House of Business. In France and generally on the European continent the same character is attributed to a shipowner or cargo-owner for the purpose of maritime capture as for other purposes. He is an enemy or a neutral according to his political nationality[6]. But the French Instructions of 25 July 1870 to naval commanders, Art. 10, say that "for the application of the principles that the neutral flag covers enemy goods and that neutral goods are free under the enemy flag, contraband of war excepted, the nationality of houses of business [*maisons de commerce*] must be determined according

[1] *The Carolina*, 6 C. Rob. 336.

[2] *The Venus*, 4 C. Rob. 355.

[3] *Crawford v. The William Penn*; Peters, Circuit Court, 106; Scott 580, 584.

[4] Despagnet, § 655.

[5] 17 *Annuaire* 284.

[6] *Le Hardy c. La Voltigeante*, 1 Pistoye et Duverdy 321.

to the place where they are established[1]. This seems to have been intended to apply to the enemy or neutral character of cargoes only, for the same article proceeds: "the nationality of ships does not result only from that of their owners, but also from their legitimate right to the flag which covers them," so that in the case of ships no mention is made of a house of business. So far as it goes, the rule of the Instructions was an innovation no doubt suggested by the Anglo-American doctrine presently to be mentioned; but Despagnet, § 651, says that the traditional jurisprudence of the French prize courts has not been modified by it, in support of which statement he quotes *The Joan*, Barboux, p. 104. In that case the court took occasion to reassert the old doctrine in strong terms[2], but the goods condemned were consigned to two Germans in neutral territory, *commanditaires of a Hamburg house of business*, so that the Instructions were not violated.

The Anglo-American system makes the enemy or neutral character of an individual, so far as it is important for the purpose of maritime capture, depend, not on his political nationality, but on his domicile in a peculiar sense known as trade domicile in war. At the same time it upholds the importance of the fact that a house of business is established in the enemy's country. Both these branches of the doctrine are defended on the ground that trade, whether industrial or commercial, is a source of wealth and therefore of strength to the country in which it is carried on, by the money spent there and the liability of the profits to taxation. It is not forgotten that it may also benefit another country in which the person to whom the trade or a share of it belongs is resident, and to which he may cause the profit or his share of it to be brought. And the combination of these points of view has led to a state of the authorities which is thus characterised by Wheaton. "Residence," he says, "in a neutral country will not protect [a merchant's]

[1] Barboux, p. 140.

[2] "Considering that Schräder and Böminger are both of German origin, and that in principle one does not cease to belong to a country because one resides in another with the object of trading in it; considering that in order to cease to belong to one's country one must have renounced it by the adoption of a new country, that is by naturalisation;" &c.

share in a house established in the enemy's country, though residence in the enemy's country will condemn his share in a house established in a neutral country. It is impossible not to see in this want of reciprocity strong marks of the partiality towards the interests of captors, which is perhaps inseparable from a prize code framed by judicial legislation in a belligerent country, and adopted to encourage its naval exertions[1]."

Without having or being a partner in a house of business established in a given country, a man may in that country make contracts or do other acts of a trader, not linked together otherwise than through his person. Then we have the state of facts with regard to which Lord Stowell said that "a man may have mercantile concerns in two countries, and if he acts as a merchant of both he must be liable to be considered as a subject of both, with regard to the transactions originating respectively in those countries[2]." And no greater extent, with regard to the rule now occupying us, can be given to what was said by Lord Lindley: "The subject of a state at war with this country, but who is carrying on business here or in a foreign neutral country, is not treated as an alien enemy. The validity of his contracts does not depend on his nationality, nor even on what is his real domicile, but on the place or places in which he carries on his business or businesses[3]."

[1] *Elements*, § 335 in Dana's numbering. In *The Antonia Johanna*, 1 Wheat. 159, it was held that the share of a partner in a neutral house is subject to confiscation when his own domicile is in a hostile country. And in *The Friendschaft* (*sic*), 4 Wheat. 105, it was held, following the opinion expressed by Lord Stowell in *The Portland*, 3 C. Rob. 44, 45, that the property of a house of trade established in the enemy's country is condemnable as prize, whatever may be the personal domicile of the partners. In *The Venus* Chief Justice Marshall, from whose judgment Wheaton was quoting almost literally in the passage in the text, said that it was impossible to consider Lord Stowell's judgments attentively without perceiving that his mind leant strongly in favour of captors; at the same time he called him a truly great man, and acknowledged that he showed no disposition to press his principles with peculiar severity against neutrals, as he certainly did not mitigate them when applying them to British subjects. 8 Cranch 299.

[2] In *The Jonge Klassina*, 5 C. Rob. 302.

[3] In *Janson v. Driefontein Consolidated Mines*, [1902] A. C. 505, 506. He referred to *Wells v. Williams*, 1 Raym. 282, 1 Salk. 46, in which case

What Lord Lindley here contrasts with real domicile is "trade domicile in war," and we have to account for the term "domicile" being used at all in connection with it. In the early times of admiralty law domicile was a familiar conception for the classification of persons, while the conception of nationality has only since been perfected along with that of the modern state. Hence admiralty judges used it as determining the enemy or neutral character of persons before they had any intention of building on the benefit derived to a given country by trade, and we may suppose that in England they were confirmed in that habit by the circumstance that prize causes here were usually assigned to the same persons who were judges in probate and matrimonial matters, in which the reference to domicile was constant and fundamental[1]. In later times the idea of the trader's place of residence being benefited by his trade came in to strengthen the connection, and has prevented domicile as referred to for war from following the development which domicile in its proper sense has undergone. For the former, as we have seen in the language quoted from Lord Stowell, still freely admits multiplicity as possible, which was the original character of all domicile, its importance in Roman law being limited to questions of jurisdiction and municipal burdens, of which there was no legal objection to a person's being subject to several. But when domicile became a criterion of law, as it now is in England for the age of majority and the intrinsic validity of a will of movable property, it was necessary in civil courts to assert its unity, and along with that necessity there has arisen in England a greater strictness in appreciating the residence necessary for its acquisition. The present English doctrine on that subject is that in order to acquire a domicile of choice in any country a person must intend to reside there in the most permanent manner, or reason must be shown for thinking that he would have formed such an intention if his thoughts had been

it was held by Treby, C. J., that "an alien enemy who is here in protection may [in his own name] sue his bond or contract, but an alien enemy abiding in his own country cannot sue here. And *Dier*, 2 b, pl. 8, and the other books ought to be understood so."

[1] See Part I. of this work—*Peace*—p. 205, and above, p. 50.

crystallised by the question being put to him[1]. But the utility to a country of the industry or commerce carried on in it depends on the actual seat of the occupation, and not on its probable continuance.

Hence our great admiralty judges have not taken a very strict view of the residence necessary for acquiring a trade domicile in war. "Time," said Lord Stowell, "is the grand ingredient in constituting domicile. I think that hardly enough is attributed to its effects. In most cases it is unavoidably conclusive. It is not unfrequently said that if a person comes only for a special purpose, *that* shall not fix a domicile. This is not to be taken in an unqualified latitude, and without some respect had to the time which such a purpose may or shall occupy....[Domicile] is to be taken in a compound ratio of the time and the occupation, with a great preponderance on the article of time: be the occupation what it may, it cannot happen but with few exceptions that mere length of time shall not constitute a domicile[2]." This doctrine he applied as well to residence in the British dominions as to residence in the enemy country, the effect in the former case being that a trade domicile in British territory brought the merchants having it under the British rule prohibiting trade with the enemy, and thereby exposed their property to capture no less, though for another reason, than if their trade domicile had been in enemy territory. He admitted a relaxation of the doctrine in favour of a person whom the outbreak of war surprises with a trade domicile in a foreign country, when by the date of the capture he has "put himself in motion, *bona fide*, to quit the country *sine animo revertendi*": then the commencement of his journey is equivalent to his arrival in his own country. But the majority of the Supreme Court of the United States, with the express concurrence of Justice Story though he did not sit in the case, refused to carry the relaxation further, and condemned the property of American citizens who had been caught by the outbreak of war

[1] See Westlake, *Private International Law*, 4th ed., pp. 334, 338. A domicile of choice is contrasted with the domicile of origin, usually that of the person's father, which is attributed to every one in order that no one may be without a domicile.

[2] In *The Harmony*, 2 C. Rob. 324, 325.

in 1812 with a trade domicile in England, notwithstanding their manifestation, without practical effect, of a desire to return to America[1]. Chief Justice Marshall dissented, holding that when a merchant establishes himself for trade in a foreign country, his intention is presumably to carry on that trade only so long as he can do so without violating his duty to his own country, which is no longer possible after a war has arisen between the two. "A continuance of trade after the war, unless perhaps under very special circumstances and for the mere purpose of closing transactions already commenced, would fix the national character and the domicile previously acquired. An immediate discontinuance of trade and arrangements for removing, followed by actual removal within a reasonable time, unless detained by causes which might sufficiently account for not removing, would fix the intention to change the domicile[2]," and should exempt the property from condemnation. And Lord Kingsdown must be reckoned as agreeing with the eminent chief justice, for he said, in delivering the judgment of the privy council in *The Gerasimo*, that "if a war breaks out, a foreign merchant carrying on trade in a belligerent country has a reasonable time allowed him for transferring himself and his property to another country[3]."

The determination of the enemy or neutral character of a house of business by its situation, or of a person by his trade domicile in war, leads to a question about the character of the territory where such situation or domicile exists, as being affected or not by events which have taken place in the course of the war. This was discussed at some length in the case of *The Gerasimo*[4], with reference to Moldavia, a friendly country which during the Crimean war was occupied by Russia: Dr Lushington deemed it to have acquired the enemy character, but he was reversed by the Judicial Committee, the judgment of which was pronounced by Lord Kingsdown. "What," they said, "are the circumstances necessary to convert friendly or neutral territory into

[1] *The Venus*, 8 Cranch 253.

[2] 8 Cranch 315.

[3] 11 Moore P. C. 96. The dictum was not necessary for the decision of the case.

[4] 11 Moore P. C. 88.

enemy's territory? For this purpose is it sufficient that the territory in question should be occupied by a hostile force, and subjected during its occupation to the control of the hostile power, so far as such power may think fit to exercise control, or is it necessary that, either by cession or conquest or some other means, it should either permanently or temporarily be incorporated with and form part of the dominions of the invader at the time when the question of national character arises?" The answer must be the same as for the conversion of enemy's territory into friendly or neutral, and for choosing the second of the alternatives which they put their lordships had the precedents of the French possessions in the island of St Domingo, which the lords of appeal in the cases of *The Dart* and *The Happy Couple*, in 1808, treated as still French although the insurgent negroes had established a government in them[1]—the Spanish ports in French occupation during the Peninsular war, which Lord Stowell considered would have to be deemed friendly[2]—and the Ionian Islands, which were held to be still distinct from Russia during the Russian occupation of them before the treaty of Tilsit[3], but to have become hostile after Russia had delivered them to France in 1807 by a voluntary transaction which was deemed to be equivalent to a cession by treaty. But although an old right to territory will be held to remain in force for the present purpose notwithstanding the temporary loss of its fruition, a new right will not for the same purpose change the character of territory till it has been followed by fruition. Spain ceded Louisiana to France in 1796, but France, not having the command of the sea, could not take possession, and a Louisianian ship captured by a British privateer was released as being Spanish and friendly. But the Danish island of Santa Cruz, having fallen under British possession during a war between England and Denmark, was classed by Chief Justice Marshall with "acquisitions made during war," so as to have become British

[1] Related in *The Manilla*, Edw. 3.

[2] In *The Santa Anna*, Edw. 182.

[3] *Donaldson v. Thompson*, 1 Camp. 429. Hamburg was similarly held not to have become hostile by the French occupation of it before its annexation to the Napoleonic empire: *Hagedorn v. Bell*, 1 M. and S. 450.

"to every commercial and belligerent purpose" of a war between England and the United States[1].

Lastly, if a person of European or American blood has a trade domicile or a house of business in an Eastern country under the protection of his consul, that is considered as a trade domicile or a house of business in his own country[2]. And a person having a trade domicile in any enemy country will not the less have the enemy character because he is consul there for his own neutral country[3].

Enemy Character of Ships. If a ship sails under the enemy flag, the character which her owner or any of her partowners may have as individuals is immaterial. By accepting the flag they have placed themselves under its protection: if that fails them she may be captured and will be condemned, and no share which a friend may have in her will be saved[4]. A mortgage or lien on a ship sailing under the enemy's flag, whether it arises by contract or by law as a factor's lien—unless it is a general law of the mercantile world, as that which gives the lien of freight—is treated as a part interest in the ship and is not saved from the condemnation[5].

The rule just stated with regard to mortgages and liens applies in England and the United States to cargoes as well as to ships, on the broad ground, stated by Lord Stowell, that "captors are supposed to lay their hands on the gross tangible property, on which there may be many just claims outstanding between other parties which can have no operation as to them.

[1] *Thirty Hogsheads of Sugar* (*Bentzon claimant*) *v. Boyle*, 9 Cranch 191, 195.

[2] Wheaton, *Elements*, § 333, Dana's numbering.

[3] *The Baltica*, Spinks P. C. 264.

[4] The Dutch colony of the Cape having fallen into British possession during the voyage, but before the capture, of a ship belonging to Cape merchants and bound from Batavia for Holland, Lord Stowell condemned her: *The Danckebaur Afrikaan*, 1 C. Rob. 107. This has been objected to by Hall, § 173, on the ground that the owners had lost their enemy character before the capture, but may be defended on the ground that the ship was still under the Dutch flag, by the protection of which she hoped to reach Holland.

[5] See, for France, *Le Turner*, 22 Dec. 1870, Barboux 75, in which the claim of the neutral mortgagee of a condemned ship was refused.

If such a rule did not exist, it would be quite impossible for captors to know upon what grounds they were proceeding to make any seizure." To which he added that it would be equally impossible for the court to decide on the question of property, because it could not know perfectly the laws of the different countries on which the interests claimed might depend[1]. These reasons can scarcely be deemed satisfactory, but the doctrine supported by them has been applied in numerous cases, in some of which the reasons have been eked out in a manner not more satisfactory by the assertion that, were it otherwise, *bona fide* neutral mortgagees could be found so easily that there would be an end of all prize condemnation[2].

The rule which forfeits the share or interest of a neutral in an enemy ship is sometimes presented as being one that a ship is in prize law an indivisible whole, but it does not avail in the Anglo-American system to free the share or interest of an enemy in a neutral ship from capture. Such share or interest will be confiscable, as we have seen is the case for property of an enemy embarked in a neutral house of business[3].

Further, a ship may have been transferred by enemies to friends with all the external completeness necessary by the laws of the neutral country for the grant of its flag, but the vendors may have retained an undisclosed interest, the apparent transaction being only a blind to avoid capture. In that case it is thought to be no want of respect to the flag she bears that it shall not protect her. Belligerents, conceiving themselves to have a right to all enemy property at sea, call the transaction a fraud on their rights, and the honour of the neutral state is not thought to be engaged in the protection of fraud. To cut short all tedious and often baffling investigations into such frauds, the French practice, dating as far back as the Réglement of 1694 and confirmed by that of 1778, ignores all sales of ships

[1] In *The Marianna*, 6 C. Rob. 25, 26.

[2] Miller, J., in *The Hampton*, 5 Wallace 374. In this case and *The Tobago*, 5 C. Rob. 218, and *The Battle*, 6 Wallace 498, the question arose about ships. In *The Marianna*, and *The Frances*, 8 Cranch 418, *The Ida*, Spinks Pr. Ca. 26, and *The Carlos v. Roses*, 177 U. S. 655, it arose about cargoes.

[3] *The Ariel*, 11 Mo. P. C. 119, as to liens.

by enemies not made by authentic acts previous to the declaration of war or the commencement of hostilities. The English practice lays down no rigid rule except one which it applies to cargoes as well as to ships, namely that "in case of war, either actual or imminent...a mere transfer by documents which would be sufficient to bind the parties is not sufficient to change the property as against captors, as long as the ship or goods remain *in transitu*....The true ground on which the rule rests...is that, while the ship is on the seas, the title of the vendee cannot be completed by actual delivery of the vessel or goods. The difficulty of detecting frauds if mere paper transfers are held sufficient is so great, that the courts have laid down that in order to defeat the captors the possession as well as the property must be changed before the seizure....The only question of law which can be raised is how long the *transitus* continues, and when and by what means it is terminated....It is true that in one sense the ship and goods may be said to be *in transitu* till they have reached their original port of destination, but" for the present purpose "the *transitus* ceases when the property has come into the actual possession of the transferee," as it may do by the ship's calling at an intermediate port where the transferee can take possession[1].

With regard to ships of war the British rule goes further. They are not allowed by it more than by the French rule to be sold at all during war. Even supposing that the ship of war of a belligerent has taken refuge in a neutral port and is there dismantled, her sale in that port would be incompatible with the duty of the neutral state to intern her. But if a private ship escapes pursuit by taking refuge in a neutral port, there seems to be no reason why she should not be sold while there, or why a person claiming her by a previous sale should not take possession of her there; and with this the English practice appears to agree[2].

[1] The extracts are from the judgment delivered by Lord Kingsdown on the appeal in *The Baltica*, 11 Moore P. C. 145, 146. Possibly the transferee might now obtain delivery or possession at sea by instructions to the master to hold on his behalf, communicated by wireless telegraphy.

[2] *The Minerva*, 6 C. Rob. 396; *The Georgia*, 7 Wallace 32.

When a transfer of a ship made earlier than the commencement of her voyage is presented to the court, "the circumstances attending a sale are severely scrutinised, and a transfer is not held to be good if it is subjected to any condition or even tacit understanding by which the vendor keeps an interest in the vessel or the profits, a control over it, a power of revocation, or a right to its restoration at the conclusion of the war[1]." Moreover the neutral "claimant shall be held to strict proof of ownership, and any circumstances of fraud or contrivance, or attempt at imposition on the court in striving to make out his title, shall be taken as fatal[2]." The court "looks for that correspondence and other evidence which naturally attends a transaction, accompanies it or follows it, and which when it bears upon the face of it the aspect of sincerity will always receive its due weight," rather than "to documents of a formal nature...often procured with extraordinary facility[3]." "The ship has been left in the trade and under the management of the former owner. Wherever that fact appears the court will hold it to be conclusive, because from the *evidentia rei* the strongest presumption necessarily arises that it is merely a covered and pretended transfer[4]."

Where the character of a ship sailing under a neutral flag is not open to question on the ground of any transfer, but the character of the persons who were and are her owners has changed during her voyage, it is their character at the time of the capture that will determine her fate[5].

[1] Hall, § 171. *The Ariel*, 11 Mo. P. C. 119, escaped condemnation although a part of her purchase money was left to be paid out of her earnings, because this was held on appeal not to create a lien on the ship and freight.

[2] So stated in *Bullen v. The Queen*, 11 Mo. P. C. 286. In that case Hall says, § 171, "the sale was genuine, but it had not been made to the persons who professed to be owners. Restitution was decreed, but without costs or damages."

[3] Dr Lushington in *The Soglasie*, Spinks 106.

[4] Lord Stowell in *The Jemmy*, 4 C. Rob. 31.

[5] *The Indian Chief*, 3 C. Rob. 12, was saved from condemnation by Mr Johnson's resuming his American domicile during her voyage. See what is said above, p. 147, note, about a seeming exception in the case of *The Danckebaar Afrikaan*.

Enemy character of cargoes. We have seen that the Anglo-American rule, adopted for the purpose of checking what are described as frauds on belligerent rights, is that the enemy character of property belonging to a hostile owner cannot be divested during a voyage by transfer to a neutral owner. It is a rule of prize law, opposed to the common law which allows transfers of property *in transitu.* A similar invalidity is asserted for a transfer made before the outbreak of the war, where consequently there could be no hostile owner at its date, if "in the clear expectation of both the contracting parties" the state to which the transferor belongs is "likely to become a belligerent before the arrival of the property which is made the subject of their agreement[1]." And a further Anglo-American prize rule lays down that "property going to be delivered in the enemy's country, and under a contract to become the property of the enemy immediately on arrival, if taken *in transitu* is to be considered as enemies' property. When the contract is made in time of peace or without any contemplation of a war, no such rule exists." This rule is saved from being opposed to the common law by the principle that "capture is considered as delivery: the captors by the rights of war stand in the place of the enemy[2]."

In France the *réglement* of 26 July 1778, arts. 2 and 11,

[1] *The Vrouw Margaretha,* 1 C. Rob. 336; *The Jan Frederick,* 5 C. Rob. 128—the words between inverted commas in the text are from Lord Stowell's judgment in this case; *The Ann Green,* 1 Gallison 274, judgment delivered by Story.

[2] The words in the text between inverted commas are from the judgment of the lords in *The Sally,* 3 C. Rob. 300, note. "The ordinary state of commerce is that goods ordered and delivered to the master are considered as delivered to the consignee, whose agent the master is in this respect; but," apart from the prize rule now under consideration, "there would unquestionably be nothing illegal in contracting that the whole risk should fall on the consignor till the goods came into possession of the consignee....If" in those circumstances, as a consequence of the capture, "the consignee refuses payment and throws" the loss "upon the shipper, the shipper must be supposed to have guarded his own interests against that hazard, or he has acted improvidently and without caution." This quotation is from Lord Stowell's judgment in *The Packet de Bilboa,* 2 C. Rob. 133. See also *The Anna Catherina,* 4 C. Rob. 107, and *The San José Indiano,* 2 Gallison 268.

provides that the neutrality of goods can be proved only by the documents on board. Apparently this must have a similar effect to the English rule ignoring the transfer *in transitu* of enemy property to neutrals, for the documents relating to what had occurred during the voyage would not be on board. But it is said that "goods sent by a neutral to a person of enemy nationality, with an agreement that their property shall pass to the latter only on delivery, are not subject to capture, with a reservation of the due appreciation of the frauds possible in such agreements[1]."

It is an Anglo-American rule that "the possession of the soil does impress upon the owner the character of the country, as far as the produce of that plantation is concerned, in its transportation to any other country, whatever the local residence of the owner may be[2]"; the consequence being that "the produce of a person's own plantation in the colony of the enemy, though shipped in time of peace, is liable to be considered as the property of the enemy[3]." The produce becomes safe from capture when sold to a friend, but is subject to capture as long as it remains the property of the owner of the soil. This is only a particular application of the doctrine which asserts the enemy character of property connected with a house of business in enemy territory, for agriculture is a business, though it is sometimes mentioned as a special rule based on some inherent tie between the soil and its produce. If during the war the other belligerent has occupied the locality in so stable a manner that its own trade with it is free, notwithstanding that there has not been cession or conquest, a third power at war with the occupying belligerent will treat the locality as a possession of its enemy, and apply the rule to justify the capture of its produce while the property of the owner who is politically its friend[4].

[1] Despagnet, § 651, quoting *The Laura-Louise*, Barboux, p. 120, in which the goods comprised in the bills of lading numbered 1, 2, 3 and 8 seem to be those referred to.

[2] Lord Stowell in *The Phœnix*, 5 C. Rob. 21, where it is stated to be an old rule, "no longer open to discussion."

[3] Lord Stowell in *The Vrow Anna Catharina*, 5 C. Rob. 167.

[4] *Thirty Hogsheads of Sugar* (*Bentzon claimant*) *v. Boyle*, 9 Cranch 191.

Enemy Character of a Ship by reason of her Service. A ship which by the criterions of character thus far discussed would be classed as neutral will be treated as hostile if she is engaged in the enemy's service. This will be the case if she is employed as a transport, as was *The Friendship*, 6 C. Rob. 420. Another example of that service, belonging not to the precedents of courts but to history, is that of the *Kow-shing*, whose British owners chartered her to the Chinese government for the carriage of troops to Korea. While so employed she was sunk by the Japanese in the first action of their war with China, which ensued on the subject of their respective relations to Korea[1]. An analogous case was that of *The Orozembo*, 6 C. Rob. 430, a neutral-owned ship hired in a neutral port by the agent of a belligerent, and employed in carrying three military and two civil officers of the latter to one of his colonies. In condemning her Lord Stowell refused to make a distinction on the ground of the small number of persons carried. Indeed the case was essentially different from that of persons being carried as passengers who fall within the description of contraband or analogues of contraband, with which we shall have to deal in explaining the laws of neutrality. The ship herself had passed into enemy service, which was enough for her condemnation whatever use the enemy had made of her.

In cases of this class if the owner or his agent is unaware of the fact that the hirer of the ship is an agent of the belligerent government, or if that government impresses the ship into its service by violence, the practice has been that she will not the less be condemned. Lord Stowell said in *The Orozembo*: "It will be sufficient if there is an injury arising to the belligerent from the employment in which the vessel is found....If imposition has been practised it operates as force; and if redress in the way of indemnification is to be sought against any person, it must be against those who have, by means either of compulsion or deceit, exposed the property to danger;...otherwise such opportunities of conveyance would be constantly used, and it would be almost impossible, in the greater number of cases, to prove the knowledge and privity of the immediate offender." And on

[1] See above, p. 25.

these principles he condemned *The Carolina*, 4 C. Rob. 256, on facts which, speaking of that case in *The Orozembo*, he thus summed up: "There was no *mens rea* in the owner or in any other person acting under his authority. The master was an involuntary agent, acting under compulsion put upon him by the officers of the French government, and, so far as intention alone is considered, perfectly innocent." Wheaton quotes this doctrine with acquiescence[1], but we agree with Hall, who says: "It is no doubt proper to throw upon the neutral the onus of proving his innocence, and to sift the evidence which he produces with the most jealous suspicion; but to punish him for the act of another person, of which he has been the unwilling or unconscious subject, is as useless as it is wrong. The belligerent cannot be intimidated by losses inflicted on his victim[2]."

Various Points of Prize Law.

Privateers. A privateer was a privately owned ship, furnished with a commission of war empowering her to carry on or act in all warlike operations, but usually confining herself to action against commerce, and commanded by officers appointed by her owners, who were however subject to be controlled by the commanders of public ships of war sailing under the same flag. Her commission was called a letter of marque, the origin of which name we have seen to have been connected with the system of reprisals[3], and her action was a part of the general reprisals which survived as an accompaniment of war; but it had the private gain of her owners as its motive, the gain made by such reprisals never being applied to the redress of the injuries deemed to have provoked the war. The first article of the Declaration of Paris in 1856 ran that "privateering is and remains abolished," but the United States declined to adhere to it on the ground that, so long as the private property of enemies remains capturable at sea, it would operate unfairly towards powers not maintaining large public navies. As between the powers which have subscribed to the Declaration, light has been thrown on its precise meaning by the regulations respectively

[1] *Elements*, § 502, Dana's numbering.

[2] § 249, note.

[3] Above, p. 9.

made for the Russian volunteer fleet, the mail steamers subsidised by this and other states, and the volunteer fleet contemplated by Prussia in 1870. None of those regulations having excited any serious remonstrance, there appears to be an understanding that what is prohibited is not the use in war of privately owned ships under commanders at least temporarily belonging to the public navy, but the combination of private ownership with private command. Privateers presenting that combination have not been employed since 1856, even by the few powers which have not adhered to the Declaration. *The Alabama* and her consorts which devastated the commerce of the United States during the great civil war were public ships of the Conferate States' navy.

Freight. We have seen the rules of the Consolat del Mar as to the freight payable in cases of maritime capture[1]. With that concerning the freight payable to a neutral shipowner for the carriage of enemy's goods we need not concern ourselves, the capture of enemy's goods under the neutral flag having been abolished[2]. The rule that the neutral owner of goods found on board a captured enemy's ship could get them only on paying the freight which would have been earned by carrying them to their destination was plainly unjust, as was pointed out by Bynkershoek[3]. It has accordingly been decided that the captor can claim the freight only when he has performed the contract of the ship, and is even then liable to have any damage which he has done to the property, or caused by his misconduct, set off[4].

[1] Above, p. 121.

[2] It may be stated that in England the neutral's lien for his freight was held to be prior to the captor's expenses, except when the ship was plying between ports of allied enemies. Where the voyage was between ports of the opposed belligerents, the captor was allowed priority for his law but not for his other expenses. *The Vrow Henrica,* 4 C. Rob. 343. And where the ship was hired for a gross sum, the captured enemy's goods were adjudged to bear only their proportion of that sum: *The Antonia Johanna,* 1 Wheaton 159.

[3] *Quæstiones Juris Publici,* l. 1, c. 13.

[4] *The Vreyheid,* decided in 1784 by the lords of appeal, as mentioned by Lord Stowell in *The Fortuna,* 4 C. Rob. 278, in which his lordship quoted Bynkershoek.

Recapture. Recapture, to which rescue as a technical term is equivalent[1], is when a ship captured by the enemy and in his power, not necessarily in his actual possession[2], is retaken by her compatriots. The question then arises whether she shall be restored to her original owner, by an application of the Roman doctrine (*postliminium*) which treated men and things recovered from the enemy as restored to their pristine condition, a reward being allowed to the recaptor as salvage, or whether she shall become the property of the recaptor, the original owner being deemed to have lost his property by her misadventure. We have seen that the Consolat del Mar adopted the latter solution[3], on condition that the first captor had brought the ship to a place of safety, *intra* or *infra præsidia* as it is expressed in subsequent technical language, which in the time of the Consolat would scarcely happen unless she had been brought to a port of the captor's country, but in the times of more developed navies might happen by her being brought within the protection of a fleet. The principle was that in order to change the property the possession resulting from the capture must be what is often described as firm, and this it was sometimes thought that the possession had not been when the recapture was immediate, although the ship had been brought *intra præsidia.* Hence it became a widely accepted rule that the original owner did not lose his right until the ship had been in the enemy's possession for twenty-four hours or during a night (*pernoctatio*)[4]. Again, after condemnation in a prize court of the enemy the ship might be taken from her new owner, whether the original captor or another, but could not be retaken

[1] *Recousse vient de* recutere, *rescousse de* reexcutere; *ces deux termes sont équipollents et signifient reprendre*: 2 Rivier 357.

[2] Wheaton, *Elements*, § 381, Dana's numbering. He quotes *The Edward and Mary*, 3 C. Rob. 305, where the captors had been prevented by the weather from sending a boat on board the prize, and *The Pensamento Feliz*, Edw. 115, where the recapture consisted in bringing a vessel out of a hostile harbour, in which however she had not been seized.

[3] Above, p. 121.

[4] Grotius, 3, 6, 3. He connects the rule of the Consolat with that of the Roman *postliminium*, by which a citizen lost his rights on being brought *intra præsidia* of the enemy, and recovered them on being brought back *intra præsidia* of Rome or her forces. Pomponius in Dig. 49, 15, 5. To

from the original captor as such, being no longer in his possession or power as such; whence it was easy to lay down condemnation as the dividing line up to which, and not beyond which, recapture for the benefit of the original owner was possible. Thus there were several systems, adopted in different countries, which limited the right of the original owner, that practised in England being the one which drew the line at condemnation[1]. But in 1786 a British act of parliament, adopting the principle of postliminy, extended the right of the original owner without limitation, the recaptors being entitled, even after the condemnation of the ship, only to salvage, fixed for ships of the navy at an eighth of the value and for privateers at a sixth; only if the ship had been "set forth by the enemy as a ship of war," she was to be the prize of the recaptors. This was re-enacted by the Naval Prize Act 1864, s. 40, with the omission of what related to privateers, which had become unnecessary, and with the provision that "where the recapture is made under circumstances of special difficulty or danger," the prize court may increase the "prize salvage" to a fourth of the value as the maximum; also the case for ousting the original owner being expressed as that when the ship has been "set forth or used" by the enemy as a ship of war. The United States act of congress of 3 March 1800 maintained the rule which drew the line between the original owner and the recaptor at condemnation, but where the ship had been "set forth and armed" as one of war it did not oust the original owner, only increased the amount payable as salvage. In France, where the twenty-four hours rule was formerly practised, the Instructions of 1870, Art. 11, maintain the right of the original owner of a rescued national ship without limit, but provide that neutral ships taken

the twenty-four hours rule Grotius attributes a German origin, quoting a Lombard law about a wounded beast, and citing Albericus Gentilis (Hisp. Adv., l. 1, c. 3) for its observance in England and Castile. Gentilis treats the common military opinion as being to the same effect. If he is right about the English rule of his time, it must have afterwards been changed.

[1] Wheaton states this; *Elements*, § 373, Dana's numbering; and it is implied in the United States act of 1800; but see Gentilis as referred to in the last note.

by the enemy, which have been more than twenty-four hours in his possession, are to be treated as enemy ships, unless in exceptional circumstances, to be appreciated by the government. The right of the original owner is also maintained without limit by the Prize Code of the Institute of International Law[1].

It may happen that the ship or goods of neutrals or other friends are recaptured. Their country may, either as an ally or separately, be at war with the same country with which we are at war, and their property may be taken by the cruisers of that country and recovered by ours. Or they may be carrying to us what our enemy captures as contraband of war, and our cruisers may recover it. And there may be other cases. Lord Stowell decided that, having regard to the diversity of the rules which are applied in different countries to the question of property between the original owner and the recaptor, he must apply the rule on that question of the country to which the recaptured property belongs, or if there should exist a country in which no such rule prevails, then the English rule[2]. If the property is adjudged to the original owner, then no salvage is due for the recapture of friend's goods which must have been liberated by our enemy's prize court if they had been carried there. But if it must be supposed that they would have been condemned by our enemy, either lawfully or because he notoriously violates international law, a service is rendered by the recapture and salvage must be paid[3].

Ransom Bills. When an enemy ship is ransomed by her captor, a ransom bill is given by her master, in which are expressed the conditions under which she is allowed to pursue her voyage without liability to molestation by any ship of her captor's or an allied nationality which she may meet, and the sum to be given for the permission. He also surrenders a hostage, who "has a right of action in the courts of his own

[1] Arts. 119–122, 9 *Annuaire* 242.

[2] *The Santa Cruz*, 1. C. Rob. 49.

[3] Wheaton, *Elements*, §§ 364–6, Dana's numbering; where it is shown that both the British and United States prize courts acted on these principles during the wars of the French revolution and first empire.

country against the master, and against the owners of the ship and cargo, to compel them to perform the conditions of the contract under which their property has been restored to them, and the due performance of which is a necessary condition for the recovery of his freedom[1]." And it is by the use of this right of the hostage that the captor has most commonly in England obtained payment of the ransom, his direct right to do so by suit on the bill being questioned on the ground of his enemy character[2].

By the Naval Prize Act 1864, s. 45, following a policy maintained by parliament from 1782, the king in council can

[1] The words are from 2 Twiss 358.

[2] The captor was allowed to recover in his own name in *Ricord v. Bettenham*, 3 Burrow 1734, and by Lord Mansfield in *Cornu v. Blackburne*, 2 Dougl. 640; but this was refused in *Anthon v. Fisher*, Dougl. 649, note, and Lord Stowell stated the law to the latter effect, in *The Hoop*, 1 C. Rob. 201. In the United States an enemy recovered in his own name on a ransom bill in *Goodrich v. Gordon*, 15 Johnson 6. In *Crawford v. The William Penn*—Peters, Circuit Court, 106; Scott 580—an alien enemy was allowed to sue in his own name on a bottomry bond given for advances made to a cartel ship, and Washington, J., after quoting *Cornu v. Blackburne* and *Anthon v. Fisher*, said: "The case of a ransom bond is very different from that of a contract arising out of a licensed trade. In the former the hostile character of the obligee is in no respect removed, on the contrary it is an act of hostility which gives rise to it. In the latter case the hostile character of the party with whom the contract is made does not attach either to him or to the contract. 'He is to be regarded,' in the words of Lord Ellenborough, 'virtually as an adopted subject of Great Britain, and his trade as British trade.'...It must nevertheless be acknowledged that in the case of *Kensington v. Inglis*, 8 East 273, the court seemed to be of opinion that, even in the case of a licensed trade, the suit cannot be maintained in the name of the alien enemy." In truth, between (1) the contracts of an enemy by nationality who, being resident in the country under express or implied permission, is a friend by the doctrine of trade domicile in war; (2) contracts of an alien enemy entered into under a license to trade; and (3) ransom bills; there may be drawn graduated distinctions, not perhaps imperceptible, but which it may be hoped that in future English judges will sweep away, allowing in every case suit in the name of the person who is allowed to contract, as is regularly done elsewhere in Europe and, it is believed, in the United States. With reference to (1) see above, pp. 50, 51, and the citation from Lord Lindley with the note on it, above, p. 142. And with reference to (2), see above, p. 139.

make such orders as he thinks fit for prohibiting or allowing the ransom of British ships taken by the enemy, and any one ransoming or contracting to ransom any ship or goods in contravention of any such order in council may be fined by the court of admiralty, in any sum not exceeding £500. By the same section all contracts and securities for ransom are placed under the exclusive jurisdiction of the court of admiralty as a prize court.

CHAPTER VII.

NEUTRALITY.

The Theory of Neutrality.

A STATE is neutral when there is a war and it is not in a state of war with either belligerent. If its conduct is unbecoming to that condition, even if it uses violence in favour of one of the belligerents, these are violations of the duties incumbent on neutrals, but its condition is still that of neutrality so long as neither its own choice nor that of the belligerent whom it has provoked has placed it in the legal condition of being at war[1]. The fact of neutrality is as old as war, but the technical term from that root is not traced by Nys further back than to treaties and edicts drawn up in French at the close of the fifteenth century, before which time we have *stille sitzen*, to sit still—*unpartyschung*, impartiality—*guerræ abstinentia*, abstinence from the war—and, especially with regard to naval war, to be *in treuga*, in truce, *in pace*, or simply a friend, *amicus*. But, once introduced, *neutralité* with the words from the same root in Latin, Italian and German were freely used, so that only their desire to maintain classical Latin caused Grotius to write *in bello medii* and Bynkershoek *non hostes*[2].

In considering the duties which are incumbent on neutrals it is important to bear in mind that they exist only so long as the neutrality is maintained. There is no general duty of maintaining the condition of neutrality. On the contrary, the general duty of every member of a society is to promote justice within it, and peace only on the footing of justice, such being

[1] See above, p. 2, for war not being set up by were acts of force without the will to set it up.

[2] Nys, *Le Droit International*, t. 3, pp. 559, 560.

the peace which alone is of much value or likely to be durable. Thus in a state the man would be a bad citizen who allowed a crime to be committed before his eyes without doing his best to prevent it, or who refused to assist the magistrates in punishing crime; and in the society of states the action of all the members in upholding its laws is the more required since an organised government is wanting. Grotius was so convinced of the evil character of studied aloofness that, as we shall see, he allowed that conviction to affect his view of the conduct to be observed by third states even while maintaining their neutrality. The general voice has not been with him to that extent, although belligerents often claim that the justice of their cause entitles them to what they call a benevolent neutrality. Bentham laid down that "a disinterested legislator would regard as a positive crime every proceeding by which a given nation should do more injury to foreign nations collectively, whose interests might be affected, than it should do good to itself.......In the same manner he would regard as a negative offence every determination by which the given nation should refuse to render positive services to a foreign nation, when rendering them would produce more good to such foreign nation than it would produce evil to itself[1]." And Lorimer has defined the cases in which neutrality is justifiable as those in which the third state has no sufficient knowledge of the merits of the quarrel, or in which it "may, from the limited character of its own resources, from its inability to secure allies, from its geographical position or other causes, be totally incapable of affecting the war one way or the other, or may be capable of affecting it only at a greater probable loss to itself than gain to the belligerent whom it knows to be in the right[2]." We may sum up by saying that neutrality is not morally justifiable unless intervention in the war is unlikely to promote justice, or could do so only at a ruinous cost to the neutral.

The duties which are incumbent on neutrals so long as they continue to be in the legal condition of neutrality are mainly founded on the importance, in international as in all other relations, of a frank sincerity. Indeed that quality is more important in international than in other relations, because states

[1] *Principles of International Law, Essay* 1.

[2] *Institutes of the Law of Nations*, vol. 2, pp. 127, 128.

over which there is no sovereign power must look chiefly to themselves for their security, and if they were harassed by doubts as to the conduct to be expected from powers not openly hostile, their situation would be so confused that they would often feel compelled to extend the area of war in a manner really needless. The reason which condemns the sudden commencement of a war which nothing had foreshadowed, namely the necessity for the sake of good order that states shall know how they stand with regard to one another, demands a loyal abstinence from real participation in a war on the part of all those who do not avowedly participate in it[1]. And the argument applies equally to the conduct which ought to be observed by states in presence of an armed civil dissension amounting to war in one of them. Neither friendship for the government which is attacked nor sympathy with the cause defended by the insurgents can justify a foreign state in a benevolent neutrality towards either, as soon as the contest has assumed such dimensions or is waged under such conditions that it can no longer be ignored as war. Civil combatants as well as international ones have a right to know how things stand with regard to every one. The duties which on the principle of avoiding all real participation in the war arise for states holding the legal condition of neutrality and their subjects, and the conduct to be observed by them, are called neutral duties and conduct.

In order to pass from the principle to rules it is necessary to seek as clear an understanding as possible of what is real participation in war, and we should launch into a vagueness productive of controversy rather than of enlightenment if we carried that notion further than participation in a specific operation of war. Hence,

Neutrality enjoins abstinence from taking part in any operation of war, and from interfering with any operation of war which is legitimate as between the belligerents, but not abstinence from any thing merely because it strengthens a belligerent.

For instance, siege being a legitimate operation of war as between the belligerents, neutrality enjoins abstinence from introducing supplies into any place which is under siege, but it

[1] There must not be *une neutralité frauduleuse, dont personne ne veut être la dupe*: Vattel, l. 3, § 104.

does not enjoin abstinence from general commerce with either belligerent, although commerce enriches and therefore strengthens those with whom it is carried on. For instance again,

A neutral state must not permit either its subjects or a belligerent to make any such use of its territory as amounts to taking part in an operation of war; a maxim which is comprised in the former one, since a state is necessarily a party to the use which it allows to be made of its territory, but which is so important as to deserve separate statement[1].

But a moment's reflection will show that, true as these statements are, they are not sufficient to remove all difficulties. When blockade is declared of a port which is not besieged, or of a line of coast not too extensive to be effectively watched but on which a landing is not being attempted, what military operation, legitimate as between the belligerents, is proceeding, with which it would be a breach of neutral duty to interfere? What is being done in that case is that a blow is being struck at the enemy's general commerce, and that neutrals are asked not to interfere with that blow, so long as their flag is not excluded from a larger area than that from which it is possible to exclude the enemy's flag also. Now this may be a good argument while the capture of enemy property at sea is maintained, but it would fall to the ground if the destruction of the enemy's commerce were decreed not to be a legitimate operation of naval war as between belligerents; and yet the demand for the abolition of the capture of enemy property at sea has not been accompanied, at least to any great extent, by a demand for restricting blockade to besieged ports. Again, it may be conceded that carrying arms or ammunition with destination to a belligerent port is taking part in an operation of war which is being prepared at that port, but is it clear that carrying arms or

[1] *L'état neutre désireux de demeurer en paix et amitié avec les belligérants, et de jouir des droits de la neutralité, a le devoir de s'abstenir de prendre à la guerre une part quelconque, par la prestation de secours militaires à l'un des belligérants ou à tous les deux, et de veiller à ce que son territoire ne serve de centre d'organisation ou de point de départ à des expéditions hostiles contre l'un d'eux ou contre tous les deux.* Resolution of the Institute of International Law, 30 August 1875, 1 *Annuaire* 139; *Tableau Général* 1873–1892, p. 162.

ammunition with destination to a belligerent country is taking part in every operation of war which may be afterwards prepared in that country? Or is it not rather a part of general commerce, whenever its connection with a particular operation cannot be pointed out? Evidently the distinction between general commerce and taking part in operations of war or interfering with them, if it is not to be made the starting point of unsatisfactory controversies, must be supplemented by positive rules, owing their obligatory force to general consent. Such are, among others, the rules relating to blockade and the carriage of contraband of war. So also rules are needed to distinguish the things done in a territory which do and do not amount to making use of it for a warlike operation. So far as rules have not been established either by express convention or by practice sufficiently constant to imply consent, neither neutrals nor belligerents can or ought to be prevented from invoking the fundamental principles of the subject, by whatever name they describe them, natural law, *droit primitif*, or justice. And there is no greater need in international law than to bring further parts of the doctrine of neutrality under the dominion of acknowledged rules.

The subject of neutral duties, especially in what concerns naval war, has often been presented as one of conflicting rights. The neutral, it is said, has a right to pursue his commerce as in time of peace, the belligerent has a right which is represented as one of self-preservation, although defeat in war is not necessarily inconsistent with self-preservation; and it is said that the latter is of a higher nature and must prevail[1]. The attempt to establish an order of precedence between these rights in the belligerent's favour, illogical as it is if the terms compared are really rights, betrays a suspicion that the rules which have received general consent lean a little to the belligerent's side, as probably they would be found to do if it were worth while to work them out from abstract considerations. The party who has arms in his hands is in a better position for bargaining than the party who, if he will not concede something, must undergo the painful

[1] *Jus commerciorum æquum est, at hoc æquius tuendæ salutis; est illud gentium jus, hoc naturæ est; est illud privatorum, est hoc regnorum.* Albericus Gentilis, *De jure belli*, l. 1, c. 21.

transition from a state of peace to one of war. In truth the case illustrates the difficulty of starting, in the construction of an ideal or so-called natural system of law, from rights to be secured to the individual man or state. The aggregate possibilities of enjoyment which any such system can furnish are inadequate to meet the demands made on them in the name of rights, and yet no right which has been recognised as primary can consistently be asked to give way to others. The very notion of a precedence among rights supposes some standard by which to judge them, lying deeper than the so-called rights and excluding them from a really primary position. And the result of a system placed on such a basis can only be a working compromise between demands, reached with reference at once to their justice and to the forces behind them, but veiled under a philosophically sounding nomenclature of rights[1].

When a positive rule of international law treats any conduct of a state as incompatible with the duties of neutrality, in a word as unneutral, it binds all the subjects of that state not to contribute to such conduct. But a positive rule of international law may treat certain conduct of an individual as unneutral, allowing the injured belligerent to repress it by action on the individual wherever such action is possible without violating neutral territory, and precluding his neutral state from defending him against such repression, while that state is not called on to join in the repression. This is the case with the rules relating to blockade and contraband of war, which the injured belligerent enforces by action at sea, not to be resented by the state of the offender so long as it is within acknowledged rules, at the same time that states not only do not punish blockade-running and the traffic in contraband but even enforce judicially contracts made for those purposes. The position of an individual who leaves his country in order to enter belligerent service is similar, the other belligerent being entitled to treat him as an unprotected enemy, while no demand is made on neutral states for more than the prevention of such enlistment on their territory as would amount to an unneutral use of it. On such cases

[1] See the section on *The alleged Inherent Rights of States* in the first part of this work—*Peace*—pp. 293-6.

however the question is often raised whether the neutral state's admission that it must not protect its subjects is not such an admission of the wrongfulness of his act as, if carried out to its logical consequences, would require it to prohibit the act and as far as possible prevent it. And it is sometimes further questioned whether the rule which obliges the neutral state to acquiesce in the belligerent's dealing with its offending subject outside neutral territory, even coupled with the general practice of not demanding active repression from that state, amounts to a renunciation of the right to demand such active repression. To these questions it appears to be a sufficient answer that the existing rules as to neutral duties embody a compromise, and that a compromise, unlike a principle, can have no logical consequences; also that where written law or convention is wanting the terms of a compromise must be sought in a practice sufficiently constant to imply consent, and not less in the practice of not demanding active repression by neutral states, because it is negative, than in the positive practice of repression by belligerents outside neutral territory. We therefore, in accordance with the general opinion, hold that a neutral state is not bound by actual international law to prohibit the export of contraband or to take any analogous action in any of the cases now under consideration. But since the opposite opinion is maintained by some jurists, and fits in with the demands sometimes made by belligerents for a benevolent neutrality, it cannot be dismissed without further mention.

"In the society of nations," says Kleen, one of the most eminent of the jurists referred to, "all neutral rights and duties pass through the state as intermediary, the state being the party immediately responsible and having rights." "Every violation of the neutrality of a citizen is at the same time a violation of the neutrality of the state." "Even when international law authorises private persons to act at their risk and peril without directly engaging the responsibility of the state (for instance, according to present usage, in the matters of contraband and blockade), it is always the state which is finally responsible, so that the belligerent *can* claim from the government of the neutral individual that it shall take measures both to prevent the violation of neutrality and to secure its maintenance, by using its coercive power over its subjects, and demand indemnity if the case requires it[1]." This is an example of the efforts to eliminate individuals from the theory even of those international relations in which they are practically concerned, which date from Rousseau's assertion that states and men are things of such different natures that no true relation can be established between them[2]. The European states which have colonial possessions know well that relations of enmity and neutrality exist between them and natives having nothing which can be treated as state life, with whom therefore they can only deal as with men to be treated with justice. If states please to arrange the duties of neutrality on a footing which allows them to leave their subjects in certain cases face to face with foreign powers, there is merely another instance of a similar kind. Impossibility in fact there is none, and to assert an impossibility in theory, to say that an individual so left to himself is incapable of interfering in a war, and that his acts can receive no legal qualification unless they are first carried up to his state and then down again to himself, is purely arbitrary. It remains true that international law is the law of states, but there is no solid reason why states should not agree by such law that the responsibility for certain acts and their repression shall rest with the individual and the state directly concerned. The only real question is whether they have done so, and of this the proof is similar in its character and equal in its cogency to that of many other international rules.

Starting from the theoretical side, we have arrived at this, that the duties of neutrals flow from the principle that they ought to avoid acts of war as long as they decline to enter on a state of war; that the hopelessness of a complete agreement on theoretical grounds between belligerents and neutrals, as to what are acts of war, makes positive rules imperatively necessary; that to a large extent such rules exist; and that some of them, for the sake of peace, throw exclusively on individuals the duties which they prescribe and the responsibility for failure in those duties, recognising in belligerents, to the extent permitted by

[1] Kleen, *Lois et Usages de la Neutralité*, t. 1, pp. 135, 133, 136. "Can" (*peut*) is in italics in the original.

[2] See above, p. 37.

the rules in question, their right of acting directly against all who interfere with their wars without state authority at their back. We have now to trace the development of the subject historically.

History of the Theory of Neutrality.

We have seen something of the mediæval attitude towards neutrality in speaking of the fate experienced by neutral cargoes and ships when involved with enemy ships and cargoes in belligerent captures. The pride and confidence in naval strength which prompted the governments of France and England, and in some measure the Hanse Towns, to reject on that question the rules of the trading communities expressed in the Consolat del Mar, showed themselves as well in other parts of what may be described as the demand that friends should be supporters and not mere spectators. To that demand there also contributed, in countries steeped in feudal ideas, a real difficulty in conceiving any political relations not personal to the rulers, or any personal relations at all not going the full length either of enmity or of declared sympathy if not of alliance. The treaty of 1303 between England and France provided that the enemies of the one should not have from the lands or dominions of the other comfort, succour or aid, whether of armed men or of victuals *or of other things whatever they might be*[1]. Later, neutral trade is denounced in less sweeping terms, but the neutral ruler is induced to lend his own law for its suppression. By a treaty of 1370 the Count of Flanders promises England to take certain measures for preventing his subjects from carrying enemy's goods, and from supplying the enemy with arms, artillery and victuals: the Flemings are then to pass without detention. In case of transgression the count shall have their goods and the punishment of their bodies, but the enemy's goods, and the arms, artillery or victuals being carried to the enemy, shall belong to the King of England and shall be delivered to his agent[2]. Later still, the language of treaties begins to be cut

[1] 2 Rymer, *Fœdera* 927.

[2] 6 Rymer, *Fœdera* 659. By the treaty of 1426, 10 Rymer, *Fœdera* 363, the Duke of Burgundy again promised England to prevent his subjects from carrying enemy's goods, but they were to be believed on their oath.

down by interpretation. Thus, the Scotch being bound by treaties not to minister any kind of aid to the enemies of England, the English government in 1543 claimed that they were thereby prohibited from trading to France in fish, as being victuals, while the Scotch government maintained that the treaties were not broken if their and the enemy's merchants continued their accustomed traffic with such merchandise as they had been used to transport to other countries in time of peace[1].

Besides treaties, the opinions and practice of the different powers as to the restrictions to which they could claim the submission of neutrals found expression in unilateral acts, such as general ordinances, notifications[2], and special instructions to their officers and prize courts. Such were the French ordinance of 1543, giving an enumeration of prohibited articles not including victuals, and the English orders in council of 1587, that some ships at Falmouth should not be allowed to sail if "laden with Spanish preparations, munitions or victuals[3]"—of 1591, that goods "manifestly of the proper natures of victuals and munitions" were to be condemned[4]—and of 1592, directing a sentence by way of compromise in certain pending prize cases because the previous understanding of the law was not clear, but providing for the future that any sort of material fit for sails or for "apparel of men's bodies," though only sometimes and not commonly used for sails, should fall under the prohibition of canvas[5]. Such also was the resolution (*placaat*) of 1599 which the Dutch states-general, whose pretensions equalled those of a feudal sovereign, "made known to all kings and nations, whereby they forbade all merchants to carry to the Spaniards provisions *or any other goods whatsoever*, under the penalty of being treated as enemies[6]." And such again was the *placaat* of the states-general in 1630, by which they declared that the whole coast of

[1] Sir Ralph Sadler's *Letters and Negotiations in Scotland*, p. 381; 2 Twiss 246.

[2] We have had occasion to refer to such notifications or *significationes*, above, p. 125.

[3] Marsden, *Six Centuries of the Admiralty Court*, 67 Nautical Magazine 394.

[4] Ib. 447.

[5] Ib. 448.

[6] 2 Twiss 247, quoting Grotius, *Hist. de Rebus Belgicis*, l. 8.

Flanders should be deemed to be under blockade, on the strength of an opinion which they had obtained from the admiralty of Amsterdam that "the rule which obtains in the case of towns, which are properly said to be besieged, and which has with good reason been applied to camps, which are as it were besieged, extends also to the enemy's ports, which when invested by ships are deemed to be besieged[1]." These acts were objectionable so far as they attempted to enforce on neutrals any restrictions not grounded in reason, but they cannot be objected to for their unilateral character, since where no positive rules have become binding by international consent, which was certainly the case at their dates, belligerents cannot be refused the right of taking their stand on the principle that neutrals ought not to participate in a war, and of interpreting that principle as their conscience dictates. At the time, unilateral acts of the nature of those which have been described appear to have carried greater weight even in determining the law than we should now be disposed to concede to similar ones. They had been considered by statesmen before they were issued, and there were few or no independent writers. Hence they attracted to themselves something of that respect which, during the two centuries following Grotius, was attributed to the eminent international jurists whose line he so magnificently inaugurated, and who, whatever their learning or their sincerity, were after all the nationals of some country or other. To this it must be added that even when a unilateral prohibition was in contradiction with the pronouncement of some other state, as we have seen was the case in the article of victuals, the sovereign who uttered it stood in the ideas of the time so immeasurably above the private person on whom he enforced it that the latter, although of another nation, seemed in infringing it to be guilty of an audacity almost wicked[2].

[1] Bynkershoek, *Quæstiones Juris Publici*, i, 11. He mentions the belief that the same opinion had been obtained from private lawyers.

[2] "Albericus Gentilis lays great stress on the fact that Queen Elizabeth had notified to the Hanse confederation not to carry provisions into Spain before she captured their vessels (*Hisp. Adv.*, l. 1, c. 20). And the Protestants are represented by De Thou to have replied to the complaints of the Portuguese, by reason of twenty-five Portuguese vessels having

The mediæval welter of ideas and facts with regard to neutral commerce, which during the sixteenth century was tending to clear itself, may be said to have come to an end with the treaty of Southampton in 1625 and the *placaat* of 1630 above mentioned. The former introduced for contraband and the latter for blockade the period in which we now live, namely one in which these two departments of maritime international law stand out as the subject of positive rules, covering a great area though not even yet completely settled, while outside them neutral maritime commerce is free from belligerent interference. At the same time, as the European monarchies were being defined and consolidated, a class of questions began to come into prominence relating less to the action of individuals than to the public political conduct of states on land as well as at sea. Grotius, whose great work *De jure belli ac pacis* was published in the year of the treaty of Southampton, wrote that "the duty of those who keep aloof from a war is to do nothing by which the one whose cause is bad may be strengthened, or the movements of him who is engaged in a just war may be impeded, but in a doubtful case to treat the two parties equally in allowing passage, in furnishing supplies to their armies, and in abstaining from the relief of besieged forces[1]." Here, failing the benevolent neutrality in favour of the most worthy which Grotius taught as the better part, the standard set up is equality of treatment in the sense of permitting or furnishing to both belligerents the same things which are permitted or furnished to either, without regard to the fact that the passage of troops through neutral territory, coaling a fleet in neutral waters, or any other thing, may mean victory or salvation to the one, while the other may be unable to avail himself of the license or may find it of no value. On the example given by Grotius, the permission of passage, we have said elsewhere: "When private war was a general evil within most mediæval monarchies, a vassal who did not oppose the march of another

been captured bound with cargoes of corn to Spanish ports, *jure belli tales spoliari naves, quippe rem edictis et constitutionibus regiis prohibitam esse.*" Twiss, *Law of Nations—War,* p. 246. And see *est illud privatorum jus, est hoc regnorum,* quoted from Gentilis, *De jure belli,* above, p. 165.

[1] L. 3, c. 17, § 3.

vassal across his fief to attack a third was not deemed to offend against the latter; the assailant was merely using the public ways of the monarchy. So when private war, put down elsewhere, became in Germany public war, it was not there deemed the duty of a neutral to prevent the passage of belligerent forces across his territory[1]." The existence of such a practice must have helped to blind the perception of right with regard to it, and a century later we find Bynkershoek still adhering to equality of treatment as the test of neutral duties[2]. It was reserved for Vattel to pronounce emphatically for entire abstinence from real participation in the war as the true test.

"Let us see," Vattel says, "in what consists the impartiality which a neutral people ought to preserve. It relates exclusively to the war and comprises two things: (1°) Not to give aid when not obliged to it; not to furnish without obligation either troops, arms, ammunition or any thing which is of direct service for the war. I say not to give aid, I do not say to give it equally, because it would be absurd for a state to aid two enemies at once. And more, it would be impossible to do so equally; the same things, the same number of troops, the same quantity of arms, of ammunition &c., furnished in different circumstances are not equivalent aid[3]." The reservation with regard to aid given under an obligation is explained in the next section by saying that "when a sovereign furnishes the moderate aid which he owes by virtue of an old defensive alliance, he does not associate himself with the war; he can therefore acquit himself of his debt and preserve an exact neutrality in other respects. The examples of this are frequent in Europe." It is true that aid so given to a belligerent will not of itself place the sovereign giving it in a state of war—no aid can do so of itself—and that, if given openly and after notice to the other belligerent, it may not involve a want of the sincerity and loyalty due from one who desires to remain a neutral. But it cannot avoid being a

[1] *Chapters on the Principles of International Law,* p. 57.

[2] *Quæst Jur. Pub.,* l. 1, c. 9.

[3] L. 3, § 104. Buddeus, in his *Elementa Philosophicæ Practicæ,* as quoted by Nys—*Le Droit International,* t. 3, p. 563—comes near to this, and makes the same reservation of aid which a neutral is authorised to furnish by a particular engagement.

real participation in the war, and the fact that the neutral had entangled himself by an alliance under which it was due cannot take from the other belligerent the right to insist that those who participate in the war shall share its responsibilities, and therefore of declaring war against the neutral who has intervened[1].

To return, however, to the former quotation, Vattel, in describing the two things comprised in true neutral impartiality, proceeds: "(2°) In every thing which does not relate to the war, a neutral and impartial nation will not refuse to one of the parties, by reason of their then quarrel, that which it grants to the other. This does not deprive it of the liberty to direct itself with a view to the greatest good of the state, in its negotiations, in the friendships which it contracts, and in its commerce. When this reason leads it to preferences in things of which every one has the free disposition, it only uses its right. There is no partiality in that. But if it were to refuse any of these things to one of the parties only because it is at war with the other, and in order to favour the former, it would no longer be observing an exact neutrality." This doctrine belongs to the region of politics, in which it is no more possible to define when the conduct of a neutral becomes justly intolerable than it is to define when the conduct of a foreign power in time of peace becomes justly intolerable. But the things to which Vattel in his (2°) no doubt intended to refer include much that relates to the use made of neutral territory, on which the doctrine is gradually passing from the region of politics to that of law, in proportion as rules are consented to under a growing sensitiveness as to what is really a participation in military operations. So far as it remains within the former region, the stress which Vattel lays on motive ought to be accompanied by a caution as to the uncertainty always attaching to suspicions of the motives of others. Still, his doctrine finds a justification in the important bearing which the neutral's motive has on the expectation which ought to be formed of his ulterior conduct, and the effect of that consideration will not always be to stimulate a belligerent to extreme measures. For instance, when France in 1905 extended in her colonies great hospitality to the Russian fleet on

[1] See the note at end of the chapter.

its way to the Far East, the behaviour of Japan must have been influenced by the persuasion that the French motive was friendship for Russia, which would have its limits in action, and not enmity to Japan. The value which governments attach to having at their disposal the means of promoting their political objects, by showing favours not involving a breach of recognised international rules, is one of the causes that have retarded the formation of such rules in what relates to the use of territory, as compared with their advanced condition in what relates to blockade and contraband. But in leaving that branch of the subject as open as it is, the risk is run that in the absence of such rules a power which feels itself to be injured may claim to fall back on principles, as the United States successfully did in the *Alabama* case.

After Vattel what chiefly remained to be supplied, in order to bring the notion of real participation in war to the degree of clearness which it has now attained, was to throw further light, from a general point of view, on the distinction between what may and may not be done in neutral territory; and important help was given in this by the appeal of Jefferson, Secretary of State of the United States under Washington as president, to the misuse or usurpation of the neutral's sovereignty as a consideration to be taken into account. It was occasioned by the incidents which occurred in America on the outbreak of the war of 1793 between England and France. To M. Genêt, the French minister in the United States, who pleaded that to grant commissions and letters of marque was one of the usual functions of French consuls in foreign ports, Jefferson wrote, 5 June 1793: "It is the right of every nation to prohibit acts of sovereignty from being exercised by any other within its limits, and the duty of a neutral nation to prohibit such as would injure one of the warring powers. The granting military commissions within the United States by any other authority than their own is an infringement of their sovereignty, and particularly so when granted to their own citizens, to lead them to commit acts contrary to the duties they owe to their country[1]." And to Mr Morris, the United States minister at Paris, he wrote, 16 August

[1] 1 *American State Papers* 67.

1793: "The right of raising troops being one of the rights of sovereignty, and consequently appertaining exclusively to the nation itself, no foreign power or person can levy men within its territory without its consent. If the United States have a right to refuse the permission to arm vessels and raise men within their ports and territories, they are bound by the laws of neutrality to exercise that right and to prohibit such armaments and enlistments[1]."

The distinction to which Jefferson points is that between the things of which, by the general usage of European and American nations, a state reserves to itself the exclusive performance within its territory, and those which the same usage allows to be done by private persons; and it would be unfair to interpret him without reference to that distinction. It is within the right of a state to reserve to itself the exclusive performance of any thing, but that does not give a belligerent the right to claim that whatever may be obnoxious to him shall not only not be done by a neutral state but shall be prohibited by that state to individuals. A belligerent however must plan his operations on the footing of what general usage leads him to expect to find in well-governed countries, and a neutral must not falsify the reasonable expectations which he so forms. It is often put that a belligerent cannot complain of commercial acts done in neutral territory by private persons, whatever their effect on the fortunes of the war. And this is true, only those who desire that the export of contraband, for example, shall be prohibited by neutral states will deny that such export is a purely commercial act. It would be difficult better to define a purely commercial act than as one containing no element of what is generally reserved for public action. Again, any act amounting to participation in a specific operation of war would certainly be one of those generally reserved for public action. We may say then that the question whether an act falls within the popular notion of a commercial act, the question whether it is a participation in a specific operation of war, and the question whether it is one of those generally reserved for state activity, furnish three lines of enquiry for determining whether it ought

[1] Ib., p. 116.

to be prohibited to private persons on neutral territory; that those lines will usually be found to lead to coincident results; but that if either the second or the third question be answered in the affirmative, the act must certainly be prohibited. And to this it must be added that since a well-governed state does not perform commercial acts except incidentally to the performance of its public duties, as in the sale of old stores, abstinence from such acts is not such a burden to it as any unfairly demanded abstinence from them would be to private persons to whom they are their living. It would therefore be highly objectionable, as an unfriendly proceeding, that a public authority should sell arms or ammunition, or lend money, to a belligerent, even when such sale or loan was within its usual course, and could not be regarded as a participation in a specific operation of war.

Note on Aid in War given in pursuance of a Treaty by a Power claiming to continue a Neutral.

It follows from what has been said above[1] that the question raised by the aid given to a belligerent by a neutral who in Vattel's language "is obliged to it" is a political one, its legal aspect, if the other belligerent chooses to insist on it, being clear. But since it figures in works on international law, it will be worth while to mention some cases of dates posterior to that of Vattel.

Russia being at war with Sweden, Denmark, in compliance with a treaty of defensive alliance, placed certain land and sea forces at her disposal. Sweden stated that if those forces acted against her in Russian provinces and waters she would not consider the peace to have been broken by Denmark, but that she would do so if they invaded Swedish territories: 11 September 1788. Denmark rejected any limitation of the sphere of their operations, and claimed to remain at peace so long as the troops and ships employed by her in the war should not exceed the force stipulated: 13 September. The Danish contingent invaded Sweden on 23 September. England, Prussia and Holland having offered their mediation, Sweden consented to regard the peace as subsisting in order to see what success the negotia-

[1] Pp. 173, 174.

tions would have: 5 October. Prussia declared that in attacking Sweden when her principal forces were employed elsewhere, with a direct tendency to crush the king of Sweden and change the form of government of that country, Denmark had far overstepped the part of an auxiliary; and that if she did not evacuate Sweden and conclude an armistice, Prussian and Hanoverian troops would occupy Holstein and Sleswick. Thereupon the king of Denmark ordered the evacuation of Sweden, 24 October; and on 5 November concluded an armistice, guaranteed by England and Prussia, to last till 13 May 1789. Russia having refused the mediation, the three mediators declared that Denmark was freed from the case of a defensive treaty, and that the junction of any of her forces with those of Russia would make her a belligerent, in which case they threatened to assist Sweden: 23 April. Denmark claimed to be allowed, before giving a definitive answer, to consult Russia, which she said had an incontestable right to demand the fulfilment of her engagements: 30 April. With the permission of Russia, Denmark promised to observe a neutrality during the continuance of the war: 9 July 1789[1]. It thus appears that England, Prussia and Holland—Russia need not be counted, being directly interested—considered that Sweden would have no legitimate ground of complaint so long as the aid given by Denmark to Russia in pursuance of a treaty should be confined within limits, as to which however they, Sweden, and Denmark were not in agreement. The want of agreement on that point emphasizes the conclusion that it was not a legal question but one of political legitimacy that was dealt with.

In 1803 and 1804 England considered that, not the succour which Spain was bound by her treaty of 1796 to give to France, but any excess of succour over what was stipulated in that treaty, would be a cause of war with Spain[2].

Canning, on the occasion of his assisting Portugal against Spain in 1826 in pursuance of old treaties, drew a distinction between a general prospective defensive alliance and a defensive alliance concluded with a power either actually at war or on the eve of a rupture with a third power[3].

[1] Martens, 1 *Causes Célèbres* 308–332.

[2] Mahan's *Sea Power, 1793–1812*, vol. 2, p. 134.

[3] Stapleton's *George Canning and his Times*, p. 535.

CHAPTER VIII.

DUTIES OF NEUTRAL STATES.

National Laws on the Subject.

In this chapter we propose to trace in detail the duties which are incumbent on neutral states, whether with regard to their own action as states, or with regard to such action of individuals as it is their duty to repress because it would amount to a violation of the neutrality of their territory. The latter point has given occasion in the United States and Great Britain to enactments covering so large a part of the whole subject, and necessarily exercising such a dominant influence on the views of American and British lawyers, that it will be convenient to take as much of the subject as we can in the order in which it appears in the latest British statute, which is called the Foreign Enlistment Act 1870, by a name derived from one of its branches and giving no adequate notion of its comprehensive character. First of all, however, it will be well to state how the series of enactments referred to arose.

In 1793, during the war between England and France, Gideon Henfield, a citizen of the United States, took service on board a French privateer, and arrived at Philadelphia as prize-master of a British ship captured by her. He was indicted under the common law, and Mr Justice Wilson charged the jury that Henfield was bound to act no part which could injure his country, and was therefore bound to keep the peace towards all nations at peace with it. To that common law doctrine he added the constitutional argument that the treaties of the United States were part of the law of the land, and that a treaty of friendship existed between them and England. The jury, after retiring several times, returned a verdict of "not guilty." Congress, thus warned of the difficulty which political sentiment might at any time place in the way of executing the law as it stood, passed the Neutrality Act of 1794 at the instance of Washington and Jefferson. This act was strengthened in 1818 in consequence of the Spanish American wars of independence, and the whole enactment now stands as one, under the head of Neutrality in the Revised Statutes of the United States. In consequence of the same wars of independence, which strongly stimulated political sympathy and commercial enterprise on both sides of the Atlantic, the first British statute on the subject was passed in 1819. The one now in force, replacing it and more stringent, was passed in 1870 in consequence of the incidents which took place during the War of Secession in the United States. On all these enactments it will be one of the matters for our consideration whether any particular provision does not go beyond what neutral duty requires. Whether in fact it does so or not, at least it is certain that no state law of the kind is a declaration to the world of what the state in question deems to be its international duty as a neutral. It is a declaration to its own subjects of the powers which it deems necessary to take over them, whether in pursuance of its own policy or in order to ensure the performance of its neutral duty; and even when no policy except such performance is concerned, the powers taken may well exceed the minimum which would be compatible with the duty. Laws often fail of their intended effect through oversight or tardiness in their administration, and the higher the standard at which they aim in the matters before us, the less likely will such slips be to bring their execution below the standard necessary for the safety and ease of the foreign relations of the state. It is true that any national enactment, whether exceeding or not the limits of international duty, must be enforced in favour of both belligerents if it is enforced in favour of either. A neutral must be impartial, though it is not enough that he should be impartial if he does not abstain from participation in the war. But he is within his right if he declines to enforce in favour of either belligerent an enactment with which he has armed himself only in pursuance of his own policy or for his own greater security.

We shall now treat of the repression by states of the unneutral action of individuals under the three heads of the Foreign Enlistment Act 1870, *Illegal Enlistment*, *Illegal Ship-building and Illegal Expeditions*, which we shall divide, and *Illegal Prize*. Lastly will come the duties of a state with regard to its own action, and with regard to any action by private persons which a state must not allow in its territory, but which in England and the United States it has not been found necessary to regulate by statute.

Illegal Enlistment.

Creating or recruiting a force to be employed in a war is clearly an operation of that war; and when it is done on neutral soil, either by a belligerent power or by private sympathisers, it is clearly a usurpation of the authority of the neutral state by or on behalf of the belligerent. On both grounds therefore it is a neutral duty of that state not to permit in its territory any thing which forms or is intended to form a part of such creation or recruiting of a force, even though it be only the enlisting of a single recruit. To enlist more, and to drill, arm and organise them, would merely be to take further steps in the same line of conduct. But that a subject, not enlisted, should go abroad with the intention of entering belligerent service would not of itself involve his state, in the territory of which nothing illegitimate would have been done, although an agency, opened or carried on within the territory for encouraging such departures in search of service, would only be a colourable avoidance of enlistment on the soil, and its case could not properly be distinguished from that of actual enlistment. All this is now generally recognised, not even Switzerland consenting any longer to furnish the recruiting-ground which she formerly supplied. Belligerent subjects who go home to perform their military duties do not fall within the scope of this doctrine. Their obligation has not been formed within the neutral territory which they leave, and it justifies their intention to take part in their country's service. Their consuls assist without offence in making the necessary arrangements for their return.

There being a civil war in Portugal between the partisans of

Don Miguel and Dona Maria, the latter of whom had the sympathy of the Liberal party in Western Europe, some of her troops, flying from Oporto, took refuge first in Spain and afterwards in England. There they were joined by other troops which had been engaged in Germany and the Netherlands, were sustained and supported by the English creditors of Dona Maria's Government, and were commanded as a body by General Stubbs. Don Pedro, the emperor of Brazil, supported the cause of his daughter Dona Maria, and his minister informed the Duke of Wellington, the English prime minister, that he intended to despatch a part of the troops in question to the Azores, where the island of Terceira still held out for her. Wellington answered that he could not recognise foreign troops in England, and that, if there were any such, they must instantly disperse and distribute themselves in the neighbouring towns; and that they would not be permitted to go in hostility to any part of the Portuguese dominions, but that they might proceed as individuals to the Azores if they pleased. The English sympathisers objecting that the men were harmless, as they were unarmed, Lord Chancellor Lyndhurst said in the House of Lords that "that argument was altogether untenable, because, as they were organised, they had no right to go there" [to the Azores][1].

The provisions of the Foreign Enlistment Act 1870 against enlisting in the active sense of that verb are that it is penal for any one, whether a British subject or not, without the royal license and within the British dominions, to induce any person (*a*) to accept or agree to accept any commission or engagement in the military or naval service of a foreign state at war with any foreign state at peace with the king (s. 4), or (*b*) to quit, or to go on board any ship with a view of quitting, the British dominions with intent to accept any such commission or engagement (s. 5); also that it is penal to induce any person to quit the British dominions, or to embark in any ship within the British dominions, under a misrepresentation or false representation of the service in which he is to be engaged, with the intent or in order that he may accept or agree to accept any

[1] *Hansard, N. S.*, xxiii., 778: see also 746, 747, 769–9. Later we shall see the further development of this Terceira affair.

such commission or engagement as aforesaid (s. 7). The provisions against enlisting in the passive or neutral sense of that verb apply to British subjects only, and are that it is penal for them, without the royal license and whether within or without the British dominions, to accept or agree to accept any commission or engagement in the military or naval service of a foreign state at war with any foreign state at peace with the king (s. 4); and without the royal license to quit, or to go on board any ship with a view of quitting, the British dominions, with intent to accept any such commission or engagement (s. 5). So far as these provisions control the action of British subjects outside the British dominions, it may be said, without controverting their political wisdom, that they are not required by the state's neutrality. And a provision against going abroad in order to enter foreign service hostile to a friendly state would not be required by the state's neutrality in the case of an isolated individual, but is useful for more certainly preventing what, if done by many individuals in combination, might amount to the departure of an expedition. Then s. 7 makes it penal for the masters or owners of ships to have or to engage to take on board, without the royal license and within the British dominions, British subjects who have been enlisted or are about to quit the British dominions, or persons who have been induced to embark, contrary to s. 4, 5 or 6; and "all illegally enlisted persons shall immediately on the discovery of the offence be taken on shore, and shall not be allowed to return to the ship." The act contains a proviso exempting from penalties persons who enter the military service of any Asiatic potentate with the license for the time being required by law (s. 33); and the interpretation clause (s. 30) puts on "foreign state" a meaning which includes parties to civil wars, so that the royal license became necessary for the formation in England of the Spanish legion, so called, which assisted under the Quadruple Alliance of 1834 in the overthrow of the Carlists in Spain.

The neutrality laws of the United States make it penal for their citizens to accept and exercise within their territory a commission to serve in war, by land or by sea, a foreign prince, state, colony, district or people against any prince, state, colony, district or people with whom the United States are at peace.

They also make it penal if within the territory any one, whether citizen or alien, enters, or hires or retains any one to enter or to go abroad with the intent of entering, the military or naval service of any foreign prince, state, colony, district or people, whether or not at war with another which is at peace with the United States. This prohibition is qualified by a proviso under which friendly ships of war or privateers, which at the time of their arrival in the United States were fitted and equipped as such, may enlist persons of their own nationality, being "transiently" within the United States, for service on board. So far as the law thus described applies to the time of peace, it furnishes another example of a national law dictated by policy and not by neutral duty. The United States law contains no provision for its relaxation by government license, and the penalty enacted by it is fine and imprisonment, while that enacted by the British law is fine and imprisonment or either, at the discretion of the court.

Illegal Shipbuilding.

When the war of the French revolution compelled the jurists of the United States, in their respective capacities of legislators and judges, to seek the right footing on which to place the law of their country with reference to its neutral duties, it was clear to them that a ship, considered in herself, however adapted she might be for war, was merely a contraband article, which a belligerent might capture as such but the trade in which it was no part of neutral duty for a state to prohibit. But the circumstances in which she set out from a neutral port might involve her in a question different from that of contraband, namely the use made of neutral territory, and for appreciating those circumstances they resorted to the legal doctrine of intent. You can intend your own actions, and you can identify yourself with another person's intention of his actions by knowingly assisting him in their performance. The actions of others with which you have not so identified yourself you may foresee with more or less certainty, and the expectation which you form of them may be your motive, but neither expectation nor motive makes their actions yours. When a ship or a cargo of arms is despatched by a neutral owner in search of a market, his motive is the expectation that it will find a belligerent purchaser who will use it in war, but the intent so to use it can only be formed by the purchaser, and remains contingent as long as the expectation exists, so that the expectation is not an assistance knowingly given to it. But when a ship is despatched from a neutral port by a belligerent owner, his intent to employ her in war has been formed while she was still in neutral territory, so that her despatch is an act of war and a usurpation of the neutral state's authority, and any one who has contracted with the belligerent owner or worked for him about the ship with knowledge of his intent has identified himself with it. Thus the line between the export of contraband and the abuse of neutral territory is drawn by the intent of unneutral employment, formed within the territory by a person whose position in relation to the thing enables him to give effect to it. And so Channell, B., interpreting the Foreign Enlistment Act of 1819 with reference to the *Alexandra*, asserted by the crown to be in building for the Confederate States as a cruiser, said: "It is, I think, agreed on both sides that the intent spoken of must be the intent of some person who has control over the vessel so as to be able to carry out his intent or purpose[1]."

The line thus drawn is consistently carried out in the Neutrality Laws of the United States, in which country building ships and sending them abroad in search of a market in time of war was then a not unimportant branch of industry. Now the increased size and cost of ships of war, the variety of their designs with the consequent importance of their being laid down to suit the party to be served, and the absence of any use for ships fitted for war in private hands, which has resulted from

[1] In *Att. Gen. v. Sillem,* 2 H. & C. 552. The difference between expectation and intent is illustrated by the cases on contracts made abroad for goods to be smuggled into England. The seller was allowed to recover their price where the delivery of the goods was complete abroad, and nothing was done by him to assist in the smuggling, though he knew that such was the buyer's intention: *Holman v. Johnson,* Cowp. 341; *Pellecat v. Angell,* 2 Cr. M. & R. 311. But he could not recover where he had packed the goods in a peculiar manner for the purpose of smuggling: *Biggs v. Lawrence* 3 T. R. 454; *Clugas v. Penaluna,* 4 T. R. 466; *Waymell v. Read,* 5 T. R. 599. See Westlake, *Private International Law,* 4th ed., p. 283.

the abolition of privateering, have practically limited the building them in private yards to building to the orders of governments. Still the American and British laws on the subject require to be thoroughly appreciated, and we will take, first, the material thing or act which they contemplate, and secondly, the state of mind in which they make it criminal to do that thing or act. First the material part of the offence stands in the Foreign Enlistment Act 1870 as building a ship or agreeing or causing her to be built, equipping her, despatching her or causing or allowing her to be despatched, or issuing or delivering any commission for her (s. 8). And the interpretation clause (s. 30) gives meanings to building and equipping which include any thing done towards either of those ends, whereby the interpretation put on the Act of 1819 in the case of the *Alexandra*[1], that the equipment must be such as would enable the ship to cruise or commit hostilities immediately on leaving port, was prevented for the future. And rightly so, for without being in a condition to fight a naval action a ship may be able to take part in some operation of war, for instance she might capture a merchantman with the small arms of her crew alone. The American law was not open to the objection which in England was remedied in 1870, since it contains the words "attempt to fit out and arm," on which it was held that "the attempt does not imply a completion of the act, or any definite progress towards it[2]." It will be noticed that the phrase "fit out and arm" corresponds to the "equip" of the British law, but the description of the material offence in the two countries is substantially equivalent, it being quite immaterial that the American law does not use the word "despatching."

Coming now to the criminal state of mind, the United States Neutrality Laws prohibit every one from committing the material offence within the territory "with intent" that the ship shall be employed in foreign service against friends[3], and they

[1] *Att. Gen. v. Sillem,* 2 H. & C. 431. The court was equally divided, Pollock, C.B., and Bramwell, B., being for the restrictive interpretation, Channell, B., and Pigott, B., against it, so that the indictment fell to the ground.

[2] *U. S. v. Quincy,* 6 Peters 445, Scott 706.

[3] In the language here abbreviated as "friends," as well as in that

prohibit any one from being "knowingly concerned" in it within the territory when committed with such intent. This simple wording covered all cases in which the intent might be formed by some one having the control of the ship, whether a foreign belligerent having her built to order or an American citizen designing to use her as a privateer or in the kind of hostility called filibustering, but it did not cover building ships to be sent in search of a market; and it corresponded accurately with a proviso that "the owners or consignees of every armed ship or vessel sailing out of the ports of the United States, belonging wholly or in part to citizens thereof," shall give bonds with sufficient sureties that she "shall not be employed *by such owners* to cruise or commit hostilities against" friends[1]. But the Foreign Enlistment Act 1870 makes the criminal state of mind to be doing the thing "with intent or knowledge, or having reasonable cause to believe," that the ship will be employed in foreign service against friends. The "reasonable cause to believe" was added in 1870 to the enactment of 1819, and brings building and despatching for a market within the act, since the intending vendor would have reasonable cause to believe that he would find a purchaser who would make the noxious use of the ship. With a view, however, to the trade of building ships to order being carried on in time of peace with reasonable security, the Foreign Enlistment Act 1870 contains in s. 8 a proviso exempting from penalty the building or equipping a ship in pursuance of a contract made before the commencement of any war in which she is intended or expected to be employed, if full notice of the facts is given to a secretary of state forthwith on a proclamation of neutrality being issued by the crown, and if the secretary of state be satisfied in respect of security to be given and measures to be taken for ensuring that the ship shall not be despatched, delivered or removed without the royal license before the end of the war. In the United States, if similar conduct were pursued

describing the service, the words "colony, district or people" were added in 1818, in order to make the attitude of the United States towards wars of insurrection the same as towards wars between recognised states.

[1] Revised Statutes, s. 5289.

in a similar case by the builder or equipper of a ship, it would evidently be sufficient of itself to negative an imputation of criminal intent.

The legislation of the United States has been consistently carried out by their courts, three leading cases in which it is desirable to mention with some particularity, since they were all prior to the arbitration at Geneva on the *Alabama* claims, and the doctrine laid down in them appears still to furnish a correct standard so far as it concerns neutral duty in the points in question. In the case of *The Santissima Trinidad*[1] a ship which had been employed as a privateer in the war of 1812 against England was sent in search of a market, armed with twelve guns and loaded with munitions of war, to Buenos Ayres, then in insurrection against Spain. There she passed into the possession of the insurgent government and received the name of the *Independencia*, after which she returned to the United States, substantially increased her crew in one of their ports by illegal enlistments in violation of their neutrality, and on the same cruise on which she left with her force so increased captured at sea the *Santissima Trinidad* and brought her into a United States port. The American court, of which Story delivered the judgment, released the prize because of the illegally augmented force with which she had been taken, but the original armament and despatch of the *Independencia* they held to have been a commercial adventure, exposing her to the risk of capture as contraband during her voyage to Buenos Ayres, but not violating the neutrality of the *United States*. The distinction between the despatch of a ship as contraband and as an unlawful expedition did not depend on her being armed.

In *United States v. Quincy*[2] the *Bolivar* was sent from Baltimore to the Danish and equally neutral island of St Thomas, with some view, the exact nature of which was disputed, to her acting as a privateer in favour of the insurgent Spanish colonies. Quincy being indicted for this under the Neutrality Laws, the court, consistently with the case of *The Santissima Trinidad*, refused to instruct the jury that the defendant must be acquitted if the *Bolivar* when she left

[1] 7 Wheaton 283, Scott 701.
[2] 6 Peters 445, Scott 706.

Baltimore, and during her voyage to St Thomas, was not in a condition to commit hostilities. As the presence of armament was not conclusive that the despatch of a ship was an unlawful expedition, so its absence was not conclusive that her despatch was merely an export of contraband. But the court instructed the jury on the one hand that the defendant must be acquitted if while in the United States he had no present or fixed intention to employ the *Bolivar* as a privateer, but only had a wish so to employ her if he could obtain funds in the West Indies for arming and preparing her, his intent in going to St Thomas being to seek funds for that purpose—and on the other hand that "if the defendant was knowingly concerned in fitting out the *Bolivar* within the United States with the intent that she should be employed as set forth in the indictment, that intention being defeated by what might afterwards take place in the West Indies would not purge the offence which was previously consummated. It is not necessary that the design or intention should be carried into execution in order to constitute the offence." On the latter part of this ruling it must be remarked that however wise it may be for a state to punish in their inception designs conceived for the violation of its neutrality, international offence can scarcely arise from a design defeated before receiving any execution.

In the third of the cases above referred to, that of *The Meteor*[1], a ship had been built in the United States in 1865, during a war between Chile and Spain, and proceedings were taken against her by the government before she could leave. Judge Betts in the lower court and Judge Nelson in the higher differed as to whether what was done by her owners towards despatching her was done in pursuance of an arrangement between them and the agents of Chile for her sale to that state, which would employ her in hostilities against Spain, or whether the negotiation for a sale to Chile had failed, and the owners had thenceforward no other purpose than to send her to a South American port in search of a market. But neither court doubted that such was the question on which the case depended.

The claims of the United States against Great Britain,

[1] 3 Wharton's Digest 561, Scott 711.

growing out of the acts of the ships which were despatched from Great Britain for the service of the Confederate States during the War of Secession, and generally known as the *Alabama* claims, were referred to arbitration by the treaty of Washington, 1871. That treaty provided, Art. 6, that "in deciding the matters submitted to the arbitrators they shall be governed by the following three rules, which are agreed upon by the high contracting parties as rules to be taken as applicable to the case, and by such principles of international law, not inconsistent therewith, as the arbitrators shall determine to have been applicable to the case." And after a declaration by the British government that it did not assent to those rules as a statement of the principles of international law which were in force at the time when the claims arose, the article proceeded: "The high contracting parties agree to observe these rules as between themselves in future, and to bring them to the knowledge of other maritime powers and to invite them to accede to them." The first of what may be called the three *Alabama* rules ran thus:

> A neutral government is bound, First: To use due diligence to prevent the fitting out, arming or equipping within its jurisdiction of any vessel which it has reasonable ground to believe is intended to cruise or to carry on war against a power with which it is at peace; and also to use like diligence to prevent the departure from its jurisdiction of any vessel intended to cruise or carry on war as above, such vessel having been specially adapted, in whole or in part, within such jurisdiction, to warlike use.

This rule, in enjoining on a state to use due diligence to prevent certain violations of its neutrality, does only what elementary common sense requires as soon as the things struck at are admitted to be violations of neutrality. Indeed it is rather favourable to the neutral state, indicating as it does that neutrality must not be construed as an insurance against every thing inconsistent with it, when there has been no failure in a reasonable endeavour to prevent any such inconsistency. In describing the violation of neutrality which due diligence is to be used in preventing, the rule follows the United States Neutrality Laws and the Foreign Enlistment Act 1870 in making it, substantially, the augmentation in neutral territory of the naval strength of a belligerent power. Sir Alexander

Cockburn, as the British arbitrator in the *Alabama* case, said that "it is the present intention of the immediate employment of the vessel for hostile purposes which makes the sending out an armed ship an offence against the law of nations." The word "immediate" marks the difference between that view and the view adopted in the rule; and on the same principle, which was that of the deciding half of the court of Exchequer in the case of the *Alexandra*[1], Sir Alexander required officers and a fighting crew, equipment and armament, for a ship the departure of which should constitute the offence. But with this view we cannot agree. No international attempt to lay down a precise rule is in favour of it, and in the absence of a precise rule generally agreed on a belligerent has the right to fall back on the fundamental principles of the subject, which raise no question of limit or degree when pointing out that a neutral who permits a belligerent to receive an augmentation of naval strength within his territory is a participant in the war.

For the rest, the first *Alabama* rule mentions "reasonable ground to believe," but as a state of mind of the neutral government, not of the culpable individual as the Foreign Enlistment Act 1870 mentions it, and therefore does not strike at building or despatching a ship of war in search of a market, could such a proceeding be now contemplated as possible. If the government has reasonable ground to believe that a culpable intent exists, it must not wait idly till the proof of it would satisfy a court of law, or it will be likely to have stirred itself too late, and it should therefore arm itself with the powers necessary for acting in time. This has been done for the British dominions by sections 23 and 24 of the Foreign Enlistment Act 1870, which provide that on having reasonable and probable cause for believing that a ship is being built or is about to be despatched contrary to the act, the secretary of state or the chief executive authority of the British dominion concerned may, and the local authority must, detain the ship. The matter is then to be put in course of trial in the Court of Admiralty, the burden of proof that nothing contrary to the act was being done or intended lying on the owner, an indemnity to whom may be ordered by the court where justice so requires.

[1] See above, p. 186.

The augmentation in a neutral port of the naval strength of a belligerent power can take place as well by augmenting the strength of one of its own ships as by building a new one for it. The legal character of both operations depends on the same principles, and the former is dealt with under the head of Shipbuilding in the Foreign Enlistment Act 1870, s. 10 of which imposes fine and imprisonment or either, at the discretion of the court, on any person who, within the British dominions and without the license of the crown,

By adding to the number of the guns, or by changing those on board for other guns, or by the addition of any equipment for war, increases or augments, or procures to be increased or augmented, or is knowingly concerned in increasing or augmenting the warlike force of any ship which at the time of her being within the dominions of [His] Majesty was a ship in the military or naval service of any foreign state at war with any friendly state.

Illegal Expeditions.

The subject of expeditions directed against a belligerent power from a neutral port, having been either originally formed there or augmented there in force after having put into it, is touched on in that part of the first *Alabama* rule which deals with the departure of ships from neutral jurisdiction. This was inevitable, although that rule seems to have been primarily designed to deal with the equipment of ships in neutral territory, because we have seen that the unneutral character of such equipment depends on an intent about what is to follow the departure of the ship. The second *Alabama* rule directly attacks the question of illegal expeditions and, with the third rule, is in these terms:

[A neutral government is bound], Secondly, Not to permit or suffer either belligerent to make use of its ports or waters as the base of naval operations against the other, or for the purpose of the renewal or augmentation of military supplies or arms, or the recruitment of men.

Thirdly, To exercise due diligence in its own ports and waters, and as to all persons within its jurisdiction, to prevent any violation of the foregoing obligation and duties.

These two rules seem to have been designed to be specially taken together, since the first rule, in which due diligence is incorporated, did not need its repetition in the third. Some doubt has been felt whether "base of operations" in the second rule was not intended to refer to a base used for large or repeated operations, the departure of a single ship from a neutral port having been dealt with in the first rule. But the term "base" does not in itself carry any implication as to the importance or number of the operations proceeding from it, and the principle is the same whether an expedition consists of a fleet or of a single ship. Nay, more, the principle is the same for expeditions starting from land or from sea frontiers. The departure of a force from either with belligerent intent is a matter which in every country is reserved for the public authority, and any private person or foreign government which presumes to despatch a force with such an intent usurps that authority, and involves the territorial government which permits such a usurpation in the charge of participating in the war. We are then entitled to omit the word "naval" from the second *Alabama* rule, and to expand "ports and waters" into "territory." We have it thus as a general rule that "a neutral government is bound not to permit either belligerent to make use of its territory as the base of operations against the other, or for the purpose of the renewal or augmentation of military supplies or arms, or the recruitment of men."

The Foreign Enlistment Act 1870 enacts as follows:

Sect. 11. If any person within the limits of H.M.'s dominions, and without the license of H.M., prepares or fits out any naval or military expedition to proceed against the dominions of any friendly state, the following consequences shall ensue:

(1) Every person engaged in such preparation or fitting out or assisting therein, or employed in any capacity in such expedition, shall be guilty of an offence against this act, and shall be punishable by fine or imprisonment or either of such punishments, at the discretion of the court before which the offender is convicted; and imprisonment, if awarded, may be eitherwith or without hard labour.

(2) All ships and their equipments, and all arms and munitions of war, used in or forming part of such expedition, shall be forfeited to H.M.

Common to this and to the enactments about illegal ship-building are the extension of "state" by the interpretation clause to include any persons exercising or assuming to exercise the powers of government, and

Sect. 12. Any person who aids, abets, counsels or procures the commission of any offence against this act shall be liable to be tried and punished as a principal offender.

A difficulty in the practical application of the doctrine as to illegal expeditions has been sometimes felt to arise when the elements of an expedition, such as ships, men and arms, are despatched from a neutral territory separately and are combined outside its limits. It would indeed be difficult to hold that the fact of combination gave a non-commercial character, in violation of neutrality, to something of which the separate elements were all of a merely commercial character; but such a case could scarcely occur in reality. If what results from the combination is a military force inspired by a belligerent intent, it can hardly be but that at least some of its elements must have been despatched from the neutral territory with that intent, so as to give to their despatch an unneutral character which, as we have seen, does not depend on the completeness of the belligerent preparations. In the case of the *Terceira* expedition in 1829, which we have already had to notice with regard to the collection and organisation of the men in England, the men sailed from Plymouth unarmed with false clearances for Brazil, the government not opposing their embarcation in consequence of an assurance given by the Brazilian minister that they were being sent to Brazil. But since the government knew that arms from England awaited them at or near Terceira, it suspected their true destination and despatched a force instructed to prevent their landing there, which it accordingly did. In the House of Commons Horace Twiss defended the action of the government by saying that "if at the end of the voyage the arms were to come into the soldiers' hands, it is no more than if the arms had come in a different vessel of the flotilla[1]." But Huskisson quoted Canning as saying that "it is only when the elements of armaments are combined that they come within the purview of the law, and if that combination does not take place till they have left this country we have no right to interfere with them[2]." Canning on the occasion so referred to was answering a complaint of Turkey about ships and other things said to have

[1] *Hansard*, N. S., xxiv, col. 165. [2] Ib., col. 209.

been supplied to the insurgent Greeks, and it is possible that nothing took place in England that did not come fairly within the description of the export of contraband, so that one of the rare cases may have been presented in which an unneutral combination of elements furnishes no ground of reproach against a country from which some of those elements have been derived. In the *Terceira* affair there can be no doubt that the collection and organisation of the men in England and their despatch from a British port were important steps taken on British soil in execution of a belligerent intent there formed, and on the true principles of neutrality were sufficient in themselves to oblige the British Government to exert itself for the frustration of that intent, although the foreseen combination with arms was appealed to in support of that action. Indeed the distinction between the export of contraband and illegal expeditions does not seem to have been clear to any one in England till the *Alabama* cases forced it into recognition. In those cases Sir Alexander Cockburn, as arbitrator, took what may be described as an intermediate view. We have seen that he held a fighting crew and armament necessary to constitute an unneutral naval expedition, but at the same time he admitted that where such an expedition was developed outside a given neutral territory, that territory might be affected by having furnished its elements. With the deference due, we are unable to see how a territory can be affected unless, within it, both an unneutral intent has been entertained and a sufficient act committed in pursuance of that intent.

The Foreign Enlistment Act 1870 places British law on a level with international requirements with relation to the elements combined to form an expedition. Sandoval purchased in England two Krupp guns and a quantity of ammunition, and sent them in a trading ship to Antwerp, where they were placed on board another ship, the *Justitia*, of which Sandoval took the command; and the expedition thus completed proceeded to America, and fought on the side of the insurgents in a civil contest which was raging in the republic of Venezuela. Sandoval reappeared in England, where he was tried, and sentenced on a finding by the jury that when he purchased the arms and ammunition he knew and expressly intended that they should form part of a naval expedition which was being prepared to proceed against a foreign friendly state[1].

In this place it will be convenient to wind up what we have to say on that part of the Foreign Enlistment Act 1870 which relates to shipbuilding and expeditions by mentioning some of the decisions on it and on the older British and United States laws. During the Franco-German war the despatch of a tug from Dover, on an engagement made with the French consul there to tow a French prize to Dunkirk Roads, was held to be illegal, and the tug was forfeited to the crown[2]. Thus neither fighting nor readiness to fight was made the exclusive test of an unneutral expedition. During the same war it was held that the despatch of a specially constructed vessel, carrying telegraph wires which an English company had contracted with the French government to lay down in France for completing the communication between two French fortresses, Dunkirk and Verdun, was innocent, her business being purely commercial although the lines to be laid might be partially used for military purposes[3]. The only intent with which the English company could fairly be identified was that of adding to the telegraphic system of France, which could not be made a participation in the war either by the fact that the addition, like the rest of the system, would be liable to military use, or by the fact that such use was the motive for which the French government desired to make the addition at that time.

But service as a transport or storeship was held under the act of 1819 to be military service[4]. And quite correctly from the international point of view, which also may be said of the American decision that converting a merchant ship into a ship of war must be deemed an original outfit[5]. In the case in question the ship's armament was added to, but it would have been sufficient that her destination was changed, for the court

1 *Reg. v. Sandoval,* 56 L. T. 526, 16 Cox C. C. 206, 3 T. L. R. 411, 436, 498.

2 *The Gauntlet,* L. R., 4 P. C. 184.

3 *The International,* L. R., 3 A. & E. 321.

4 *The Salvador,* L. R., 3 P. C. 218. And see *Burton v. Pinkerton,* L. R., 2 Exch. 340.

5 *United States v. Guinet,* 2 Dallas 328.

held that it was the conversion from a peaceable to a warlike purpose which constituted the offence.

The arbitrators on the *Alabama* cases based their award against Great Britain, commonly known as the Geneva award, so far as concerned negligence in preventing the building, equipment and armament of cruisers for the Confederate States, on the facts relative to three ships: the *Alabama* herself, originally number 290, with regard both to her construction at Liverpool and her equipment and armament in the vicinity of Terceira; the *Oreto* or *Florida*, with regard to the occurrences at Liverpool, Nassau and Green Cay; and the *Shenandoah*, with regard to the occurrences at Melbourne. And for the purpose of appreciating the negligence charged they laid down these two canons:

> And whereas the due diligence referred to in the first and third of the said [*Alabama*] rules ought to be exercised by neutral governments in exact proportion to the risks to which either of the belligerents may be exposed from a failure to fulfil the obligations of neutrality on their part;.........
>
> And whereas the government of Her Britannic Majesty cannot justify itself for a failure in due diligence on the plea of insufficiency of the legal means of action which it possessed.

The first of these canons must not be understood as carrying due diligence to a point at which it would be equivalent to insurance. It merely applies to the conduct of governments where the interests of others are concerned the maxim on which every one would act where his own interests were concerned, namely that the more important are the issues at stake the greater ought to be the care taken. The second canon results from the independence of states, which draws a sharp line between their internal and their international affairs. For the ascertainment of their international duties they present themselves to one another as units. Each such unit must regulate as it deems best the rights and functions of the individuals and authorities which compose it, subject to the condition that the resulting action of the international unit shall not fall below the standard which experience shows to be reasonably attainable. Where that standard is not attained, the internal conditions to which the unit has submitted itself are not quotable in its defence.

We have now examined the three famous rules in respect both of the things which they declare ought to be prevented, and of the vigilance which they declare ought to be used in their prevention, and they appear to us to be sound in both respects. We do not think that there was any miscarriage in their application to the case presented at Geneva, but, however that may be, the possibility of miscarriage is incident to all judicial proceedings, to international arbitrations not less than to others; and England, which has been so often successful in international arbitrations—notably in the Behring's Sea and, practically, the Venezuelan boundary cases, besides many of less importance—can look on their total result with equanimity. The rules are law by treaty as between the British empire and the United States, together no small part of the world. We are not aware of any objection being taken to their substance by cultivated international opinion. And we look forward to their being adopted, with whatever improvement in expression it may be possible to give them, among the definitions of neutral duty which it is greatly to be desired should be laid down by a general conference. They will always be memorable in the history of international law, not only as having been the means of settling a threatening dispute, but as a first and not unsuccessful attempt to supply some of the *axiomata media* which Bacon taught the necessity of interposing between the first principles and the detailed results of any science, and the want of which is conspicuous in the theory of neutral duties.

Illegal Prize.

A prize may be brought into a port of a neutral country after being taken on the high sea by means obtained through a breach in that country of some neutral duty comprised under one of the foregoing heads of *Illegal Enlistment, Shipbuilding or Expedition.* Along with that case, as depending on the same principles, may be grouped the case of a prize taken in the territorial waters of a neutral country, and remaining or after being carried off being brought back within them, so as to be within the power of the country of which its capture violated the neutrality. And a third case which it will be convenient to mention at the same time is that of a prize taken in the territorial waters of a neutral country and brought into a port of the captor's country. In all these cases a state is called on to declare, either directly by its executive or through its courts, the attitude which it assumes towards a breach of the neutrality either of itself or of some other state.

One point is common to all three cases, namely that no breach of neutrality invalidates a capture as between the belligerents. Hence in a belligerent court an enemy cannot object to the condemnation of a prize on the ground that she was captured in violation of the neutrality of a third state. The sovereign of that state may intervene in the proceedings, and then restitution of the prize will be decreed to him, but failing such intervention she will be condemned[1]. If the ship is sold to a third party after such condemnation or at a prize sale ordered by the court, it has been thought in the United States that the purchaser obtains a title which cannot be impeached even in the country of which the neutrality was infringed, and even when the infraction consisted in a breach of the laws of that country. He is personally innocent, and has acquired title by a lawful proceeding[2]. Ortolan dissents from that view, saying that a neutral government of which the territory has been violated is not obliged to subordinate its right to the decision of a foreign tribunal and submit to the consequences of such

[1] *The Etrusco*, Lords, 1795, and other cases, cited in a note to *The Anna*, 5 C. Rob. 373. In *The Anna* the claim was made by the United States minister, in *The Eliza Ann*, 1 Dodson 244, by the Swedish consul, and in *The Twee Gebroeders*, 3 C. Rob. 162, by the Prussian consul under the direction of the Prussian *chargé d'affaires*. In a United States case, *The Anne*, 3 Wheaton 435, it was held that a consul cannot intervene in a case of this kind without the special authority of his government.

[2] In *La Nereyda*, 8 Wheaton 108, the United States court restored to the King of Spain a prize taken by a ship illegally fitted out in a United States port and sailing under a commission from an insurgent republic; but this was because the prize, although condemned, was still controlled by the original wrongdoer, and the claimant was unable to prove his purchase of her. Wheaton treats it as doubtful whether the ship ought not equally to be restored when through her condemnation she has passed into the hands of a *bona fide* purchaser without notice of the unlawfulness of the capture: *Elements*, § 433, Dana's numbering.

decision; and Hall agrees with him, as we also do[1]. However that may be, it is agreed by all that the captor's own position is not improved by the condemnation of the illegitimate prize, or by his purchasing her at a prize sale[2]. A proceeding instituted by him must, so far at any rate as he is concerned, be no more than a continuation of his offence.

The precise extent of the relief which ought to be given against the offending captor in the court of the injured country, when the prize is found in its waters in his possession, was considered in the case of *La Amistad de Rues*, in which a Spanish vessel captured by a Venezuelan privateer, alleged to have increased its force within the United States in breach of their neutrality laws, had been brought into New Orleans[3]. The incriminating allegation was not proved, but Story, in delivering the judgment of the Supreme Court, laid down the doctrine which he would have applied if it had been proved. The owner would have been entitled to the restitution of the prize, but not to damages for the loss occasioned by the capture. He might have demanded that the act which offended the sovereignty of the state should be undone by restoring the prize to him, and this would have been granted, solely in order to vindicate the offended sovereignty. But the demand for damages, as for a capture made without probable cause or otherwise illegal, would have involved an enquiry into the validity of the capture as between the parties, which the court could not make. The remedy which the Foreign Jurisdiction Act 1870 gives in this class of cases is limited to the restitution which Story thus deemed to be alone proper, and is as follows:

Sect. 14. If, during the continuance of any war in which H.M. may be neutral, any ship, goods or merchandise, captured as prize of war within the territorial jurisdiction of H.M. in violation of the neutrality of this realm,

or captured by any ship which may have been built, equipped, commissioned or despatched, or the force of which may have been augmented, contrary to the provisions of this act,

are brought within the limits of H.M.'s dominions by the captor or any

[1] Ortolan, *Diplomatie de la mer*, t. 2, p. 302; Hall, § 227.

[2] Wheaton agrees in this: u. s.

[3] 5 Wheaton 385, Freeman Snow 406.

agent of the captor, or by any person having come into possession thereof with knowledge that the same was prize of war so captured as aforesaid,

it shall be lawful for the original owner of such prize or his agent, or for any person authorised in that behalf by the government of the foreign state to which such owner belongs, to make application to the Court of Admiralty for seizure and detention of such prize,

and the court shall, on due proof of the facts, order such prize to be restored.

The language of this section most easily accommodates itself to the view which we have expressed, that in the violated neutral territory the legal situation of a prize is not altered by the judgment of a belligerent prize court, since it does not except persons claiming under such a judgment from the description of persons having come into possession of the prize. Perhaps however the language might not be incapable of a different interpretation if held to be required by principle.

The United States neutrality laws enact that "the District Courts shall take cognisance of complaints, by whomsoever instituted, in cases of captures made within the waters of the United States, or within a marine league of the coasts or shores thereof[1]."

Of course the government of which the neutrality has been violated must do what it can to enforce the restitution of the peccant prize, being within its jurisdiction. When a French privateer captured the British ship *Grange* in Delaware Bay, the United States Government required the French consul Genêt to restore it, which he did[2]. When the United States man of war *Wachusett* forcibly carried off the Confederate cruiser *Florida* from the Brazilian port of Bahia, the Brazilian Government demanded reparation and obtained the release of her crew, but the *Florida* sank in Hampton Roads "by an unforeseen accident."

The legal extent of the protection against belligerent capture

[1] Sect. 7 of the act of 1818.

[2] *The Estrella*, 4 Wheaton 298, was the case of a prize taken and brought into United States waters by a privateer which had unlawfully augmented her force in them. She was recaptured in those waters by a United States cruiser, and the government libelled her, but for some reason which does not appear the proceedings were left to be fought out between the owner and the captor.

which the neutrality of territorial waters affords was discussed by Lord Stowell in the case of *The Anna*[1], the same in which he reckoned its geographical extent as being measured from the mud islands off the mouth of the Mississippi and not from the bank of the stream. "It is said that the act of capture is to be carried back to the commencement of the pursuit, and that if a contest begins before, it is lawful for a belligerent cruiser to follow, and to seize his prize within the territory of a neutral state; and the authority of Bynkershoek is cited on this point," [the *dum fervet opus* doctrine]. "True it is that that great man does intimate an opinion of his own to that effect, but with many qualifications, and as an opinion which he did not find to have been adopted by any other writers. I confess I should have been inclined to have gone along with him to this extent, that if a cruiser, which had before acted in a manner entirely unexceptionable and free from all violation of territory, had summoned a vessel to submit to examination and search, and that vessel had fled to such places as these" [the mud islands], "entirely uninhabited—and the cruiser had, without injury or annoyance to any person whatever, quietly taken possession of his prey—it would be stretching the point too hardly against the captor to say that on this account only it should be held an illegal capture." It will be observed that Lord Stowell stops far short of allowing a fight commenced outside territorial waters to be continued within them, which the danger thereby caused to neutral persons and property would render quite inadmissible.

As to the nature of the acts done by a cruiser in neutral waters which will invalidate a capture, Lord Stowell in *The Twee Gebroeders*[2] had laid down that no proximate act of war is to originate in them in any manner, and had applied that principle to the case in which a cruiser had stationed herself in neutral waters and sent her boats to make captures outside them. In another case of the same name[3] he refused to apply it to the case of a cruiser merely passing through neutral waters in order to make a capture, without stationing herself in them; but in *The Anna* he applied it in circumstances which he thus characterised.

[1] 5 C. Rob. 373.
[2] 3 C. Rob. 162.
[3] *The Twee Gebroeders* (2), 3 C. Rob. 336.

"The captors appear by their own description to have been standing off and on, obtaining information at the Balise, overhauling vessels in their course down the river, and making the river as much subservient to the purposes of war as if it had been a river of their own country. This," he said, "is an inconvenience which the states of America are called upon to resist, and which this court is bound on every principle to discourage and correct."

That a prize cannot lawfully be made in neutral waters does not depend on whether they were furnished with forts or other means of defence. There were none in the cases before Lord Stowell which have been cited, and in the case of *La Perle*[1] Portalis observed that it is the neutral territory which must be respected, without regard to its strength, and for its own sake.

But the prize which is to benefit by the fact that she was taken in neutral waters must not have begun the hostilities, although if attacked there she does not lose her right by defending herself[2]. And she must apply to the neutral authorities for protection, if she has the opportunity to do so before being attacked, and this even although those authorities may have no force at the spot capable of preventing the capture, for it is always possible that an intervention by a civil representative of the neutral state may be effectual. This ground was taken in 1851 by the president of the French republic as arbiter between the United States and Portugal, the latter power being alleged by the former to have failed in its duty as a neutral by not preventing the capture of an American privateer, the *General Armstrong*, in the harbour of Fayal, by an English Squadron in 1814. The privateer not having applied at the beginning to the local authorities, Portugal was not responsible for the result of the collision[3]. It needs scarcely be said that no complaint lies against the neutral power if it does all that it can to prevent an outrage being committed in its waters.

[1] 1 Pistoye et Duverdy 100, Freeman Snow 398.

[2] *The Anne*, 3 Wheaton 435, Scott 688.

[3] 2 Moore's *International Arbitrations of the United States* 1071–1132, 2 Wharton 604. The capture of the *Modeste* in the port of Genoa in 1793 is sometimes quoted as if at that time Great Britain held imperfect views about the inviolability of neutral waters. In truth it arose from a studied

Duties of Neutral States in their Public Action.

We now come to those duties of neutral states which do not consist in regulating the action of individuals, but in themselves doing certain things or avoiding them, granting certain things to a belligerent state or withholding them from it. Some parts of such conduct, especially in what concerns the land territory of a neutral, are so obviously dictated by the principle of not taking part in any operation of war that all question about them has long ago been settled. Thus, a belligerent must not be allowed to march his troops across neutral territory, and if any of them enter it, whether of free choice or in flight from an enemy, they must be interned[1]. That they should use the territory by recovering their strength in it, or by waiting in it for a favourable opportunity of returning to the theatre of war, or to their own country where they might be available for war, would clearly be to bring the neutral soil within the range of military operations. There can be no question about it of equal permission to both belligerents: it must be permitted to neither. But to other parts of the public conduct of states similar reasoning has not been worked out to universally accepted conclusions, and these parts will especially be found in what concerns the water territory of a neutral. Thus it has not been agreed that the entrance of a belligerent force into the ports of a neutral must be followed by its internment as absolutely as its entrance on his soil, and practice has not been uniform as to the limits of the difference. This is an example of the truth that the public action to be required of neutral states has not been reduced to rule with so near an approach to completeness as the action to be required of neutral individuals. That this is so is partly due to the difficulty inherent in some of the cases which arise, but partly also to the desire of governments to hold at their disposal a field which

disregard of the neutrality of Genoa, which it was desired to force into taking part with the allies. See Botta, *Storia d' Italia* 1789–1814, ed. 1824, v. I, pp. 171–4 and 206.

[1] See the rules about internment among the Hague laws of land war, above, p. 107.

they may use for promoting their political objects, and to the jealousy with which all depositaries of power regard any restraint on their conduct towards their equals, though they are often willing enough to legislate in restraint of their subjects. It may be doubted whether neutrals gain more by the liberty so claimed than they lose by the resentment which political motives cause, and sometimes by the undue imputation of such motives. The extension of rules appears to be desirable on every ground, and in the meantime belligerents are not bound to wait for their establishment. The area is covered by the elementary principles which underlie rules, namely that a neutral must take no part in any operation of a war, and that he must not interfere with any operation of war which is legitimate as between the belligerents. On those principles a belligerent may take his stand. Such assent of nations as makes international law is necessary for his being bound by any interpretation of them which does not commend itself to his own judgment, or by any exception to their application. He is not morally obliged to tolerate any conduct of a neutral by which his enemy may profit, if it cannot be justified by any interpretation or exception reposing on such assent. He may think it safer to endure it than by resenting it to add to the number of his antagonists, or on grounds of humanity he may think that its importance does not warrant his entering on a new war. But that is all.

Use of Neutral Waters by Belligerents.

In the detailed consideration of the duties of neutral states in their public action we will first take the subject to which in the preceding general observations we have referred as illustrative. The rules laid down by the British Government for the conduct of all its departments, at the outbreak of the war between Spain and the United States in 1898 and at that of the war between Russia and Japan in 1904[1], are expressed to be applicable to the ships of war of either belligerent "in any waters subject to the territorial jurisdiction of the British crown." No distinction is made in them between littoral waters and ports or roadsteads. We have already seen that the right

[1] *London Gazettes Extraordinary,* 26 April 1898 and 11 February 1904.

of innocent passage through the littoral waters of a neutral state extends to belligerent ships of war, subject to the neutral's right to regulate it, and so long as it is used truly for passage and not for anchoring or hovering[1]. To that extent the neutral power makes no concession to the belligerent by not interfering with his right of passage, but the regulations which the neutral has to make in order to prevent the abuse of that right are substantially the same as those required for ports and roadsteads, although their enforcement may not be always practicable, so the comprehension of both in one set of rules is convenient. The questions do not include in either case the absolute exclusion of belligerent ships of war, which in littoral waters would be theoretically inadmissible and in ports and roadsteads has not practically been suggested, while in both cases it has to be considered whether and how the stay of a belligerent ship of war shall be limited—to what purposes she may put any communication which she has with the shore—whether, in those purposes or in the duration of her stay, any larger favour shall be extended to her on the ground of distress—and whether, on the other hand, she is to be treated with peculiar strictness when the distress from which she seeks refuge is pursuit by her enemy.

The British rules begin by laying down that belligerent ships of war may not use British waters "as a station or place of resort for any warlike purpose, or for the purpose of obtaining any facilities for warlike equipment," which is a statement of principles that a belligerent may fall back on when regulations for carrying them out are wanting or insufficient, whenever they are violated either by or to the profit of his enemy.

Rule of 24 hours' interval.

Then Rule 1 proceeds to say that "no ship of war of either belligerent shall be permitted to leave any [British] port, roadstead or waters from which any vessel of the other belligerent, whether the same shall be a ship of war or a merchant ship, shall have previously departed, until after the expiration of at least 24 hours from the departure of such last mentioned vessel beyond the territorial jurisdiction of H. M." This is a reasonable precaution for securing that the stay of a ship of war in neutral waters shall not be abused by making them a sallying point for captures, and

[1] Part I, *Peace*, pp. 189, 192.

is referred to as a rule of the law of nations in a letter from a French captain to the governor of Cadiz in 1759[1]. In the regulations voted by the Institute of International Law in 1898, Art. 42, it is extended to the case in which the ship secondly departing is a merchantman, so as to make the 24 hours' interval apply between any two ships of mutually enemy character, and the local authority is to increase the interval if necessary, as is implied by the phrase "at least" in the British rule. And the rule of the Institute provides, in accordance as may be believed with general practice, that "the right of first departing belongs to the ship which first entered, or, if she does not wish to exercise it, to the other, who has to claim it from the local authority, which delivers the permission if the adversary, duly notified, persists in remaining[2]." We thus have what may be called "the rule of 24 hours' interval," to distinguish it from "the rule of 24 hours' stay" with which we shall meet. It has been adopted in recent declarations of neutrality or other official documents as follows. As between any two ships of mutually enemy character, in 1898 by Brazil (with the addition that the interval shall be 72 hours if the ship first departing is a sailing vessel and that secondly departing a steamer), China, Italy (which also has the rule in Art. 250 of its Mercantile Marine Code), the Netherlands and Russia, and in 1904 by France; also by the Belgian decree of 18 February 1901, Art. 19. Where the ship secondly departing is one of war, by Great Britain and Denmark in 1898 and 1904, Portugal in 1898, and Sweden and Norway and Egypt in 1904 (the latter with the addition that no vessel of one of the belligerents shall leave either of the terminal ports of the Suez Canal less than 24 hours after a ship of war of the other belligerent has left the same port); also by Spain in 1863[3]. And in 1898 Haiti and Japan promulgated the 24 hours' interval only as between the departures of mutually enemy ships of war.

A still greater care for the safety of departing vessels is shown by a clause in the regulations of the Institute of International Law, to the effect that if at the departure of a vessel

[1] Ortolan 292.

[2] 17 *Annuaire* 286.

[3] Correspondence with Great Britain, 2 Ortolan 297.

belonging to a belligerent one or more enemy ships are signalled, the departing ship must be notified, and may be readmitted to the port to await the entry or disappearance of the others[1]. And the French instructions of 1904 provide that belligerent ships in a French port must abstain from all enquiry as to the forces, position or resources of their enemies, and must not put to sea hastily (*brusquement*) in order to pursue those which may be signalled.

We may sum up by saying that the rule of 24 hours' interval is advanced far enough towards universal acceptance for a belligerent to have just cause of complaint against a neutral, if a vessel of his should be captured by a ship of war of his enemy which had been allowed to depart from a port of that power within 24 hours after her.

Rule of 24 hours' stay.

We now come to the rule of 24 hours' stay as the limit of the hospitality accorded to belligerent ships of war in neutral waters. The form in which this is received in Great Britain is found in Rule 2 of the instructions of 1898 and 1904, which requires that any ship of war of either belligerent "shall depart and put to sea within 24 hours after her entrance into any [British] port, roadstead or waters, except in case of stress of weather, or of her requiring provisions or things necessary for the subsistence of her crew or repairs; in either of which cases the authorities of the port or of the nearest port, as the case may be, shall require her to put to sea as soon as possible after the expiration of such period of 24 hours, without permitting her to take in supplies beyond what may be necessary for her immediate use; and no such vessel which may have been allowed to remain within British waters for the purpose of repairs shall continue in [them] for a longer period than 24 hours after her necessary repairs shall have been completed: provided that......the time hereby limited......shall always in case of necessity be extended so far as may be requisite for giving effect to [the rule of 24 hours' interval], but no further or otherwise."

[1] In the regulations made by the neutral states of Italy in 1778 it is put that in such a case the departing ship shall be obliged to return to the port: 2 Ortolan 292 note.

Flight from the enemy.

The first remark on this is that no distinction is made in it between the cases of a belligerent ship of war entering neutral waters in flight from an enemy, to escape from peril of the sea, or for any reason lying within her free choice. Yet these cases may be distinguished in principle. When refuge is given even for a limited time to a ship of war flying from an enemy, in which must be included the case of escape after defeat although no pursuer may be following close, we have not to do with that aid of a merely general nature which cannot fail to be received from any use of a neutral port, but with the interruption of a specific operation of war to the advantage of the belligerent who is received but not interned. Accordingly the Institute of International Law has justly laid down that "a belligerent ship taking refuge in a neutral port from pursuit, or after being defeated by the enemy, or for want of a sufficient crew to keep the sea, must remain there till the end of the war. The same applies if she conveys there any sick or wounded, and is in a condition for fighting when she has landed them. The sick or wounded, although received and succoured, must equally be interned after being healed, unless judged to be unfit for military service[1]." The want of a sufficient crew to keep the sea is here put on a level with flight from the enemy, because to permit the recruitment of men would be a more obvious and flagrant breach of neutrality than to permit the receipt of supplies and repairs. In comparing the rule of the Institute with the British rule it must be borne in mind that the latter only limits the stay of a belligerent ship of war, not recognising or conferring on her a right even to the hospitality so limited, and that an intention cannot be presumed to surrender or fetter the power of the crown to deal with any case as the principles of neutral duty may require. The British rule is not therefore to be read as ensuring a 24 hours' stay, free from internment, to a ship of war flying from her enemy, or wanting a sufficient crew to

[1] 17 *Annuaire* 285. Although *un navire belligérant* is a term comprising merchantmen, this can scarcely have been intended, since their internment has never been proposed, and persons crossing a land frontier with their goods in order to escape requisition or pillage are not interned.

keep the sea, and we cannot believe that such would be granted to her. After the sea fight of 10 August 1904 several Russian ships fled to Chinese ports, and in the cases of the *Askold* and the *Grosovoi*, which reached Shanghai, the duty of disarming them was finally admitted and performed, though the crews were not placed under proper guard. The *Reshitelni*, which reached Chifu, was cut out by the Japanese after she had been subjected to a disarmament which her captors found not to be complete; and it seems to us impossible to assert that the Japanese exceeded their rights in this, although it was an extreme exercise of them.

Repairs and supplies in other cases, especially coal.

In every other case but those just considered a belligerent ship of war may need repair or supply, and it has never been claimed that so much repair or supply must be refused her as will enable her to keep the sea. The analogy to a force crossing his land frontier, which a neutral must intern whether or not it was flying from an enemy, is here departed from, and in that fact it is impossible not to see an effect of the desire of governments to retain in their hands the power to oblige their friends, and to avoid establishing a rule which may one day tell against themselves. Humanity is invoked, but since there would be no inhumanity in internment the only ground for the plea is the fear that, rather than be interned, a ship might try to keep the sea too long[1]. It is however agreed that a belligerent ship of war must not enlist men in a neutral port[2], make it the base of an investigation

[1] See a similar plea in favour of a belligerent's merchantmen driven into enemy waters by peril of the sea: above, p. 140. The Institute of International Law, which admits it in that case, does not admit it in favour of enemy ships of war except as addressed to generosity: 17 *Annuaire* 285. Ortolan gives examples of immunity generously allowed to enemy ships of war in distress, by French and Spanish authorities, a British example being of the opposite character: t. 2, pp. 321–5. But in dealing with neutral duties it must not be forgotten that generosity to one belligerent is exercised at the expense of the other.

[2] In the regulations of some countries, as Brazil (1898), Belgium (1901) and France (1904), the prohibition is expressly declared to include enlisting the ship's own nationals, and this is the effect of the Foreign Enlistment Act 1870 when a royal license has not been obtained to the

into the force, situation or resources of the enemy[1], or receive in it such repairs or supplies as will increase her fighting strength beyond what it was when she came in. She may be made seaworthy, and the British and usual rule extends the limit of her stay to "24 hours after her necessary repairs shall have been completed." In that time she may take in, under Rule 3 of the British instructions, only "provisions and such other things as may be requisite for the subsistence of her crew, and so much coal as may be sufficient to carry [her] to the nearest port of her own country or to some nearer named neutral[2] destination; and no coal shall again be supplied to [her] in the same or any other port, roadstead or waters subject to the territorial jurisdiction of H.M., without special permission, until after the expiration of three months from the time when such coal may have been last supplied to her within British waters." It is understood that the coal supplied under such a rule shall be used in proceeding to the destination which the commander of the ship named as being that of which the distance authorised the supply, and it may fairly be argued that in proceeding to that destination she shall make no captures, since her making any during a voyage which she had been expressly coaled for would constitute the neutral port her base of operations for the specific operation of war constituted by them; only if she is attacked during that voyage she may of course defend herself. But the legiti-

contrary; but the neutrality laws of the United States allow enlisting nationals transiently within the territory. See above, pp. 182, 184. In theory the more stringent rule seems to be more in accordance with the principles enunciated above, p. 181, lest the ship should become the equivalent of a recruiting agency set up within the territory.

[1] *Ils* [the belligerent ships of war] *doivent s'abstenir de tout acte ayant pour but de faire du lieu d'asile la base d'une opération quelconque contre leurs ennemis, comme aussi de toute investigation sur les ressources, les forces et l'emplacement de leurs ennemis:* Belgian decree of 1901, Art. 15. The French instructions of 1904 are in nearly the same terms. The Institute of International Law merely requires abstinence from *tout espionnage*: 17 *Annuaire* 286. The larger form of the rule seems to be right in principle, but in any form the rule must be difficult to enforce without a strict control of the communication between the ship and the shore.

[2] The words "named neutral" were added in 1904.

mation by international practice, however faulty in principle, of the mere receipt of supplies without a specification of the use to which they are to be put, must imply the legitimation of any use to which they may be put[1].

The rules which have been thus far treated of, except the three months' interval between supplies of coal—which however has been adopted by the Netherlands, Denmark, Belgium, Japan and China besides Great Britain—have been adopted by numerous states as the standard of their conduct, and are substantially incorporated in the naval code recommended by the Institute of International Law[2]. When the Russian Baltic fleet was about to undertake a voyage to the Sea of Japan, Great Britain took a further step in advance by the instructions of 8 August 1904[3], which appear to us to have been not only justifiable but a necessary corollary from admitted principles. After reciting that the principle of the previous British regulations "does not extend to enable belligerent ships of war to utilise neutral ports directly for the purpose of hostile operations," it was directed that the rule which "refers to the extent of coal which may be supplied to belligerent ships of war in British ports during the [then] war shall not be understood as having any application to the case of a belligerent fleet proceeding either to the seat of war, or to any position or positions on the line of route with the object of intercepting neutral ships on suspicion of carrying contraband of war; and that such fleets shall not be permitted to make use in any way of any port, roadstead or waters subject to the jurisdiction

[1] The supplying and coaling the Confederate cruisers in British ports which entered into the grounds of the award in the *Alabama* case must not be and were not judged by the better practice which has since so widely arisen. The Confederate ports being closed by blockade, a proposed voyage to them would not have been a justification of coaling the cruisers even had the practice then existed. But in the award the coaling and other supplies were connected with previous failures in neutral duty, which the entry of the cruisers into British ports gave the opportunity of correcting by detaining the ships, or with repetitions of supply, sufficient, without specification of its purpose, to make the ports a base of operations.

[2] 17 *Annuaire* 285.

[3] Parliamentary Paper, Russia No. 1 (1905), p. 15, and Malta Government Gazette of 12 August 1904.

of H.M. for the purpose of coaling, either directly from the shore or from colliers accompanying such fleet, whether vessels of such fleet present themselves to such port or roadstead or within the said waters at the same time or successively; and that the same practice shall be pursued with reference to single belligerent ships of war proceeding for the purpose of belligerent operations as above defined; provided that this is not to be applied to the case of vessels putting in on account of actual distress at sea." France stands at the other extreme of the scale of advance in the definition of neutral duties, not only not following England in treating the voyage to a scene of action as a special case to which all assistance in coal ought to be denied, but not even limiting the stay in her ports of belligerent ships of war not accompanied by prizes to 24 hours or any other time; while she limits the supplies and repairs which such ships may receive in her ports only to the subsistence of their crews and the safety of their navigation, without any reference to the quarter towards which such navigation may be directed[1]. We must therefore admit that the rule of 24 hours' stay, and the limits which as above mentioned have been set by many states to their supply of coal, are not yet a part of international law; but the amount of recognition which they have received would lend very great weight to any complaint which a belligerent might make on principle of conduct by a neutral power not in conformity with them.

Prizes in neutral ports.

A prize sailing under the war flag of her captors stands in principle, for the purpose of her reception into a neutral port, on the same footing as if she had originally belonged to her captors. But there is always the danger of a conflict on board her between her own crew and the prize crew, and, if she is accompanied by a ship of war, of a conflict between the two ships; and this furnishes a sufficient reason for a special objection being taken by neutrals to the reception of prizes in their ports. Indeed, even if the captors are so superior that no such danger

[1] Instructions of February 1904: 11 *Revue Générale de D. I. P., Documents*, p. 2. See above, p. 174. It is not the practice of Germany to issue detailed general instructions for the conduct of her forces and authorities with regard to a war in which she is neutral.

practically exists, their retention of the prize is a continuous exercise of force over the captured crew[1], and no exercise of force between belligerents can in theory be permitted in neutral waters. It was not however from these considerations but because of the injury done to commerce by the illegal practices of privateers and pirates, that the regulations of 1650 and ordinance of 1681 prohibited the stay of prizes in French ports for more than 24 hours, except for stress of weather or if they had been captured from enemies of France, the property of French subjects to be taken out of them before their departure and restored[2]. It is possible that this regulation of 24 hours' stay for prizes suggested the similar regulations in different countries for belligerent ships of war generally, but by many powers prizes are now treated as exceptions and ships of war are prohibited from taking them at all into their ports when neutral except in case of distress. Notably this is the case in Great Britain[3], Italy[4], Belgium[5], the Netherlands, Denmark and Japan[6]. France, Spain and Brazil adhere to the older system of applying the rule of 24 hours' stay to ships with prizes and not to other ships of war, but they prohibit altogether the disposal of prizes or of articles coming out of them, a prohibition which is implicitly contained in the refusal of entry to the prizes though often expressed in addition to it. Of course all this paragraph refers to prizes which have not been judicially condemned by the proper court or sold by its direction. Once that has been done the vessel is the property of the new owner and is no longer a prize.

[1] Vattel observes that *garder et retenir des prisonniers de guerre est une continuation d'hostilités*: l. 3, § 132. But the use which he makes of this principle is to prohibit a privateer from landing his prisoners and keeping them captive on shore. He does not perceive that it equally condemns what he describes without disapproval as being the practice, namely that *un armateur conduit sa prise dans le premier port neutre et l'y vend librement.* The explanation may be that he appears from the context to have been thinking of the case only as it affects property.

[2] 2 Ortolan 303 note.

[3] Art. 4 of the instructions of 1898 and 1904.

[4] Art. 246 of the Marine Code.

[5] Art. 10 of the decree of 18 February 1891.

[6] The last three by their regulations of 1898 or 1904.

Even when a prize lies in a neutral port, the belligerent power whose cruisers have captured her cannot set up a court there to try the capture. The exercise of jurisdiction being a right attached to sovereignty, to attempt it anywhere without the permission of the territorial sovereign would be a usurpation, and for that sovereign to grant the permission would be an unneutral loan of his sovereignty to the belligerent. The same reasoning does not apply to an ally, but the general sentiment is opposed to his allowing a court to be set up in his territory. It is, says Ortolan, "the general rule among all maritime powers that captors are bound to take or send their prizes to the ports of the state to which they belong, and as far as possible to the ports where they were equipped"—the last clause refers to privateers—"and that, under severe penalties, nothing shall be removed from the prize or alienated before a definitive judgment of a special court, sitting in the territory of that state, has pronounced the validity of the capture[1]." The rule however does not appear to require the presence of the prize in the ports of the state where the court is held. Phillimore, quoted with acquiescence by Hall, says that "an attentive review of all the cases decided in the courts of England and the North American United States during the last war, 1793–1815, leads to the conclusion that the condemnation of a capture by a regular prize court, sitting in the country of the belligerent, of a prize lying at the time of the sentence in a neutral port, is irregular but clearly valid[2]." This, if established in practice, seems to be unsound in principle. To be a proper subject of adjudication a prize must have been brought *intra praesidia*, which is not the case while she lies in a neutral port, in which any forcible control of her ought not to be allowed by the territorial sovereign.

No asylum where previous breach of neutrality.

It remains to be considered whether any asylum at all ought to be given in neutral waters to belligerent ships of war or their prizes when the former have been fitted out or the latter taken in breach of the neutrality of the very state under the protection

[1] *Diplomatie de la mer*, t. 2, p. 313.

[2] Phillimore, v. 3, § 379, quoted by Hall, § 226.

of which they seek to shelter. We have seen that by British law and United States' practice the prize which is in such a case is so far from enjoying an asylum that she ought to be seized and restored[1]. It has been thought that from a ship of war the stain of violated neutrality is wiped away by her commission. Accordingly the Confederate cruisers which had been illegally despatched from English ports were afterwards treated by the British authorities as if there was nothing against them. That view was not accepted by the arbitrators at Geneva, who found that "the *Alabama* was on several occasions freely admitted into the ports of the colonies of Great Britain, instead of being proceeded against as it ought to have been in any and every port within British jurisdiction in which it might have been found;" a finding of similar purport being made as to the *Florida*, with the addition, "nor can the fact of the entry of the *Florida* into the Confederate port of Mobile, and of its stay there during four months, extinguish the responsibility previously to that time incurred by Great Britain." This appears to be the correct reasoning. A state which has not adequately enforced the observance of its neutrality is bound to take every opportunity of stopping the mischievous consequences of its slip, nor can its doing so be rightfully complained of by a foreign sovereign who has granted a commission only rendered possible by the violation of neutrality. At least the obligation resulting from the slip cannot be destroyed by the circumstance that it may involve the state to which the slip is imputable in a difficulty with a third party. To intern the offending ship without insisting on her forfeiture would seem to conciliate as far as possible the duty of stopping her career with respect to a foreign flag[2].

[1] Above, pp. 200, 201.

[2] It is desirable to take every opportunity of effacing the prejudice against international arbitration which the Geneva award has created in this country. We will therefore observe that even if the wrath of a state of which the neutrality has been infringed ought to be diverted by a commission granted by a friendly power into seeking redress by diplomatic channels, still diplomatic channels were not open in the cases of the *Alabama* and *Florida*, the Confederate States not having been recognised as a power. They had only been recognised as having

Use of Neutral Soil by Belligerents.

Any question about illegitimate advantage to be obtained by a belligerent on neutral soil can scarcely arise except where the immediate source of the advantage is the action of individuals or that of the territorial sovereign: the action of the belligerent state is excluded by the fact of the soil being foreign to it, with no such exception as in the case of neutral harbours arises by the customary admission of the belligerent flag under certain conditions. Consequently most of the possible cases have already been dealt with in going through the various heads under which the British Foreign Enlistment Act and the United States Neutrality Laws repress the unneutral action of individuals. The principal matters which remain to be noticed are the loan of money, which has not fallen under legislation in the English-speaking countries, and the use which the territorial sovereign may fairly permit to be made of his postal and telegraphic services.

Loans to belligerent states.

I. Since money is truly described as the sinews of war, and it is no part of the business of a state to deal in money, its loan by a neutral state to a belligerent would necessarily have a special character, not only as aiding the latter in fact but also as disclosing an intent to aid him in his war. It would therefore be an unneutral act. If by the law of the neutral state the consent of the executive is required to loans by individuals to foreign powers, or if the executive is in the habit of practically controlling such operations by the exercise of its influence, a loan by individuals to a belligerent which is allowed to slip through the meshes will have an international character not distinguishable from a loan by the state. But in countries where, as in England, the loan market is free in time of peace, the question arises whether the state is bound to interfere with it in time of war by a prohibition to lend to belligerents. In such a country loans to foreign states are not political but commercial acts, falling within the daily

belligerent rights; therefore, if the ships were not liable to be stopped, Great Britain was defenceless against the wrong done her by the continuance of their depredations—*quod est absurdum*.

habits of persons engaged in business, not implying any intent by those persons as to the use to be made of the money by the governments assisted, and such that to prevent them just when the greatest profit is likely to be obtained from them would be felt to be an onerous interposition. They do not constitute a participation in any specific operation of war, nor is the branch of business to which they belong reserved for public action by the general understanding of the civilised world. Tried therefore by the tests which have been suggested as imposed by the theory of neutrality[1], loans by neutral individuals to belligerent states must be pronounced legitimate, and such they are in fact held to be. During the Franco-German war of 1870, large parts of the loans contracted by both belligerents were raised without objection in England.

The case has by some writers been confounded with that of loans to unrecognised insurgents against friendly powers, which in England and the United States are illegal. But those operations do not fall under the principles relating to neutrality, since, even when separation is the object of the insurrection, it is only after the new state has been recognised as independent by the state in which the loan is made that there are in the eyes of the latter two friendly powers between which there can be neutrality. Even the recognition that the insurgents have established so solid a military position as to be entitled to the rights of belligerents will not affect the question. Such recognition will ensure respect for their acts of war, and will impose duties on the recognising state and its subjects, but it does not raise the insurgents to the position of friends, and assistance given to them remains assistance given against the only friends whom either international law or the law of the land sees in the case. Nor can it be said that loans to insurgents are a part of any regular financial business. They are very special operations, the motive of which is seldom free from the ingredient of political intent[2].

[1] Above, p. 176.

[2] See *De Wütz v. Hardricks*, 9 Moore C. P. 586, and *Kennett v. Chambers*, 14 Howard 38, Scott 723. In the last mentioned case the District Court of the United States held a contract illegal which was

Use of postal and telegraph services.

II. There is no doubt that a state is bound in principle not knowingly to allow the use of its services for the reception and transmission of letters or telegrams, the latter whether wireless or not, in furtherance of belligerent interests; and where any such service is not a state monopoly, its exercise in the territory by a private undertaking ought to be subject to a similar restraint[1]. Such use of the service would be a direct aid to the belligerent, an implication in the operations which were combined by means of it, and would make the territory a base of operations to that extent. There is however great difficulty in making any practical application of the principle. The contents of letters cannot be known without an intolerable violation of the secrecy of the post office, and the true meaning of telegrams may be concealed by cipher, or by the employment of common words and names arranged to convey to the recipient a sense which others cannot penetrate. It does not seem possible for a neutral state to do more than to refuse for itself, and prohibit for the private undertakings in its territory, the reception and transmission of messages in cipher, or in common language which from its want of apparent sense may be inferred to be the equivalent of cipher, when those messages appear from their address to be intended for the benefit of a belligerent operation. In the instructions issued in 1898 by Brazil, Art. 5 ran that "it is prohibited to citizens, or aliens residing in Brazil, to announce by telegraph the departure or near arrival of any ship, merchant or war, of the belligerents, or to give them any orders, instructions or warnings with the purpose of prejudicing the enemy." This seems to go too far, since suppression of the information usually given of the movement

made with the object of assisting in the equipment of the army of the insurgent Mexican province of Texas, at a time when it had not been acknowledged by the United States as the independent state of that name, but when the establishment of its independence was hardly doubtful.

[1] *Il est entendu que la liberté de l'état neutre de transmettre des dépêches n'implique pas la faculté d'en user, ou d'en permettre l'usage, manifestement pour prêter assistance à l'un des belligérants*: Art. 4 of the resolutions of the Institute of International Law on submarine cables, 19 *Annuaire* 332.

of shipping, however intended to deny assistance to one belligerent, might operate as an assistance to the other.

Of course a neutral state must not allow a belligerent to have in its territory an establishment of his own for postal or telegraphic service, as Russia was too long allowed by China to have a station near Chifu for maintaining wireless communication between Port Arthur, besieged, and the outer world. But a neutral state cannot be bound to prohibit or prevent the passage of wireless messages across its territory. Just as there is a right of innocent passage through the littoral sea, there must be a right of innocent passage through the vertically littoral air, which before long it may become necessary to define, but which certainly must not be so limited as to impose too heavy a burden on the sovereign of the ground.

CHAPTER IX.

BLOCKADE.

FROM immemorial antiquity the operations of a siege have included preventing communication between the besieged place and the outside, by ingress, egress, or transport inwards or outwards. Every attempt by neutrals to cross the line of investment is a palpable interference with a specific operation of war, incompatible as such with their duties as neutrals, and has always been sternly repressed by the besiegers. This is equally true when the besieged place is on the coast and the line of investment partly on the sea, and in that case it has been made the basis of extensions which have resulted in the international doctrine of blockade. To understand those extensions it must be borne in mind that the word "blockade" originally meant "siege by investment," and must not, when first met with, be taken in the technical sense which has grown up along with the technical doctrine[1]. The history commences

[1] "The word *blocus* or *blockade* is neither to be found in Du Cange nor in the vocabulary of barbarous Latinity appended to Facciolati. *Bloc*, in the language of the Walloon country, signified a high mound; whence persons who had died under sentence of excommunication, and whom it was not lawful to bury beneath the soil, were said to be *imblocati* because the earth was heaped over their bodies as they lay on the surface: Du Cange, v. *Imblocatus*. We are brought still nearer to the root by *bloche*, which in the dialect of Champagne signified a clod of earth: Du Cange, v. *Blesta*. And *blocage* even now denotes in France the rubblework often used to fill up the interior of walls, or a rough wall itself when entirely composed of such work. Our own *block* is obviously allied, though we do not use it of stones or nodules so small as to serve for rubblework. Thus a stone, nodule, clod or mass, smaller or larger—a funereal barrow, a dyke or mound, themselves

with 1584, in which year the Dutch government issued a *placaat* declaring all the ports of Flanders then remaining in the power of Spain to be blockaded. Those ports were not many, they must at that time have all been more or less strongly fortified, and the naval power of the Dutch was already considerable. It is consequently quite intelligible that a real attack on them all may have been intended, or at least such an intention professed; and we must not assume that the term "blockade" was used so early in any other sense than that of "siege." We should rather understand that the intention was to use the right of siege on an unprecedented scale. For nearly half a century the Dutch did not advance further in the particular direction thus entered on, probably because they boldly tried to prevent all commerce whatever with their enemies[1], but a significant development appeared in the great work of Grotius, published in 1625. After mentioning objects of use only in war and those which are of use only in peace, the former of which are declared to be always capturable, the latter never, he says about objects which are of use in both war and peace (*ancipitis usus*) that "if the introduction of the supplies impeded me in the pursuit of my right, and this was open to the knowledge of the person who introduced them, as if I was keeping a town besieged or ports closed, and a surrender or peace was already looked for, he will be bound to repay me for the damage occasioned by his fault[2]." Here the condition that a surrender or peace seems near, and the circumstance that a right of capturing objects of no use in war is not given at all, were limitations of which belligerent governments disposed to close the ports of their enemies to neutrals took no account. But the mention of the closure of ports as a distinct case from

large blocks or masses and piled up of smaller clods and rubble—even, if occasion serves, a rough and ready wall, built with the unwrought materials obtainable on the spot—lastly, a circumvallation: such is the series of ideas presented to us by the words of this family." Westlake, on *Commercial Blockades*, in the *Transactions of the Juridical Society, 1858–1863*, vol. 2, p. 701.

[1] See the *placaat* of 1599, mentioned above, p. 170.

[2] *De jure belli ac pacis*, l. 3, c. 1, § 5. And see the passage quoted above, p. 172, from l. 3, c. 17, § 3.

siege, operating in the opposite direction as an encouragement, was availed of with all the more freedom since Grotius had placed his opinion on the ground of the law of nature, finding, as he says, nothing settled about the matter by agreement. The need of that encouragement must have been felt by the Dutch because since 1584 Ostend had passed into the hands of the Spaniards, and England from a co-belligerent had become a neutral power, so that siege of all the Flemish enemy ports was not to be thought of. Within five years from the appearance of the *De jure belli ac pacis* the government obtained opinions from the admiralty of Amsterdam and, as Bynkershoek believed, from private lawyers, to the effect that "the rule which obtains in the case of towns, which are properly said to be besieged, and which has with good reason been applied to camps, which are as it were besieged, extends also to the enemy's ports, which when invested by ships are deemed to be besieged[1]." On the strength of these opinions the States General in 1630 issued a *placaat* in which they announced their intention to confiscate neutral ships caught at any distance sailing for the enemy's ports in Flanders, as also those which, having broken the blockade, should be caught at any time before the completion of their voyage. This they justified by the declaration that "their High Mightinesses keep the said ports continually blockaded by their vessels of war at an excessive charge to the state, in order to hinder all transport to and commerce with the enemy, and because those ports and places are reputed to be besieged, which has from all time been an ancient usage after the example of all kings, princes, powers and other republics, which have exercised the same right on similar occasions[2]." For the real absence of settled usage we may safely accept the statement of Grotius in preference to the phrases of official style asserting its existence. What is important in the *placaat* is that investment by sea takes the place of any necessity for true siege. In other words blockade as a

[1] Bynkershoek, *Quæstiones juris publici*, i, 11. That great jurist passed lightly over the equivalence of investment to siege, which by his time had been settled, but wished that Grotius "had not added the condition that a surrender or peace is already looked for."

[2] Robinson's *Collectanea Maritima*, p. 158.

technical institution, with its interception of all commerce and not merely of contraband goods, is officially adopted by Holland, and thenceforward stands out distinctly from the confused ideas of previous ages[1]. That the investment should be real, as in the actual instance the *placaat* asserted it to be, the authority from which that document emanated could not take from neutrals the right to judge for themselves. If it was alleged by them not to be real, that would be a dispute between the governments concerned.

The new institution however did not immediately find acceptance outside Holland. The Dutch government did not help to smooth the difficulty over by showing much practical moderation, for in 1652 it proclaimed a blockade of all the coasts of the British Isles, of which it would be absurd to imagine any real investment. But it was capable of adapting its course to the pursuit of diplomatic advantage, and it did not renew the *placaat* of 1630 on the occasion of its decreeing a blockade of Flanders in 1645, and in its treaty of 1646 with France, while obtaining (as it believed) the concession of the rule "free ships free goods," it did not insist on the equivalence of investment to siege, but acquiesced in the confiscation of ship and cargo being denounced against those who shall have succoured or thrown men, grain or provisions into a place attacked by his majesty's armies[2]. And this provision was substantially repeated in the Anglo-French treaty of 1655[3]. The Franco-Spanish treaty of the Pyrenees in 1659 prohibited commerce

[1] See above, p. 172; also p. 171, as to the influence of such unilateral acts in developing the law.

[2] Dumont, t. 6, pt. 1, p. 342. See above, p. 127, as to the efforts of the Dutch in favour of the rule "free ships free goods." "The language of this treaty [of 1646] would seem to support the construction put upon it by De Witt, that it provided for the perfect freedom of the Dutch carrying trade; but De Witt found to his surprise that the French interpreted the treaty merely to provide for the temporary suspension of the ordinance of king Henry III (A.D. 1584), according to which enemy's goods forming part of the cargo of a neutral vessel infected the remainder of the cargo and the vessel itself, and led to the condemnation of both as good prize." Twiss, *War*, § 81. But the Dutch obtained from France the concession of "free ships free goods" in 1662.

[3] Dumont, t. 6, pt. 2, p. 121.

of all kinds with towns and places "besieged, blockaded or invested," but added an express prohibition of French commerce with Portugal, as being a revolted province of Spain, the whole Portuguese coast being apparently regarded as too extensive for the Spanish blockade to be relied on for legally sealing it[1]. But the Anglo-Swedish treaty of 1661, while also prohibiting the entry of all kinds of articles into besieged places, restricted the right of capturing them to cases of contraband: if goods not contraband should be carried by either party to ports or places besieged by the other, they might either be sold to the besiegers or carried away freely to ports not besieged[2]. In the Dutch-Algerine treaty of 1662[3] and the Dutch-Swedish one of 1667[4] the prohibition of commerce with besieged places extends to contraband and articles which may tend to the convenience or assistance of the enemy, which, if not intended as a euphemism for all articles, would probably be interpreted as such by the Dutch admiralty. And this is the last which we hear of any limitation, even veiled, of the kind of commerce obnoxious to blockade. But both the treaties in question insist on the limitation of blockade to siege—the Algerine one prohibiting the commerce with "towns actually besieged in regular form (*obsidione justa realiter cinctis*) either by sea or land, and by no means in any other case"—and the Swedish one prohibiting it with "fortresses, towns or places having military garrisons, so long as it shall happen that they are under siege or attack by an armed force with the intention of reducing them into the power of such force, and, in respect of places situate on the coast, by land as well as by sea." Such careful phraseology begets the suspicion that the governments and admiralties of naval powers were beginning to assume the equivalence of investment to siege with a freedom which the simple word "siege" in a treaty could not be trusted to prevent. The new institution had indeed nearly reached its maturity, and it was finally recognised by the Anglo-Dutch treaty of 1674[5], the Franco-Dutch one of 1678[6] and the Dutch-Swedish one of 1679[7], in all which commerce in articles not contraband is

[1] Ib., p. 264. [2] Ib., p. 384. [3] Ib., p. 445.
[4] Dumont, t. 7, pt. 1, p. 37.
[5] Ib., p. 282. [6] Ib., p. 357. [7] Ib., p. 437.

declared to be free "except with towns or places besieged, shut in or invested (*obsidione cinctis, circumseptis vel investitis*)," to which the first of the three adds "*Gallice, blocquées ou investies.*"

That before the end of the seventeenth century blockade had acquired the definite meaning of a lawful exclusion of all commerce from an invested place, subject to the question of what might be a real investment, may be concluded further from the fact that, in contrast with the extravagant use of the term in 1652[1], it was not used in the Anglo-Dutch convention of 1689, notified by the parties to all the European powers. That document did not profess to exercise a belligerent right against neutrals but, in effect, to forbid neutrality. It dwelt on the necessity of destroying the commerce of France in order to prevent a great effusion of blood, and recited that many sovereigns had prohibited trade with France and that others would soon prohibit it, wherefore the two allies prohibited commerce with the whole coast of France and with all French possessions in every part of the world, and announced their intention of seizing on the high seas, at any distance from France, any ship which might be found sailing for her ports[2]. This was an extraordinary stroke of policy, and, as the *placaat* of 1599[3] and the similar attempt in 1793, outside law even in the ideas of those who resorted to it; and was marked as such by the separate article by which the two allies promised to aid each other in suppressing the resistance which they expected that their action would arouse. There are reasons for thinking that the interdiction so fulminated was not attempted to be enforced for more than a few months, and that the armed neutrality of 1693 was caused by other infractions of maritime law.

The question of the equivalence of investment by sea to siege as conferring a right to cut off neutral commerce, of which we have traced the history, was nearly equivalent to that which has been raised in more modern times of the legitimacy of commercial blockades. Of a port neither fortified nor garrisoned but purely commercial there cannot be real siege: such a port can be occupied from the sea whenever desired. On the other hand a naval force which desires to cut off neutral

[1] See above, p. 224.

[2] Dumont, t. 7, pt. 2, p. 238.

[3] Above, p. 170.

commerce from a port not purely commercial can have little difficulty in giving a colour of attack to a maritime investment of it. It was in the form of an objection to commercial blockades that the question of the seventeenth century was revived in the nineteenth. In the preamble to the Berlin decree of 1806 Napoleon, with a lofty disregard of more than a century of intervening history, complained that "Great Britain extends the right of blockade to unfortified towns and commercial ports, to harbours and the mouths of rivers, though according to right reason and the usage of all civilised nations it is only applicable to strong places." And in 1859 President Buchanan of the United States added the abolition of commercial blockades, as a condition for adhering to the Declaration of Paris, to the immunity of private enemy property at sea which had at first been made the only condition[1]. Secretary Cass wrote that "the investment of a place by sea and land with a view to its reduction, preventing it from receiving supplies of men and material necessary for its defence, is a legitimate mode of prosecuting hostilities, which cannot be objected to so long as war is required as an arbiter of national disputes. But the blockade of a coast or of commercial positions along it, without any regard to ulterior military operations and with the real design of carrying on a war against trade, and from its very nature against the trade of peaceable and friendly powers, instead of a war against armed men, is a proceeding which it is difficult to reconcile with reason or with the opinions of modern times[2]." The same view was supported in England by Cobden[3], but the tendency of the times has been against it, and we must be content with the compromise between the exigencies of belligerents and the just claims of neutrals which by tacit international agreement has been effected in the matter

[1] See above, pp. 129, 154.

[2] Circular to the powers, among others to Mr Dallas, minister to Great Britain, under date of 29 June 1859: 3 Wharton 373, 7 Moore 450, 781.

[3] The abolition of commercial blockades was advocated by us in *Papers read before the Juridical Society, 1858–1863*, vol. 2, pp. 681–721, and in a pamphlet entitled *Commercial Blockades considered with reference to Law and Policy*, 1862.

of blockade. The right of a belligerent to establish a commercial blockade cannot be based on any theory of neutral duty which will not set him free from any limitation of the articles which he may please to consider as contraband of war. It may be put on the alleged superiority of the belligerent's exigencies, called rights, our condemnation of which has been expressed above[1]. Or it may be put, as Hautefeuille and others have done, on a ground which applies only to one of the interpretations of the compromise, in connection with which we shall mention it[2].

The compromise between belligerents and neutrals which is all that can be called law in the matter of blockade is subject to the interpretation of a real investment—in other words, to the question what is the character of the investment which neutrals have accepted as equivalent to siege. One point in that compromise may be regarded as certain, namely that there must be a real danger to the blockade-runner in crossing the line of the investment, independent of any danger which he may run of being caught earlier with the intention of crossing it, or later after having crossed it. A blockade which it is not in itself highly dangerous to try to break can affect with technical guilt neither the intention of the blockade-runner to break it nor the fact of his having broken it. This is expressed as follows by the Declaration of Paris:

> 4. Blockades, in order to be binding, must be effective[3], that is to say, maintained by a force sufficient really to prevent access to the coast of the enemy.

If "really to prevent access" were taken literally, the successful crossing the line by one blockade-runner would prove the blockade to be void, which has never been contended. The meaning therefore must be, "to make the attempt at access highly dangerous." But, this being so, a question of interpretation still remains. The continental powers, including Holland

[1] P. 165. [2] See below, p. 230.

[3] *Effectifs* in the original, which means "real," not "producing an effect," as effective means in English. But the official translation is "effective," and the meaning of an "effective blockade," so often spoken of by English writers, may be taken as fixed by this declaration.

herself after her relative decline in naval power, have usually maintained that a blockade is only valid in law if the danger of ingress or egress arises from the cannon either of ships, stationary or sufficiently near one another, or of works on land. This is laid down, with more or less variety of expression, in the treaty of 1742 between France and Denmark, in that of 1753 between Holland and the Two Sicilies, in the declarations and treaties of armed neutrality in 1780, in the various adhesions of other continental states to that armed neutrality or its rules, and in the declarations and treaties of armed neutrality in 1800[1]. When Russia, by a change of policy consequent on the battle of Copenhagen and the death of the emperor Paul, abandoned the armed neutrality of 1800, her treaty of 1801 with England required for a blockade the presence only of ships stationary *or*, instead of *and*, sufficiently near to create an evident danger of entering. Yet in 1823 she assured the United States that she no longer held herself bound by that engagement[2].

On the other hand Great Britain ever since the institution of blockade as a technical procedure, and the United States ever since their independence, have acted on the view that the real danger necessary to make a blockade effective may be created by cruisers, agreeing in that with the practice of Holland in the age when she founded the institution. This does not assert the sufficiency of the danger arising from

[1] In several of these pieces the place to be blockaded is described as attacked, but, considering the practice of the eighteenth century, it must be admitted that this arose only from habit, or at least was done without an intention to require a real attack. An exception to that interpretation is however furnished by the treaty of 1787 between France and Russia, in which the rule of the armed neutrality of 1780 is reproduced with a variation requiring an attack by a number of ships proportioned to the strength of the place, and Napoleon or his advisers may have had that treaty in their mind when drafting the Berlin decree. But that will not excuse the transparently false assertion about "the usage of all civilised nations." See above, p. 227. Again, many of the treaties, ending with that between Russia and Denmark in 1818, require the line of investment to be formed by a certain number of ships, usually two. That of 1753, mentioned in the text, requires six ships, which may lie a little outside the range of the shore batteries, but which must expose blockade-runners to danger from their cannon.

[2] Lawrence's *Wheaton*, edition of 1863, editor's note 235.

liability to capture at any distance for intended or accomplished breach of the blockade, which at the hands of a power having what is called the command of the sea may be very real. There must be a distinct blockading squadron, which however need not be stationary. The Lords of Appeals, of whom Sir William Grant was the chief, expressed themselves in language which is thus reported in substance. "It was the duty of the blockaders to maintain such a force as would be of itself sufficient to enforce the blockade. This could only be effected by keeping a number of vessels on the different stations, so communicating with each other as to be able to intercept all vessels attempting to enter the ports of the [blockaded] island[1]."

Those who accept the continental doctrine may support it, as is done by Hautefeuille and others, on the right acquired by a line of ships whose fires cross. That right cannot indeed be described as conquest, which is not now admitted except as arising by the terms of peace or by the extinction of the enemy state, nor even in those cases could conquest be asserted of any but littoral waters, outside which the blockading squadron may happen to lie. But whether within littoral waters or without them stationary ships with crossing fires may be held to have established an occupation, giving a right of control analogous to that exercised by a belligerent in the district occupied by him on land. Even so however the argument only reinforces the right of blockading by means of a stationary squadron. It does not put out of court the claim to a larger right of blockading based on international practice embodying and sanctioning a compromise between the opposing claims. And when we remember that the Anglo-American doctrine has been acted on for more than two centuries, and during all that time, except for the short periods covered by the two armed neutralities, has been acquiesced in *de facto* even by those powers which have disputed it as a matter of law—also that the Declaration of Paris was so worded as not to exclude it—it seems to us that, in spite of the invidious name of "paper blockade" which has been given to it[2], it cannot at this time

[1] In *The Nancy,* 1 Acton 57.

[2] The name "paper blockade" properly describes any blockade which

of day be refused an authority equal to that of the other doctrine. It is a case in which neither a belligerent taking the line which suits him, nor a neutral resenting that line, can lightly be stigmatised as a law-breaker, and for the solution of which some express international agreement is desirable.

The question just discussed seems at present to go to the root of blockade itself, for the danger to a stationary squadron from torpedoes and submarine boats would be so great at night that such a squadron could not keep its station except by day. On the other hand blockade by cruisers, if admitted, seems still to have a great part to play in the future. Captain Mahan has written: "Is it necessary, to constitute a real danger to blockade-runners, that the blockading fleet should be in sight? Half a dozen fast steamers, cruising twenty miles off shore between the New Jersey and Long Island coasts, would be a very real danger to ships seeking to go in or out by the principal entrance to New York; and similar positions might effectually blockade Boston, the Delaware and the Chesapeake....It seems probable in these days of submarine" [and we may now add wireless] "telegraphs, that the blockading forces in shore and off shore, and from one port to another, might be in telegraphic communication with one another along the whole coast of the United States, readily giving mutual support; and if by some fortunate military combination one detachment were attacked in force, it could warn the others and retreat upon them. Granting that such a blockade off one port were broken on one day by fairly driving away the ships maintaining it, the notification of its being reestablished would be cabled all over the world the next. To avoid such blockades there must be a military force afloat that will at all times so endanger a blockading fleet that it can by no means keep its place[1]." In these circumstances it seems likely that, so far as blockade may be employed in the future, the argument of necessity will induce even those powers whose

it is attempted to impose by notification without reality, but since Great Britain never attempted this without reality in her sense, the opprobrious name practically signifies want of reality in the continental sense.

[1] *The Influence of the Sea Power upon History, 1660–1783*; edition of 1890, pp. 85, 86.

theory has been that of blockade only by stationary ships to give it in practice the form of blockade by cruisers. The Danish government blockaded the ports of Northern Germany in 1864 by cruisers, though in its regulation of 15 February 1864, published expressly for that war, it had maintained its view of 1780 and 1800[1].

Although a blockade may be established on his own authority by the belligerent commander on the spot, he more usually establishes it on the instructions of his government, which notifies expressly to neutral powers, as well as announces in some public manner at home, the blockades which it directs, or which it adopts on information being given of them by its commanders. The notification or announcement is not sufficient without the reality of the blockade, but it is important on the question of the knowledge which is necessary for culpability. The neutral power which has received notification of a blockade is bound and presumed to publish the information throughout its dominions, and the announcement of a blockade by a belligerent power may be the subject of notoriety. A vessel sailing from a port belonging to a state to which a blockade has been notified by a belligerent government, or from a port at which it was

[1] Gessner, *Le Droit des Neutres sur Mer*, 2e éd., p. 184. He quotes thus the Danish regulation referred to in the text: "*Un port ennemi est bloqué quand il est cerné par un ou plusieurs vaisseaux de guerre, de manière à ce qu'aucun bâtiment merchand ne puisse entrer dans ce port ou en sortir sans un danger évident d'être saisi.*" *Cerné* implies investment by a closed line, and the same necessity results from the requirement that the danger must be evident. It is common on the continent to treat the Declaration of Paris as having consecrated the doctrine of the armed neutralities on blockade, but that declaration does not reproduce the condition of *evident* or *manifest* danger. It says that the blockade must be real (*effectif*), and if on the one hand that means that there must be a real investment, on the other hand it tests the reality of the investment by its being maintained by a force sufficient *really* to prevent access. Such a form allowed Great Britain to sign without abandoning blockade by cruisers when strict enough to be real, though the force so applied may not be evident to a vessel which has arrived near the entrance of the port. It is needless to say that the great blockade of the Confederate coast by the United States was enforced by cruisers. Its legality as such was questioned by no neutrals, a fact which must have its weight as a nearly contemporary exposition of the declaration.

notorious that a belligerent government had directed or adopted a blockade, or to whose owner or master the knowledge that a blockade had been so directed or adopted can be brought home by any kind of proof, may under the Anglo-American system be captured at any point of her voyage to the blockaded port, and will be condemned, provided that the blockade really existed at the moment of her capture. The offence not being deemed to consist in passing a line of investment but in communicating with a prohibited spot, its commission dates from the commencement of the attempt to communicate with knowledge of the prohibition. The only exception is when the vessel has sailed from a port so distant that her owner or master may have had ground for thinking that the blockade might be raised before her arrival, through a change in the plans of the belligerent government. Then, when met by a cruiser, she will be justified in having prosecuted her voyage with a view to enquiry, but such enquiry ought to be made, and she ought to intend making it, at a neighbouring port and not at the blockaded one. If the blockade of which the owner or master had knowledge was established by a commander on the spot, and had not to the knowledge of the former been adopted by the government of the latter, its continuance is regarded as less certain, and enquiry at the spot will be allowed. If on such enquiry it is found that the blockade continues, the vessel will be dismissed with a warning, and will not be allowed to plead enquiry as her purpose if she appears a second time at or on her way to the blockaded spot. Under the continental system, which does not admit blockade by cruisers, there can be no real blockade if there is not a ship at the spot of which enquiry can be made. Hence an enquiry is always allowed on the first visit to the spot, but after the warning then given the next visit will be punished by capture and confiscation, the illegitimate intention being deemed to be manifest.

The notification or announcement of a blockade, whether by a government or by a commander on the spot, must not embrace a larger extent of coast than is really blockaded, since otherwise, by its deterrent effect on the sailings of neutrals, it would gain some of the advantage of blockade where the reality which is the only justification of that advantage was wanting. Such an excess in the notification would vitiate the blockade even of those parts of the coast on which it was really established. In the American civil war President Lincoln's proclamation notified the intention to blockade the whole Confederate coast, and the actual blockade was announced by the different commanders as different parts of that coast were considered by them to be really blockaded. Each neutral vessel attempting ingress was therefore entitled to receive and received a warning, as in the case of a blockade by a commander which no government notification had introduced; only this ceased when the blockade had become notorious at the ports from which the blockade-runners sailed, as though the fact and its notoriety related to the proclamation. Some of the announcements by the commanders were more extensive than they had forces to support, and the mixed commission under the treaty of Washington awarded damages to the *Monmouth* for being warned off the whole coast.

A blockade is broken and the penalties for its breach are incurred as well by egress from the blockaded port as by entering it, and the shipping in that port are presumed to have notice of the blockade as soon as it is really laid. But in all recent wars a time has been fixed by the blockading government within which neutral vessels may leave the port with their cargoes, and even after that time they may leave in ballast or with cargoes loaded on board before the commencement of the blockade[1]. The time during which a vessel which has broken a blockade by egress, whether she was in the port at the commencement of the blockade or had entered that port by a successful breach of it, may be captured with condemnation as the result, is subject to a difference between the Anglo-American and the continental schools analogous to that which we have seen to exist as to the commencement of the liability for a breach by ingress. Those who hold that a blockade can only be maintained by a stationary squadron restrict to that squadron the right of vindicating a breach of it. A ship of that squadron may pursue the blockade-runner who has succeeded in passing its line to any distance compatible with the maintenance of the blockade by

[1] See in Twiss, *War*, § 113, peculiar cases in which the prohibition of egress is held not to apply to neutral vessels.

the remainder of the force, but when he has once entered a neutral port the affair is closed and he is free. Those who hold that a blockade may be maintained by cruisers allow any ship of war, whether she has or not been a member of the blockading squadron, to capture the offender at any distance from the blockaded port until his destined voyage is ended, supposing always that the blockade is really in existence at the time of the capture. In the opinion of that school the blockade-runner has not got rid of his culpability, deposited it as the phrase is, by entering a neutral port not that of his destination in order to escape pursuit or under stress of weather. On his leaving it the chase can be renewed or taken up by some other ship[1].

The blockade once established must be continuously maintained. If its reality is interrupted, even for a short time, subject to the question to be mentioned about interruption by weather, the legal effect will not be merely to free from penalties the vessels which have entered or left the port during that time, but to render necessary the re-establishment of the blockade in the manner necessary for the first establishment of one. This was questioned by the United States in their great blockade of the Confederate coast, in a case of which Mr Seward wrote to Lord Lyons, 27 May 1861: "We are informed that the *Niagara*," blockading Charleston, "was replaced by the steamer *Harriet Lane*, but that owing to some accident the latter vessel failed to reach the station as ordered until a day or two after the *Niagara* had left....This government holds that the blockade took effect at Charleston on the 11th day of this month, and that it will continually be in effect until notice of its relinquishment shall be given by proclamation of the President of the United States." Professor Bernard, on this, expresses the contrary view as follows. "Mr Seward was mistaken.... The temporary absence of the blockading force, if it be such an absence as to remove the risk of capture, not only impairs the blockade but discontinues it, unless the absence be involuntary and caused by stress of weather. If the blockading ships be blown off by a gale, the reasonable presumption is that they will return as soon

[1] Ortolan (4me édition, t. 2, p. 354) seems to approve the Anglo-American doctrine, but he is an exception to the general continental view.

as weather permits, and the neutral trader is therefore bound by that presumption. But no such presumption arises when they are sent away on other service, nor even where without orders they chase to a distance from the port. Nor is the neutral bound to enquire whether the intermission is due to a miscalculation on the part of the government, or to mistake or disobedience on the part of its officers, or to any accidental cause[1]." The doubt here is whether the exception of interruption by weather can be admitted. It is affirmed by Lord Stowell[2], and admitted by Ortolan[3] and by Pillet, the latter of whom adds that Stowell's decision on the point "has been received without difficulty[4]," but it is not admitted by Gessner[5]. The only difference to a neutral between interruption of a blockade by weather and by any other cause is that, in the former case, he has before his senses a reason for rejecting the supposition that the interruption arises from an intention to discontinue: but what is the importance of the belligerent's intention, if the rule is that the blockade must be real? And Gessner urges that the consequences of chance and the fortune of war must be borne by the party on whom the blow falls. The exception appears to us to be maintainable on the ground that blockade would be almost an absurdity if weather were not understood to be allowed for, but we deprecate maintaining it on the ground of intention, which would favour serious tampering with the necessary reality of blockades.

A blockade may be limited, so long, first, as the belligerent power enforcing it does not reserve for its own subjects any means of access or of commerce which it forbids to neutrals; secondly, the relaxations of the general rules of blockade are not inconsistent with the existence of any blockade at all; thirdly, the relaxations are notified to neutral states, so that their

[1] *Neutrality of Great Britain during the American Civil War*, p. 239. Mr Seward's despatch is on p. 238.

[2] *The Hoffnung*, 6 C. Rob. 112.

[3] T. 2, p. 344. He adds what we suppose is generally held by partisans of the exception, that ingress during the actual interruption by weather will not be culpable.

[4] *Lois Actuelles de la Guerre*, p. 137.

[5] P. 209.

subjects may be fully apprised of what they may or may not do[1]. The object of a blockade being the interruption of commerce, one can scarcely quote as an example of a limited blockade the fact that during the American civil war neutral ships of war had free access to the blockaded coast. A good example of one was furnished in the Crimean war by the Anglo-French blockade of the Danube, declared "in order to stop all transport of provisions to the Russian armies," which was held not to affect the export of cereals from the Danube, such being "in furtherance of the objects of the allies and to the prejudice of the Russians[2]." And another may be found in the British blockade of all the coast from Brest to the Elbe in 1806, that of the part from the Seine to Ostend being more rigorous than that of the other parts of the line[3]. Licenses to particular persons, in cases of blockade and others, were granted by Great Britain during the wars of the French revolution and empire, in favour as well of belligerent as of neutral individuals, and caused great offence. Such licenses in case of blockade appear to be indefensible.

Since the material part of the offence of blockade-running consists in the ingress or egress, or attempted ingress or egress, of a ship, and the master, by whom the course of the ship is directed, is the agent of her owner, the master's knowledge of the blockade binds the owner, and the ship is confiscable independently of the latter's personal knowledge. Where the ship and cargo belong to the same persons, the knowledge of the master, as their agent, affects them to the extent of all their property concerned in the transaction, and the cargo also is confiscable. Where the ship and cargo belong to different persons, it has been "established that when the blockade was known or might have been known to the owners of the cargo at the time when the shipment was made, and they might therefore by possibility be privy to an intention of violating the blockade, such privity shall be assumed as an irresistible inference of law, and it shall not be competent to them to rebut it by evidence....The necessity of acting upon these rules

[1] See the judgment of the Privy Council in *The Franciska*, 10 Moore P. C. 37, Scott 804.

[2] *The Gerasimo*, 11 Moore P. C. 88, Scott 811.

[3] Manning's *Law of Nations* 332; Twiss, *War*, § 118.

is rested by Lord Stowell on the notoriety of the fact that in almost all cases of breach of blockade the attempt is made for the benefit and with the privity of the owners of the cargo; that if they were at liberty to allege their innocence of the act of the master, it would always be easy to manufacture evidence for the purpose which the captors would have no means of disproving[1]." The owners of the cargo, if the penalty was really incurred without their privity, must seek their remedy against the master or owners of the ship. It may however happen that the blockade was known to the master but not to the owners of the cargo, whose property will then escape condemnation[2].

Since blockade-running is not a hostile proceeding, and the belligerent's rights with regard to it are limited to those which the accepted compromise gives him over the ship and cargo, the crew of a captured blockade-runner must not be treated as enemies and prisoners. They are bound not to resist the vessel's being taken to a port of the captors for adjudication, but if they rise and rescue her their state will not be obliged to restore her or visit the crew with any punishment. If however she falls again into the power of the captors' state before her offence has been deposited by the completion of her voyage, she will be condemned with her cargo, which suffers for the deeds of the master to which it was entrusted, whatever may be the merits of her case in other respects[3].

Limitation of Blockade by the rights of Neutral Territory.

Where the mouth of a river divides a belligerent from a neutral state, the enemy of the former does not lose his right of blockading the shore belonging to it, but he cannot interfere with the trade of the other shore. In 1870 the French blockaded the Prussian but not the Hanoverian shore of the Ems, treating the latter as neutral from political motives, though Hanover

[1] Lord Kingsdown, in *The Panaghia Rhomba*, 12 Moore P. C. 168, Scott 800.

[2] Some cases of this kind are mentioned by Twiss, *War*, § 116.

[3] See Bernard, *Neutrality &c.*, pp. 323–9, for various incidents connected with the matter of this paragraph.

had been conquered by Prussia four years before. This during the American civil war was conceded as to the mouth of the Rio Grande, dividing Mexico from Texas, one of the Confederate States; "but the Supreme Court [of the United States] laid down the rule that it was a duty incumbent on vessels with the neutral destination to keep south of the dividing line between the Mexican and Texan [water] territory, and in the case of vessels captured for being north of that line [without being driven across it by weather] refused, while restoring them, to allow their costs and expenses." We agree with Hall that "it is to be hoped that a rule so little consistent with the right of neutrals to uninterrupted commerce with each other will not be drawn into a precedent[1]."

Where there are neutral states on the upper waters of a river, it is clear on principle that a belligerent's right of blockading either the whole or one side of its mouth cannot entitle him to interfere with the commerce of those states, though the rule has not perhaps been always respected.

A blockade cannot affect the commerce which the blockaded port carries on through a neutral port with which it has inland communication[2].

We reserve the question of continuous voyages in connection with blockade till we can treat it as a whole in connection with contraband.

[1] Hall, from whom the quotations are taken, § 266. See Bernard, *Neutrality &c.*, note on p. 318.

[2] *The Ocean*, 3 C. Rob. 297, Scott 819.

CHAPTER X.

CONTRABAND OF WAR.

CONTRABAND of war are those articles which belligerents prohibit neutrals from carrying to their enemies, not in connection with a blockade but because they are regarded as being objectionable in themselves, either generally or in the particular circumstances of a war. It may here be mentioned once for all that although the terms used with reference to contraband in public documents, by authors or in these pages, often seem to contemplate only things carried in ships, which of course present the commonest case, ships themselves, when suitable for any warlike use and on their voyage with a view to sale in a hostile port or for delivery to the enemy, fall under the same principles and are contraband. No one contests this, and in the British view, to be developed later, they are absolute contraband.

On some of the prohibited articles there is a settled agreement between belligerents and neutrals, with regard to others there is much variation in the pretensions of belligerents and the submission of neutrals to those pretensions. But however indeterminate the class of contraband may be, its existence is recognised by all authorities on international law, a fact which amounts to a double understanding. One face of that understanding is that the commerce of neutrals with a belligerent is not necessarily to be free whenever it cannot be connected with a specific operation of war, even by so loose a deduction as that which has expanded siege into blockade. The other is that it is not to be entirely suppressed. Between those two poles what international law there is on the subject began to arise in the sixteenth century, on the foundation of the more moderate of the warnings given by belligerents to neutrals. The name of contraband was derived from those warnings, its literal sense being that which is contrary to the ban or edict, and it having already, before its use in war, been applied to trade which contravened national or municipal regulations[1].

In the earliest of the more moderate unilateral acts to which we have referred we can trace two opposite tendencies which have never ceased to divide the world on the subject, the one pointing to a more restricted prohibition of neutral commerce, the other to a prohibition at once larger and not definitely limited. Thus the French ordinance of 1543 prohibited only munitions of war, while England prohibited victuals in 1587 and 1591, and in 1592 gave a very wide definition of canvas as a prohibited article[2]. In 1589 England condemned corn in Hanseatic ships and in 1597 in Polish, as being aid or supplies, alleging that the Hanse towns, Poland and Sweden had done the same[3]. Spain condemned tobacco in English ships as victuals, on the ground that by the use of tobacco the consumption of victuals might be prolonged, and Elizabeth granted letters of reprisal only on the ground that the inference as to tobacco was erroneous[4]. Thus at this time France stood very much alone for the restricted form of prohibition, and she took the same line in negotiation. In the arrangement of May 1599 between Elizabeth and Henri Quatre the former had to exempt French subjects from search, on Henri's undertaking that they should not carry enemy's goods, or carry to the Spaniards "arms,

[1] Twiss quotes from Ducange an Italian charter of 1445, in which a trade in salt contravening municipal regulations is called *contrabannum*, but its use in the treaty of Southampton between England and the United Provinces, 1625, seems to be the first appearance of the word in relation to the laws of war which he could trace: *War*, § 121.

[2] As early as 1370, as well as in the treaty with Scotland of which the application was questioned in 1543, she had obtained the prohibition of victuals by treaty. See above, pp. 169, 170.

[3] Letter of Secretary Cecil to Sir Henry Neville, 2 July 1599, in Winwood's *Memorials*, v. 1, p. 57; Camden, *Hist. Eliz.*, anno 1597; Zouch, *Fetial Law*, p. 128: all quoted by Twiss, *War*, § 124.

[4] Zouch, *Fetial Law*, part 2, § 8, and *De Judicio inter Gentes*, § 8, part 2, p. 132; quoted by Twiss, *War*, §§ 123, 127. See also what is related by De Thou, above, p. 171, note 2.

munitions or other instruments or materials of war, either by land or sea," the French representatives being expressly unwilling to include provisions in the list[1]. And in the abortive negotiations of 1602 the draft, probably emanating from the French side, which was discussed by the English and French commissioners, proposed by its Art. 6 only to prohibit carrying any kind of arms to the enemy, though accompanying this with a proviso that the liberty of commerce should not be abused by the subjects of either power to the prejudice of the other[2]. A similar contrast may be remarked in that Henri Quatre was less tolerant than Elizabeth of the principle of the *placaat* of 1599 by which the Dutch prohibited the carriage of all goods whatever to the Spaniards. He directed his subjects to submit to it for the limited term of six months, while her government held it to be "an effect of great necessity which had no law[3]," and the other powers of Europe passed it over in silence.

This first stage in the history of special commerce prohibited to neutrals ends with the treaty of Southampton, an offensive and defensive alliance concluded 17 September 1625 between Charles I and the United Provinces. That treaty declared that "all contraband goods, as are victuals and munitions of war, ships, arms, sails, cordage, gold, silver, copper, iron, lead and the like, whencesoever they are carried to Spain or to any other country subject to the King of Spain or his adherents, shall be good prize together with the ships and the men that they shall carry." And on 4 March 1626 an English proclamation, rather to be regarded as explaining than as extending the clause of the treaty, gives what is probably the earliest detailed enumeration of prohibited articles, especially detailed with regard to what in a previous proclamation of 31 December 1625 had been summarily described as materials for ships or munitions of war. In these provisions we have the less restrictive of the two tendencies previously traceable embodied in what may be described as the first sketch of a law on the subject, with the name of contraband and a specification doubtless derived

[1] Winwood's *Memorials*, v. 1, pp. 19, 22, 23.

[2] Ib., p. 392.

[3] Sir Henry Neville's letter of 15 May 1599 to Secretary Cecil, Winwood's *Memorials*, v. 1, p. 23; quoted by Twiss, *War*, § 126.

from the practice then most widely prevailing, especially that which had grown up in the English admiralty. The proclamations base themselves on "the rules of policy," "the law of nations," the quality of Charles as "a monarch and prince sovereign," "former declarations and acts of state made in this behalf in the time of Queen Elizabeth of famous memory," and the practice of "other states and princes upon the like occasions, avowed and maintained by public writings and apologies[1]." At the same time the right of states and princes to add to the specification was not understood to be relinquished. On the contrary, in 1674, during a war between France and Spain, a Spanish privateer having captured pitch and tar belonging to English subjects on board a Swedish ship bound to Rouen, Sir Leoline Jenkins, in an opinion which he gave to Charles II, began by pointing out that such goods were not made contraband by the Anglo-Spanish treaty of 1667. He went on to say that unless they were affected by being in the Swedish ship, they "cannot be judged by any other law but by the general law of nations; and then I am humbly of opinion that nothing ought to be judged contraband by that law in this case but what is directly and immediately subservient to the uses of war, except in the case of besieged places"—meaning blockade—"or of a general notification made by Spain to all the world that they will condemn all the pitch and tar they meet with[2]."

France however did not abandon the position which at that time was almost special to her, and she obtained the assent of Spain to it by the treaty of the Pyrenees in 1659[3]. Art. 12 of that treaty prohibited as contraband a list of things which may be described as arms, adding *et autres assortiments servants à l'usage de la guerre*, but no materials except saltpetre; and Art. 13 declared that victuals should be free except when carried to Portugal, an exception dictated by the policy of the moment,

[1] The clause of the treaty and the proclamations may conveniently be seen in Twiss, *War*, §§ 121, 122, 123. The belief in a law of nations on interference with neutral commerce can be traced as early as the *Hispanicae Advocationes* of Albericus Gentilis.

[2] *Life and Correspondence of Sir Leoline Jenkins*, v. 2, p. 751.

[3] Dumont, t. 6, part 2, p. 266.

or to blockaded places. Two years later the more widely received understanding received a fuller development in the treaty of Whitehall between England and Sweden[1], 1661, so that these two treaties may be opposed to one another as being at their date the standards on their respective sides. The Anglo-Swedish Art. 11 prohibited a list of things which may be described as arms, adding *et quæcunque alia bellica instrumenta*, and money, *commeatus*—by which victuals for military or naval use appear to be intended—saltpetre, horses, horse furniture, ships of war and guardships, all under pain of confiscation. A stipulation followed in the same article that "neither of the confederates shall suffer any of his subjects to give aid, sell or lend ships, or be in any way useful to the enemies or rebels of the other to his prejudice or detriment." Under that clause the English prize court held that pitch, tar and other materials for building and equipping ships, the produce of Sweden, found in Swedish vessels bound for the enemy, could be brought in, but for preemption and not for confiscation. This practice was confirmed by the Anglo-Swedish convention of 1803, which fixed the price for preemption at the invoice price in Sweden or the market price in England at the choice of the owner, with ten per cent. additional and an indemnity for detention and necessary costs[2].

The treaty of Whitehall shows marks of the influence of Grotius. Writing when no clear doctrine either of contraband or of blockade had emerged from the medieval welter, for his great work was published in the year of the treaty of Southampton, Grotius mentions neither of those terms—which might be partly due to his studied classical style[3]—and mixes the two subjects in what he says about belligerent interference with neutral commerce. Things which are of use only in war he holds to rank the neutral as being on the side of the belligerent to whom he supplies them, and they can always be confiscated by the enemy. Of supplying things which serve only for pleasure no complaint can be made. For a judgment on the

[1] Ib., p. 385; Hertslet, v. 2, p. 329.

[2] Martens, *Recueil*, t. 8, p. 92. See Lord Stowell in *The Zacheman*, 5 C. Rob. 152.

[3] See above, p. 161.

supply of things useful both in war and in peace, such as money, provisions (*commeatus*), ships and what belongs to ships—*res usus ancipitis*—the grounds which he selects are the belligerent's necessity, the neutral's knowledge of his necessity, and the justice of his cause. The first standing alone, will authorise the belligerent who meets with the goods to intercept them subject to an obligation to indemnify the neutral. The second makes the neutral culpable, with a liability, if harm to the belligerent who meets with the goods has not yet followed, to their being detained and security for the future exacted from him, but if the surrender of a place or the conclusion of peace has been hindered, then to their confiscation by way of redress[1]. And when the justice of the belligerent with whom he meets on his way is very evident, the neutral will be liable not only civilly but criminally, to punishment which in practice must depend on that belligerent's discretion. This doctrine of Grotius met with an imperfect and indirect success. Although the expression *res usus ancipitis* has come to be loosely used, the distinction which Grotius employed it to express has never been accurately applied as the test for a practical distinction; nor has recognition of the self-alleged justice of each belligerent's cause been accepted as a neutral duty. But the recognition of the belligerent's necessity by a philosophical writer, and the example set by him of not treating all cases of contraband alike, must have contributed to the birth of a system in which a belligerent was allowed to consult his necessity on condition of preemption.

The view of contraband which found one of its earliest expressions in the treaty of Whitehall may, from the state most eminent among its authors and upholders, be called the British view. Its most remarkable features are, first, the assertion of a class of conditional or occasional contraband, or contraband of circumstance, never including any thing solely of peaceful use, but in which things of use both in peace and in war, on their way to a hostile destination, may be placed as occasion requires, being otherwise entirely free; secondly, a milder treatment, by way of preemption, in certain cases roughly corresponding to that class. Goods *usus ancipitis* may be contraband of the con-

[1] We have seen this under the head of blockade, above, p. 222.

ditional class either by virtue of an express declaration by the belligerent government, based on the circumstances of the war, or by the judgment of its prize court, when that court sees reason for believing or presuming that they are intended to be used for purposes of war. The Admiralty *Manual*, embodying the British practice, declares that such a "presumption arises when the hostile destination of the vessel [carrying the goods] is either the enemy's fleet at sea, or a hostile port used exclusively or mainly for naval or military equipment[1]." An example is furnished by the well known case of the Dutch cheeses, fit for naval use, which Lord Stowell condemned when taken on their way to Brest, where an expedition was known to be in preparation[2]. Goods *usus ancipitis* not classed as conditional contraband may either escape altogether or be placed in a class regarded as more highly noxious. "All goods fit for purposes of war only, and certain other goods which, though fit also for the purposes of peace, are in their nature peculiarly serviceable to the enemy in war, on board a vessel which has a hostile destination, are absolutely contraband[3]." Into this class the crown claims the power of elevating any description of goods, subject to its treaty engagements, a condition which equally applies to the power of classing the less noxious goods *usus ancipitis* as conditional contraband[4]. The goods at present regarded by Great Britain as absolutely contraband are enumerated in the Admiralty *Manual*, and are arms and machinery for manufacturing them—ammunition and materials for it—gunpowder and its materials and gun-cotton—military equipments, clothing and stores—and naval stores, specified with great detail and including the requirements for building and equipping merchantmen as well as ships of war[5]. The present

[1] *Manual of Naval Prize Law*, prepared by Professor Holland on the foundation of that prepared by Sir Godfrey Lushington in 1866, and issued in 1888 by the authority of the Admiralty: Art. 63. "If the commander is satisfied that the goods on board the vessel are fit for purposes of peace exclusively, he should allow the vessel to proceed on her course": ib., Art. 66.

[2] *The Jonge Margaretha*, 1 C. Rob. 189, Scott 762.

[3] Admiralty *Manual*, Art. 61.

[4] Ib., Art. 65.

[5] Ib., Art. 62.

list of "goods conditionally contraband" is given in another article, and is evidently intended to be read as subject on the one hand to the prize court's being satisfied of the destination of the goods for purposes of war, and on the other hand to the power of the prize court to condemn goods *usus ancipitis* not mentioned in the list if satisfied of their being so destined[1]. The difference of treatment made by British practice cannot be better or more shortly put than in the words of the Admiralty *Manual*.

82. The penalty for carrying goods absolutely contraband is, in general, the confiscation of such goods and also of any interest which the owner of such goods may have in the rest of the cargo.

84. The carriage of goods conditionally contraband, and of such absolutely contraband goods as are in an unmanufactured state and are the produce of the country exporting them, is usually followed only by the preemption of such goods by the British government, which then pays freight to the vessel carrying the goods[2].

The United States maintain the British view on contraband, which they inherited. The Jay treaty between the two countries, 1796, after giving an enumeration of contraband articles, meets "the difficulty of agreeing on the precise cases in which alone provisions and other articles not generally contraband may be regarded as such" by stipulating preemption, "with a reasonable mercantile profit," freight and demurrage, "whenever any

[1] Ib., Art. 64.

[2] In this article attention must be paid to the limitation contained in the word "usually." The cheeses going to Brest which have been mentioned furnish an example of the confiscation of conditional contraband, though the case was so far from being one of extreme culpability that Lord Stowell said: "as the party has acted without dissimulation in the case, and may have been misled by an inattention to circumstances to which in strictness he ought to have adverted, as well as something like an irregular indulgence on which he has relied, I shall content myself with pronouncing the cargo to be contraband without enforcing the usual penalty of the confiscation of the ship belonging to the same proprietor." It seems that the military importance of the supply will affect the question: *The Edward*, 4 C. Rob. 68, 70. The privilege allowed to the produce of the exporting country is not lost by the ship's not belonging to that country if the goods are its property: *The Apollo*, 4 C. Rob. 158. And for the purpose of that privilege neighbouring districts usually exporting through the Hanse towns were reckoned as one country with them: *The Evert*, 4 C. Rob. 354.

such articles so becoming contraband according to the existing law of nations shall for that reason be seized."

The school of thought whose view on contraband was embodied in the treaty of the Pyrenees objects to conditional contraband as opening a door to arbitrary behaviour on the part of belligerent governments and their prize courts, and declines to see an alleviation in bringing in neutral cargoes for preemption only, which in practice can scarcely fail to cause some molestation to neutral commerce, and in theory conflicts with the view that a neutral ought not to be touched at all when his innocence is admitted by not condemning him. In the treaties concluded under the influence of that school the enumerations of contraband have often included articles *usus ancipitis*, which were thereby exposed to confiscation when under the British system they would have escaped with preemption. And states which take this line, having deprived themselves of a class of conditional contraband in which to place branches of neutral commerce only occasionally in conflict with their belligerent interest, have been the more impelled to save that interest by excessive extensions of absolute contraband. Thus France in 1885, in spite of her traditional policy as to victuals, declared rice destined for any Chinese port north of Canton to be contraband of war, and justified herself, in answer to the British remonstrance, by the importance of rice in feeding the Chinese population as well as the Chinese armies[1]. Thus also Russia, which up to the time of her war with Japan did not admit conditional contraband, and, which during the African conference at Berlin declared that she would refuse her consent to any inclusion of coal among contraband, issued at the commencement of that war a list of contraband including rice, provisions, horses, and "every kind of fuel, such as coal, naphtha, alcohol and other similar materials[2]." Afterwards

[1] *Parliamentary Papers, France No. 1, 1885.* Lord Granville notified that Great Britain would not consider herself bound by any decision of a French prize court giving effect to the declaration, but the case did not arise, as the war was short and shipments of rice appear to have been stopped by the threat.

[2] Russian Regulations of 28 February 1904, in the *London Gazette* of 11 March 1904. Provisions, horses and coal are all named as conditionally contraband in Art. 64 of the British admiralty *Manual.*

however, in deference to the protests of Great Britain and the United States, she consented that rice and provisions should be regarded only as conditionally contraband, according to the use to which they were to be applied[1]. It remains to be seen what may be the consequence of the check so given to the school which we are criticising. In the mean time it must be noted that the Institute of International Law has taken a line not entirely in accordance with either school. In 1895 a commission adopted a resolution approving conditional contraband when resulting from an immediate and special destination to the military or naval forces or the military operations of the enemy, and declared in advance by the belligerent government. But in 1896 the Institute as a whole substituted an emphatic condemnation of conditional contraband, at the same time proposing for a belligerent a right of sequestration or preemption, at his pleasure and subject to an equitable indemnity, over all goods, being on their way to a port of his enemy, which can serve equally for warlike or peaceful uses. The change was made in spite of strong opposition from the late Dr Perels, who held an eminent position in international law both from his talents and from his being a director in the German ministry of Marine. And we are thus entitled to say that if the doctrine which had its origin in France has become widely spread, at least it cannot claim to be regarded as that of the whole continent[2].

The treaties in which contraband of war is mentioned, except the great ones which launched the subject, present little interest except for ascertaining by what engagements each state is actually bound. Stipulations on contraband, like all political stipulations, are not extended beyond the original parties by a most favoured nation clause. Like all stipulations as to the rights of neutrals which do not take the form of declarations of law, such as the Declaration of Paris, they are cancelled by war between the parties. Even while they endure they have no effect unless one party is a belligerent and the other

[1] Lord Lansdowne's letter of 2 November 1904 to the London Chamber of Commerce, in *Times* of the 4th.

[2] The discussions and resolutions of the Institute on contraband of war are in the *Annuaire*, vols: 13, 14, 15.

a neutral, and so many European wars have been general ones as seriously to affect the number of cases in which that situation has existed. Whether these facts have led to their being rather carelessly entered into or from any other causes, the mind of England on the subject of contraband would be erroneously judged if her treaties during a century and a half were taken as showing it. What that mind really was is shown by her practice so far as she was free, and by her resistance to the Armed Neutralities. In fact England adopted the system of the treaty of the Pyrenees, sometimes with slight variations, in treaties of 1667 with Spain and Holland, and of 1677 with France—instances which are remarkable for coming so soon after the Anglo-Swedish treaty of 1661 of opposite character—and again in treaties of 1713 and 1786 with France. Nor were these the only instances, and Hall, speaking of the eighteenth century, says that treaties embodying the French doctrine of contraband bound England at different times with France, Spain, Sweden, Russia, Denmark and the United States[1]. The fact goes far to undermine the reliance placed by many jurists on treaties, as testimony to a public conviction on litigated points of international law.

Penalty for the Carriage of Contraband of War.

The penalty for carrying contraband goods, so far as it was necessary to mention it in order to explain the difference between the British and French views of the general subject, with which the existence of a class of cases visited only with preemption is intimately connected, has been already discussed[2]. The Admiralty *Manual* further deals with it as follows.

83. The vessel which carries [contraband] goods, if not owned by the owner of such goods, is not confiscated but forfeits her freight for such goods and all right to expenses the result of her detention.

85. The penalty for carrying contraband goods with simulated papers, or in disregard of express stipulations by treaty, is confiscation not only of the contraband goods but also of the vessel, and of any interest which her owner has in the rest of the cargo.

87. A vessel which is herself contraband is liable to be confiscated, together with such part of her cargo as belongs to her owner.

[1] § 238.

[2] Above, p. 247.

The vessel is also confiscated if she resisted capture or search, or if her owner was privy to the carriage of the contraband goods though not their owner. She is confiscable in Germany and Denmark if all her cargo, in France if three fourths of her cargo, are contraband, and by the Italian code of mercantile marine when any part is confiscable contraband.

The time during which the penalty for the carriage of contraband is enforceable is, in general, from the moment of the ship's quitting port with the goods having a hostile destination on board to that when the goods are unloaded. On the return voyage the ship is free. But where a ship succeeded in carrying contraband to a hostile destination with false papers, and was taken on the return voyage, Lord Stowell and Sir William Grant condemned her with her return cargo, whether it had been purchased with the proceeds of the outward contraband cargo or several intermediate transactions had been interposed; and the Admiralty *Manual* approves[1]. Gessner on the other hand strongly objects[2], and in our judgment he is right. It is contended that in such cases the offence of the ship is not deposited with the goods, but the offence of the ship is not punished on the return voyage when it consists in the shipowner's being privy to the carriage of the contraband, and it is difficult to see how the use of false papers, though a graver offence, brings in a different principle.

At the other limit of the time during which the penalty is enforceable, namely its commencement, there is no legal difficulty but there is one of convenience. When the penalty may be enforced there is a right of visit and search, the exercise of which at a great distance from the port to which the contraband, if any, is suspected to be in course of transport, may seriously disturb commerce bound to a variety of destinations.

[1] Art. 80, quoting *The Nancy*, 3 C. Rob. 122 and *The Margaret*, 1 Acton 333. Even independently of false papers Lord Stowell held that "in distant voyages the different parts are not to be considered as two voyages but as one entire transaction," where those parts are "formed upon one original plan, conducted by the same persons and under one set of instructions, *ab ovo usque ad mala*": in *The Nancy*, 3 C. Rob. 126. This doctrine is ignored by Art. 80, rightly as we think.

[2] P. 141.

The distance from the port of destination, Delagoa Bay, at which Great Britain claimed the right during the South African war, the cargo of the mail steamer *General* being examined at Aden, contributed with other incidents to a diplomatic discussion with Germany. In the course of it the German chancellor, Prince von Bülow, speaking in the Reichstag on 19 January 1900 and reviewing the chief points of the law of contraband, said: "The right of visit and search naturally applies to waters which are not too distant from the theatre of war. For mail steamers there are at present no special understandings." The incident passed off, the British government agreeing that there should be no search at places more remote than Aden. It would scarcely be possible to limit the distance by any general rule, and it must perhaps be always left to the discretion of the belligerent and neutral governments interested.

Continuous Voyage and Rule of War of 1756.

We have repeatedly had to speak of a destination to the enemy as being a condition of goods being contraband, and subject as such to confiscation or preemption. It might be thought clear enough that the destination in question is simply that of the goods, and abroad this has always been the most general opinion. But in England it has been generally maintained by systematic writers that a destination to a hostile port of the ship which carries the goods is further necessary for the belligerent's right to interfere with the latter. If she is bound for a neutral port—at least if such is her ultimate destination and not merely to be used by her as a port of call—the goods are not within the prohibition of contraband and cannot be captured, although their destination may be to the enemy. With this we cannot agree. The difference between the doctrines will appear from the following considerations.

Goods on board a ship destined to a neutral port may be consigned to purchasers in that port or to agents who are to offer them for sale there, in either of which cases what further becomes of them will depend on the consignee purchasers or on the purchasers from the agents. Such goods before arriving at the neutral port have only a neutral destination. On arriving there they are, in Lord Stowell's language, imported into the common stock of the country. If they ultimately find their way to a belligerent port, or to a belligerent army or navy, it will be in consequence of a new destination given them, and this notwithstanding that the neutral port may be a well known market for the belligerent in question to seek supplies in, and that the goods may notoriously have been attracted to it by the existence of such a market. The consignors of the goods to the neutral port may have had an expectation that they would reach the belligerent, but not an intention to that effect, for a person can form an intention only about his own acts, and a belligerent destination was to be impressed on the goods, if at all, by other persons. Therefore it is not contended by any one that on the way to the neutral port there will be a right of capture, whatever the character of the goods.

On the other hand goods on board a ship destined to a neutral port may be under orders from their owners to be forwarded thence to a belligerent port, army or navy, either by a further voyage of the same ship, or by transhipment, or even by land carriage. Such goods are to reach the belligerent without the intervention of a new commercial transaction, in pursuance of the intention formed with regard to them by the persons who are their owners during the voyage to the neutral port. Therefore even during that voyage they have a belligerent destination, although the ship which carries them may have only a neutral one. If that destination is combined with the character required for their being contraband the mischief exists against which a belligerent is allowed to protect himself, his cruiser falls in with the *corpus delicti* at sea, which is the recognised arena for his self-protection, and the voyage of the goods to the neutral port must be regarded in law as being continuous with their voyage or other transit from that port to their final destination. *La destination pour l'ennemi est présumée lorsque le transport va à un de ses ports, ou bien à un port neutre qui, d'après des preuves évidentes et de fait incontestable, n'est qu'une étape pour l'ennemi comme but final de la mêmeo pération commerciale*[1].

[1] Resolution of the Institute of International Law in 1896, 15 *Annuaire* 231.

The first recorded notice by a British prize court of the possibility that voyages distinct in fact may be continuous in law occurs in connection with what is called the rule of the war of 1756, which for that reason, though having no other connection with the doctrine of contraband, may be conveniently dealt with in this place. "During the war of 1756," if we may borrow Wheaton's words, "the French government, finding the trade with their colonies almost entirely cut off by the maritime superiority of Great Britain, relaxed their monopoly of that trade, and allowed the Dutch, then neutral, to carry on the commerce between the mother country and her colonies under special licenses or passes, granted for this particular purpose, excluding at the same time all other neutrals from the same trade[1]." This was held by the British prize court to amount, on the part of the Dutch acting on the licenses, to be such an identification of themselves with the enemy that both ships and cargoes were captured and condemned; nor in our opinion can any fault be found with that view, which commends itself both to Wheaton and to Hall, unless it should be held that a merely implied identification with the enemy is now excluded by the Declaration of Paris. Before the outbreak of the war of 1778 France, probably to avoid similar consequences, announced that trade with her West Indian colonies would thenceforth be permanently open: accordingly the neutrals who engaged in it were not interfered with by Great Britain, except so far as they might be carrying contraband. "In 1793 however, the French having opened their coasting and colonial trade to neutrals, the latter were not only forbidden by England to carry French goods between the mother country and her colonies, but they were also exposed to penalties for conveying neutral goods from their own ports to those of a belligerent colony, or from any one port to another belonging to the belligerent country[2]."

This extension of the practice of 1756 to all the trade which was not open to neutrals in time of peace, though commonly included in the term "rule of the war of 1756," has always been

[1] *Elements*, § 508, Dana's numbering.

[2] Here we borrow Hall's compendious statement: § 234.

generally condemned both on the continent and in the United States, in spite of the great authority of Lord Stowell. The reasons adduced for it are variations of circumstance on the theme that all trade strengthens a belligerent. Or if they are based on the familiar plea that the true test of a trade's being compatible with neutrality is its being carried on during peace, then it must be remembered that belligerents have never admitted that plea in a neutral's favour, so as to exempt articles belonging to his ordinary trade from being classed as contraband, and that therefore they ought not to invoke it when it tells against him. We agree with Hall in condemning the extended doctrine, of which the Declaration of Paris seems sufficient to prevent any application in future, even were not the colonial trade of the world as open as it now generally is.

It was in connection with the extended rule of the war of 1756 that Lord Stowell and Sir William Grant applied the principle of continuous voyage. Neutrals carrying on the trade between an enemy colony and its mother country would unship the cargo brought from the former at a neutral port, reload it —perhaps with some addition, or after payment of the customs duties in order to give further colour to the pretence of importation there—and then complete its transport to the enemy mother country on the same or another ship. Condemnation followed on capture during the latter part of the voyage or transport, which was held to be continuous with the former part, so as to constitute one transport between the places between which the trade was prohibited by Great Britain to neutrals[1]. The same principle must have applied if the capture had been made during the first part of the transport, supposing the intention to be proved, but the case does not seem to have happened. This being so, it seems impossible to believe that Lord Stowell would have objected to applying the principle of continuous voyage to the carriage of contraband. And indeed in *The Rapid*[2], which was the case of a ship carrying a despatch addressed to a hostile minister, he said: "It is to be observed that where the commencement of the voyage is in a

[1] *The Maria,* 5 C. Rob. 365; *The William,* ib. 385; *The Thomyris,* a case of transhipment, Edwards 17.

[2] Edwards 228.

neutral country and it is to terminate at a neutral port, or as in this instance at a port to which though not neutral an open trade is allowed, in such a case there is less to excite his [the master's] vigilance, and therefore it may be proper to make some allowance for any imposition which may be practised upon him." This distinctly gave it to be understood that the carriage of despatches—which is at least analogous to that of contraband goods if the despatches, being things and not persons, are not rather contraband than analogues of contraband—would not necessarily be held innocent because the ship's voyage was to terminate at a neutral port. We cannot therefore agree with those who maintain that Lord Stowell considered the important destination to be not that of the goods but that of the ship, because he happened to say that "the articles must be taken *in delicto*, in the actual prosecution of the voyage to an enemy's port." In the case before him the destination both of the ship and of the goods had been to an enemy's port, but on learning that that port was blockaded the master changed his course for a neutral port, and no proof was offered that the owner of the goods had any agent there charged with forwarding them to the enemy[1]. And now the British government has adopted the doctrine of continuous voyage by searching for contraband, during the South African war, ships bound for the Portuguese neutral port of Lourenço Marques in Delagoa Bay, from which the goods would proceed by inland carriage to the enemy South African Republic[2].

In the United States during the civil war the carriage of contraband was generally presented to the courts in connection

[1] *The Imina,* 3 C. Rob. 167. The judgments of the court of Common Pleas on insurances effected during the American civil war were in favour of the doctrine of continuous voyage: *Hobbs v. Henning,* 17 C. B., N. S., 791, 34 L. J., C. P., 117; *Seymour v. London and Provincial Marine Insurance Company,* 41 L. J., C. P., 193, confirmed in the Exchequer Chamber, 42 L. J., C. P., 111. See the former judgment explained in articles by us, 15 L. Q. 424, and by Mr E. L. de Hart, 23 L. Q. R. 199.

[2] These ships were the *Bundesrath,* the *Herzog* and the *General.* No contraband being found in them, indemnities were paid. The correspondence between Great Britain and Germany about them is in the Bluebook Cd. 33 (1900), and extracts from it are given by Mr J. Dundas White in 17 L. Q. R. 12.

with blockade-running, to which the doctrine of continuous voyage does not apply. The offence of blockade-running, consisting in the attempt to communicate with a prohibited port and not in the introduction of a prohibited class of goods, is essentially one of the ship, and not an offence of the goods except as derived from that of the ship. If a ship is bound for a neutral port, not as a port of call, no blockade-running has been attempted by her, and her cargo, still innocent, cannot connect her with any such attempt which the ship into which it may be removed may afterwards commit. The United States judgments however did not always distinguish sufficiently between the two conditions. But in the case of *The Peterhoff*, which was independent of blockade, since the sea carriage of the goods was to terminate at the Mexican port of Matamoras, from which there was communication with the Confederate territory by land or inland navigation, it was clearly laid down that the confiscation of the goods depended on whether they were intended to make part of the general stock in trade at Matamoras or for further transport to the enemy in the vicinity[1]. In France the doctrine of continuous voyage was applied to contraband during the Crimean war in the case of the *Frau Howina*[2]. In Italy it was judicially affirmed during the Abyssinian war in the case of the *Doelwyk*[3], though confiscation was refused on the ground that before the trial peace had been established. In Germany it has the support of Gessner[4] and Perels[5], and of the Prussian regulations of 1864[6], although the German government, in complaining of the search for contraband on the way to Delagoa Bay, attempted to show that British authority was against it. On the whole then it must be recognised as the reigning view

[1] See *The Bermuda*, 3 Wallace 514; *The Stephen Hart*, Blatchford's Prize Cases 387, 3 Wallace 559, Freeman Snow 509, Scott 852; *The Springbok*, 5 Wallace 1; *The Peterhoff*, 5 Wallace 28, Freeman Snow 465.

[2] Calvo, édn 3me, § 2476; édn 4me, § 2767; 17 L. Q. R. 194.

[3] *Archives Diplomatiques*, January 1879, p. 81; 4 *Revue Générale de Droit International Public* 157, 298.

[4] *Le Droit des Neutres sur Mer*, p. 137.

[5] *Das Internationale Oeffentliche Seerecht*, p. 159; 14 *Annuaire de l'Institut de Droit International* 63.

[6] As pointed out by Mr E. L. de Hart in 17 L. Q. R. 197.

that the critical destination in matter of contraband is that of the goods and not that of the ship.

Export of Contraband and Convoy.

We have seen that the export or carriage of contraband of war, like blockade-running, is in general left by international law to be repressed by the belligerent whom it damages[1]. A state which attempted to prevent it by its own law would not only be gratuitously outrunning its neutral duty, but would be assuming a task very difficult to perform without so strict a supervision of its subjects' business as in most countries would be felt to be intolerably onerous. In return it would scarcely fail to meet from belligerents with complaints of imperfect and partial fulfilment of the duty undertaken, which it would be more difficult to answer than it would have been to maintain the true line of neutral conduct. Nevertheless some states have entered on the dangerous course. On the outbreak of the Spanish-American war the export to the belligerents of every thing capable of immediate use in war was prohibited by the Netherlands, and of material of war by Brazil; and on the outbreak of the Russo-Japanese war Sweden notified the liberty of the belligerents to export from her all goods "except those which are considered to be contraband of war." These steps may have been prompted by what we should hold to be a mistaken caution on the part of powers not of the first rank, or by that view of the position of individuals in the question which we have rejected[2].

When however the export of contraband amounts in its peculiar circumstances to participation in a specific operation of war, it no longer falls within the conditions under which a state can tolerate it without a disregard of the neutrality due from its territory. We have seen this in the case of despatching ships in belligerent service or control, and a similar case is presented by the export of coal to a war fleet at sea. That would amount to a participation in the operations which the

[1] See above, pp. 166–168, 176. For the legality in England and the United States of contracts entered into for the purposes here in question, see *exp. Chavasse, re Grazebrook*, 34 L. J., N. S., Bk. 17; *The Helen*, 35 L. J., N. S., Adm. 2; *Seton v. Low*, 1 Johnson 1; Scott 798, 799 n.

[2] See above, p. 167.

supply of coal rendered possible, and Great Britain accordingly prohibited the export of coal to the French fleet in the North Sea during the war of 1870, but refused to prohibit its export to France, though strongly pressed to do so by Germany, which power did not place the demand so much on general grounds as on the equally inadmissible claim to a benevolent neutrality on the part of Great Britain.

Closely connected with the question of government interference with the export of contraband is that of convoy. So far as a belligerent is empowered by the convention of nations, tacitly contained in customary international law, to repress any traffic at sea, he must be authorised to visit and search the ships which he has reasonable ground to suspect of being engaged in that traffic. An important field for the exercise of this authority, as claimed and practised by British cruisers and privateers, was at one time the search for enemy's goods on board neutral shipping, but since the Declaration of Paris has freed such goods from capture the search for contraband is the chief, though not quite the only, remaining field for it. As early as 1653, during a war between England and Holland, Queen Christina of Sweden employed her ships of war in convoying Swedish merchantmen, with instructions "to decline in all possible ways that they or any of those that belong to them be searched." And from that time downwards the right of convoy has been in dispute, often by force, between Great Britain on the one hand and the Baltic powers and the Netherlands on the other hand. Those who claim the right require that the declaration of the commander of a ship of war shall be accepted by the belligerent commanders whom he meets, as sufficient evidence that the merchantmen sailing under his protection have only innocent goods on board, and are not avowedly or constructively in the enemy's service, or engaged in any enterprise, such as blockade-running, which a belligerent is entitled to prevent. This view has obtained so wide a currency that now the United States, France, Germany, Austria, Spain, Italy, Japan and the Baltic powers provide by their naval regulations that the declaration of a convoying officer shall be accepted. Great Britain on the other hand adheres to the practice upon which she has always acted.

In defence of the British contention it may be urged that, as long as international law does not make it the duty of a neutral state to prohibit the export of contraband, or otherwise to supervise in belligerent interest the commercial activity of its subjects, so far as that activity does not involve the use of its territory by a foreign power or its agents—so long a belligerent is not bound to accept the offer of a neutral state to undertake such supervision, and to substitute its own responsibility for that of the individuals with whom international law has left him to deal. Further, since any administrative procedures which the neutral government might adopt in its ports and markets would in the long run be conducted by methods of routine, and would usually be unaccompanied by such knowledge of suspicious circumstances as self-interest would prompt a belligerent to be diligent in acquiring, the declaration of the convoying officer would in practice mean little more than that the papers of the vessels under his protection showed no cause for belligerent interference on their face. Again, in the matter of contraband, the system of convoy would in effect compel the belligerent to be content with the neutral's definition of the articles to be considered as such. In truth the efforts of the Baltic powers to establish that system have been closely connected with their efforts to eliminate the naval materials which they produced from the list of contraband. But, well grounded as the British objection to the system of convoy appears to us, it must be admitted that in the present state of foreign opinion it may be difficult to maintain it in practice. While we write the British government has proposed at the Hague Conference to abolish the doctrine of contraband, and in our judgment it is one of the merits of that proposal that, as a consequence, the importance both of convoy and of the objection to it would almost entirely fall to the ground.

In the mean time, since resistance by a neutral merchantman to search, and even sailing with instructions to make such resistance, is a cause for condemning both her and her cargo, it is held in England that sailing under neutral convoy, whether of the merchantman's own of any other neutral state, carries the same consequence, because it is thereby sought to profit by the convoying ship's unlawful employment of force[1]. Whether

[1] Admiralty *Manual*, Arts. 147, 148, 149; *The Maria*, 1 C. Rob. 340, Scott 858; *The Franklin*, 2 Acton 106; *The Elsebe*, 5 C. Rob. 173.

a neutral merchantman incurs condemnation by attaching herself to a war fleet or ship of the enemy, thereby resorting to what is called belligerent convoy, is a question on which the British and United States prize courts have differed. The former decide in the affirmative, on the ground that by so doing she seeks to profit by the enemy's employment of force. In the United States the negative has been held, on the ground that the enemy's force of which advantage is sought to be taken is lawful. Each answer must be and is given in the same sense in the case of a neutral cargo embarked in an armed ship of the enemy, but the British court has held that neutral cargo does not suffer for being embarked in an enemy private ship which makes resistance[1].

Analogues of Contraband: Men and Despatches.

When a neutral ship is chartered by a belligerent government or its agent for the purpose of conveying men or despatches, she is subject to capture and confiscation as being in belligerent service, so that there is no need to invoke an analogy to the law of contraband, and the importance of the men or despatches conveyed is immaterial[2]. Where the service of a neutral ship was obtained under duress applied by a belligerent, Lord Stowell equally condemned her[3]; but it is widely, and in our opinion justly, thought that this was wrong, since the condemnation cannot operate as a lesson to neutrals in a similar case.

When a neutral ship has not placed herself in such a relation to a belligerent government as to be virtually in its service, and has a belligerent's men or despatches on board her, either by special contract or because advantage has been taken of her functions as a regular passenger ship or of the mail bags which

[1] For Great Britain, Admiralty *Manual*, Arts. 147, 150; *The Catharina Elizabeth*, 5 C. Rob. 232; *The Fanny*, 1 Dodson 443. For the United States, *The Néréide*, 9 Cranch 441, Scott 884, in which Chief Justice Marshall delivered the opinion of the majority, Justice Story dissenting; *The Atalanta*, 3 Wheaton 409, Scott 894 note.

[2] *The Orozembo*, 6 C. Rob. 430, Scott 785. The result will be the same if she is chartered as a transport: *The Friendship*, 6 C. Rob. 420; or for any other service. And see above, p. 153.

[3] *The Carolina*, 4 C. Rob. 256, alluded to in the judgment in *The Orozembo* as "the Swedish vessel." And see above, p. 154.

she carries, the question as it affects men must be kept separate from that concerning despatches. Men present no real analogy to contraband, although they as well as despatches are often spoken of as its analogues. Men cannot be forwarded like goods, in pursuance of an intention formed about them by some one else. All that can be done is to give them facilities for locomotion, and the question is what facilities of the kind the customary law of nations does not allow a neutral ship to afford. Accordingly the carriage of men has not been usually coupled in treaties with the carriage of contraband but with the clauses stipulating the rule "free ships free goods," in which it is common to find it laid down that the freedom of the flag covers all persons on board except those in the enemy's military service. And by the resolutions of the Institute of International Law on "transport service," which it passed at the same time as those on contraband, the only persons whom it is forbidden to neutrals to carry are those in a belligerent's military service and his diplomatists credited to his ally[1]. The British Admiralty *Manual* includes in the prohibition "civil officials sent out on the public service and at the public expense[2]." The persons carried in the *Orozembo* were three military men and two going to be employed in civil capacities in a colonial government of the enemy. Lord Stowell did not feel it necessary to determine whether the principle on which he condemned her would apply to the latter alone, but he thought it reasonable that it should apply whenever the enemy thought it worth while to send out such persons at the public expense. We agree in theory, and that condemnation of the ship should follow, when the enemy has sent out the persons, military or civil, by special arrangement. But that is a case no longer likely to happen, so abundant have regular passenger ships become in all seas. When they travel as passengers in the ordinary course, it must be remembered that the customary right to capture even military officers has not been accompanied by any relaxation of the duty to send every neutral ship that is interfered with in for adjudication, and that to arrest a passenger liner and send her in for adjudication would be an intolerable nuisance. The duty referred to cannot

[1] 15 *Annuaire* 123. [2] Art. 89.

properly be relaxed, for those who capture the men cannot be allowed to be judges in their own cause, and an adjudication on the ship is the only means of submitting their act to legal decision.

Accordingly when Messieurs Mason and Slidell, sent by the Confederate States to attempt the opening of diplomatic relations with Great Britain and France, were taken by a United States naval commander out of the British passenger steamer *Trent* on a voyage between two neutral ports, the United States surrendered them to Great Britain on the ground that the *Trent* had been allowed to pursue her course. There remains the nuisance which bringing her in would have caused, and this has suggested that the right to capture any persons whatever, military or civil, being carried in a neutral ship bound for a neutral port, had better be abandoned, except when the ship is in the enemy's service either openly by hiring, or virtually by rendering such service as is rendered by a transport. Mr Mountague Bernard, who makes this suggestion, with which we agree, adds: "The number of the persons conveyed, the nature of their employment, their importance, their immediate or ultimate destination, may then become material elements of proof; and there should be evidence of intention, or of knowledge from which intention may be reasonably inferred, on the part of the owner or his agent the master[1]." Where the proof is thus fully made, the inconvenience of interrupting the regular passenger service by sending the ship in for adjudication must be faced; but where it can be made, there can hardly fail to have been indications warning the public that on that trip she was not acting in her ordinary capacity.

Despatches, on the other hand, being things, present a real analogy to contraband: they might have been classed as such, but for the attention having been concentrated on the commercial aspect of contraband. As early as the year 1636 the right of the French to visit English ships, in order to prevent the carriage of their enemies' "advices and directions," was admitted[2]. The rule is that carrying the despatches of the

[1] *Neutrality of Great Britain during the American Civil War*, p. 224.
[2] Robinson's *Collectanea Maritima*, p. 46, quoting 2 Sydn. Lett. 436.

enemy government, unless the master can show that he was justifiably ignorant of their noxious character, is a cause of confiscation for the ship, and for the cargo so far as belonging to the owners of the ship, *ob continentiam delicti* as Lord Stowell expressed it[1]. An exception is made for despatches sent in order to maintain communication between the enemy state and neutral ones, for such communication is the right of the neutral states, however valuable it may be to the enemy. On this principle the carriage of despatches from the enemy government to its own consul in a neutral country, not known to contain any thing hurtful to England, was held innocent, since the office of a consul relates to international trade, in which the country where he is stationed is interested as well as that to which he belongs[2]. But despatches sent in the course of communication between different parts of the enemy's dominions are held to be noxious even if they relate only to civil business[3]. To paralyse the enemy's government in all its operations is a legitimate means of compelling it to submit to the terms of peace demanded. Even private letters may be "of an injurious tendency," and so "give the captors the right of enquiry," apparently whether they ought not in the circumstances to be regarded as really public communications, for which purpose they may bring in the ship carrying them; but if the communications are not found to be public she will not be condemned[4].

Where the despatches which under the general rules thus far laid down would be ranked as noxious are carried in neutral mail bags, it is worthy of serious consideration whether those rules at all apply to them. Since neither the master nor the owners of a ship have any knowledge of the contents of a mail bag put on board her by a postoffice, the guilty knowledge or *mens rea* necessary for the condemnation of the ship must always be wanting in that case. There can therefore be no justification

[1] *The Atalanta*, 6 C. Rob. 440, Scott 780; *The Rapid*, Edwards 228, Scott 782. The master's ignorance will not be justifiable unless he has made "the utmost exertions of caution and good faith": *The Susan*, 6 C. Rob. 461 note.

[2] *The Madison*, Edwards 224, Scott 785.

[3] *The Atalanta*, u. s.

[4] Lord Stowell in *The Caroline*, 6 C. Rob. 469.

for bringing in the ship for adjudication, on the sole ground of her carrying such bags; and examination of the bags on board her without bringing her in cannot be justified. During the American civil war mail bags found in ships searched on suspicion of blockade-running or carrying contraband were the subject of correspondence between the British and United States governments. Earl Russell wrote, 10 October 1862:

> Her Majesty's government cannot doubt that the government of the United States are prepared to concede that all mail bags, clearly certified to be such, shall be exempt from seizure or visitation, and that some arrangement shall be made for immediately forwarding such bags to their destination, in the event of the ship which carries them being detained. If this is done, the necessity for discussing the claim, as a matter of strict right, that Her Majesty's mails on board a private vessel should be exempted from visitation or detention, might be avoided.

Mr Seward, by way of reply, gave the following directions, addressed to the Secretary of the Navy, 31 October 1862:

> It is thought expedient that instructions be given to the blockading and naval officers that, in case of capture of merchant-vessels suspected or found to be vessels of the insurgents or contraband, the public mails of any friendly or neutral power, duly certified and authenticated as such, shall not be searched or opened, but be put as speedily as may be convenient on their way to their designated destinations. This instruction however will not be deemed to protect simulated mail bags, verified by forged certificates or counterfeited seals[1].

[1] M. Bernard's *Neutrality of Great Britain during the American Civil War*, pp. 322, 323.

CHAPTER XI.

THE HAGUE CONFERENCE OF 1907.

All the preceding chapters of this volume were printed before the meeting of the second Hague Conference, and its completion was postponed until it should be possible to give the results of that Conference so far as the international law of war is concerned. This we now proceed to do, combining with those results what we had reserved on points of which the Conference was expected to treat. We have not in this volume to deal with matters discussed at the Conference which belong to the international law of peace, or to the political arrangement of foreign affairs rather than to either branch of international law properly so called.

The regulations which we shall have to quote as adopted at full sittings of the Conference will have to be embodied in conventions in order to become binding, so far as the reservations made at the Conference by particular powers will allow them to become binding. The publication of those conventions in England will no doubt be accompanied by official translations. Our translations have been made from the French texts on which the discussions and votes took place, and we have mentioned the most important reservations.

Declaration of War.

A regulation on the commencement of hostilities, expressed as the contract which it is intended to become by a convention, was adopted in the following form at the full sitting of the second Hague Conference on 7 September 1907.

I. The contracting powers recognise that hostilities between them ought not to commence without a preceding and unequivocal notice, which shall have the form either of a declaration of war expressing its motives, or of an ultimatum with a conditional declaration of war.

II. The state of war must be notified without delay to the neutral powers, and will produce no effect with relation to them until their receipt of a notification which may even be made by telegraph. It is however understood that neutral powers will not be able to plead the absence of a notification, if it is established in no doubtful manner that in fact they knew of the state of war.

This regulation coincides with the doctrine which we have laid down above, pp. 18—28. Only two remarks are needed in order to put the matter in a clear light. One is that the declaration of war is now expressly required to be *motivée*, which the declarants have always made it for their own justification[1]. The other is that the commencement of hostilities without a preceding declaration, in such peculiar cases as are contemplated above, p. 24, is left possible by the fact that the parties are not made to contract that they will not commence hostilities against one another otherwise than is described, but recognise that hostilities ought not (*ne doivent pas*) to be otherwise commenced.

Nothing can more clearly show the impossibility of insisting on an interval of notice between a declaration of war and a commencement of hostilities under it, than the fact that the very moderate proposal of a 24 hours' interval, made by the delegation of the Netherlands, was not accepted. The Conference has therefore rather confirmed than weakened the necessity that, in order not to be taken unprepared, every nation must rely on its own vigilance and on no formal rule.

[1] The qualification *motivée* is not applied in the regulation to the conditional declaration of war accompanying an ultimatum, doubtless because in that case the demands which are considered to justify war are contained in the ultimatum.

The Laws of Land War, as revised at the Hague in 1907.

The Regulations which the Hague Conference of 1907 adopted at its full sitting on 17 August embody the following principal amendments of the Regulations of 1899, set forth in Chapter IV above.

Art. II: above, p. 62. As another condition to be satisfied by a population which rises spontaneously on the approach of the enemy, there is added that it must carry arms openly. Switzerland and Montenegro alone voted in the negative.

Art. V: above, p. 63. The confinement of prisoners cannot last longer than the circumstances which make it indispensable for safety. Voted unanimously.

A discussion took place on the confinement of a population or portions of it in what in Cuba and South Africa were known as concentration camps, which was remarkable for the opinion expressed by the eminent Belgian delegate M. Beernaert, to the effect that Arts. III and V are to be construed as covering the whole ground of internment, so that no so-called concentration not authorised by them is allowable. We cannot subscribe to that opinion. The Articles in question only profess to deal with the armed forces of the belligerent parties.

Art. VI: above, p. 63. Officers who are prisoners of war cannot be compelled to work, and non-commissioned officers and privates can only be compelled to do work which corresponds with their rank and aptitude.

Art. XIV: above, p. 66. The individual returns mentioned in the first paragraph is to include certain particulars and to be delivered to the other belligerent after the conclusion of peace. The second paragraph is to apply also to the effects of prisoners who have been set free on their parole, have been exchanged or have escaped.

Art. XVII: above, p. 67. The scale of pay to be allowed to officers who are prisoners is to be that of the captor state.

Art. XXI: above, p. 68. This Article has become obsolete by the conclusion of the amended Geneva Convention of 1906, which we deal with in the next section under the heading *The Red Cross in Land War*.

Art. XXIII : above, p. 72. To the prohibitions contained in this Article there was added, on the proposition of Germany: *To declare that private claims of the subjects of the enemy are extinguished, suspended, or not admissible.*

Art. XXII A. *Any compulsion of the nationals of the enemy to take part in the operations of war directed against their country, even in the case of their having taken service before the outbreak of war, is prohibited.*

This new Article, which was proposed by Germany, would seem to have its proper place after Art. XXIII, but was referred to in the proceedings at the Hague as XXII A, perhaps on the assumption that in the new code XXIII would become XXII by XXI dropping out as obsolete. It is also intimately connected with the subject of XLIV and XLIV A, together with which it will be noticed in the order of the latter.

Art. XXVII : above, p. 78. On the proposition of Greece, historical monuments were added to the edifices protected by this Article.

Art. XLIV A. *Any compulsion of the population of an occupied territory to give information concerning their own army or the means of defence of their country is prohibited.*

Great Britain and Austria-Hungary were among the powers which reserved their assent to this new Article.

The old Art. XLIV—above, p. 91—is more than covered by the new XXII A, which prohibits compelling the occupied population to take part, not merely in "military operations" as did H XLIV, but in "the operations of war," and it may be supposed that in the new code it will be omitted, and XLIV A, so referred to in the proceedings at the Hague, become XLIV. Austria-Hungary desired to limit XXII A by adding "as combatants," which would have reduced it to the measure of H XLIV. The rejection of that limitation, as well as the terms of XLIV A so far as that Article shall ultimately be found acceptable, ought to be decisive against the forced employment of enemy subjects as guides, which we have discussed on p. 91, and which in the discussion of XXII A was specially mentioned with reprobation by the German and French delegations.

Art. LII : above, p. 96. The last paragraph of this Article

has been amplified as follows, the addition being shown by italics: "What is furnished in kind shall as far as possible be paid for in ready money; if not, the fact of furnishing shall be recorded by receipts, *of which the amount shall be satisfied as soon as possible, even before the close of hostilities, so far as the military authority of the belligerent shall have the necessary pecuniary means in its power.*" This addition leaves the matter much as it stood before. No obligation of the invading government to furnish its military authority with the means of satisfying the receipts is expressed, and mere inference would certainly be insufficient to charge that government with any obligation towards the subjects of the invaded state, strong enough not to be wiped out by the treaty of peace together with all other claims connected with or arising out of the war. The fact that the addition has been made and not carried further only proves that an uneasy conscience is left by the vaunted superiority of land war to naval war in the matter of the respect paid to private property.

Art. LIII: above, p. 102. *All means of communication or transport, by land, sea or air, which are destined for the transmission of persons, things or news*, are to be included in the second paragraph of this Article.

Lastly, a sanction was provided for the code by the following new Article: LXI. *A belligerent party which violates the dispositions of the present Regulations shall pay an indemnity if there be occasion, and shall be responsible for all acts committed by persons forming part of its armed forces.*

The Red Cross in Land War.

Pages 68—72 of this volume, in which the Geneva Convention of 22 August 1864 is given at length with a commentary, in consequence of its having been incorporated in the Hague Laws of War as H XXI, were printed before that convention was superseded by the new one of 6 July 1906. The recency of that revision rendered any reconsideration of the subject by the Hague Conference of 1907 unnecessary. Unlike its predecessor, which laid down general rules, the new convention contains in 33 Articles a full code of the law relating to the sick and wounded in land war, and therefore comprises too much technical detail to be suited for reproduction here. It has not affected principles, and the old articles with our commentary, combined with the additions and corrections which we shall proceed to make, will still convey such information on the subject as is suitable to the design and dimensions of this book.

The Red Cross societies, or societies for the succour of the wounded, are now mentioned, taking their place alongside of the medical, called in the convention the sanitary, service of the armies to which they are attached. Both are to bear the distinctive flag and arm-badge of the convention, and to carry also the national flag of the belligerent. By the new Art. 16 the material belongings of the societies are "considered as private property, and as such are respected in all circumstances, saving the belligerents' right of requisitioning acknowledged by the laws and customs of war."

The term "neutrality" entirely disappears. The medical service, including that of the societies, is to be "protected and respected by the belligerents."

The ambulances and hospitals of the old convention are now described as "the movable formations and fixed establishments of the medical [sanitary] service."

The guards mentioned in our comment on the old Art. 1, if they fall into the hands of the enemy, are not to be treated as prisoners of war: new Arts. 8, 9.

With reference to our comment on the old Art. 2, it is now provided that "the chaplains attached to the armies" are included among those who are not to be treated as prisoners of war: new Art. 9.

The limitation in the old Art. 2, "so long as there remain any wounded to bring in or to succour," does not reappear.

The persons, of whom it is said in the old Art. 3 that they "may continue to fulfil their duties etc.," now are bound to continue the fulfilment of their duties as long as their assistance is indispensable: new Art. 12.

In place of the old Art. 5, which as we observed went too far, we have the following new Art. 5: "The military authority may appeal to the charitable zeal of the inhabitants to receive the wounded and sick of the armies, and take care of them under its control, granting a special protection and certain immunities to the persons who shall have responded to that appeal."

In place of the 2nd, 3rd and 4th paragraphs of the old Art. 6, all such matters relating to the wounded are now referred to the agreements which may be made between the belligerents: new Art. 2.

Lastly, it was decided not to allow any variation from the adopted cross, the true significance of which, in order to obviate any friction with the religious sentiments of non-Christian states, was thus explained:

ART. 18. As a homage to Switzerland, the heraldic sign of a red cross on a white ground, formed by the interchange of the federal colours, is maintained as the emblem and distinctive sign of the medical [sanitary] service of armies.

The representatives of Japan, Persia and Siam declared their satisfaction with this, and to treat Turkey differently would have been open to grave objection. As M. Moynier, one of the eminent founders of the Red Cross movement, pointed out long ago, the crescent cannot serve as a sign of the medical service unless its use in other branches of the Turkish army is prohibited, and even were this done the soldiers could not be expected to change all at once their associations with the crescent, and to understand it as the symbol of a new military morality. Nevertheless the Turkish delegate, this time together with the Persian, renewed the objection to the cross in the discussion in 1907 on the amendment of the convention for the adaptation of the Geneva principles to maritime war. He was supported by the Russian delegate, who brought forward the fact that the Red Cross and Red Crescent had cooperated successfully during the Russo-Turkish war of 1877; and we may therefore expect to see a similar variation of fact in the future, both by land and by sea, from the rule of law laid down.

The Three Hague Declarations of 1899.

The three declarations made at the Hague Conference in 1899 which are mentioned on p. 110, above, were renewed at the Conference of 1907, Great Britain being a party to them all. On the latter occasion the United States proposed the interdiction of "balls which inflict uselessly cruel wounds, such as explosive balls, and generally every kind of ball which goes beyond the limit necessary for putting a man immediately out of action." This proposal was not discussed because, for some reason not easy to understand, it was held not to be within the scope of the Conference.

A curious point is that the duration of the declaration against launching projectiles and explosives from balloons, for which a limit is made necessary by the rapid progress of aerostatic science, was declared to be "till the end of the next Conference," on a British proposal adopted by 26 votes against 9 with 8 abstentions, while the Belgian proposal, to make it five years as in 1899, was also adopted by 28 votes against 9 with 8 abstentions. It is therefore necessary to await the form in which the declaration will be signed by any power, in order to be certain as to the duration of its obligation.

The Red Cross in Naval[1] War.

The Hague Conference of 1899 produced a *Convention for the Adaptation to Naval War of the principles of the Geneva Convention of* 1864[2]. An amended form was voted by the Hague Conference of 1907, and will no doubt be embodied in a new convention. We shall here state the substance of the most important articles of that form.

Hospital-ships may be either belligerent or neutral. The former may either be military, that is public, hospital-ships, having been constructed or assigned by a belligerent state specially and solely for the purpose of assisting the wounded, sick, or shipwrecked—or private ones, having been equipped wholly or in part at the cost of private individuals or officially recognised relief societies, but these must be furnished with an official commission from a belligerent state, and with a certificate from the competent authorities declaring that they had been under their control while fitting out and on their final departure. The names of both must be notified by the belligerent to the hostile power at the commencement or during the course of hostilities, and in any case before they are employed. Both classes are to be respected, even during fighting as far as possible, and cannot be captured while hostilities last, and military hospital-ships will not be on the same footing as men-of-war as regards their stay in neutral ports.

Neutral hospital-ships are those equipped wholly or in part at the cost of private individuals or officially recognised societies of neutral countries, and in order that they may be entitled to the same rights as belligerent ones they must have placed themselves under the direction of one of the belligerents, with its authority and the previous consent of their own government, the former being obliged to notify their names to its adversary as in the case of its own hospital-ships.

All hospital-ships are to be painted white outside, with a horizontal band about a metre and a half in breadth which is

[1] *Guerre maritime* in the French text, but in English "maritime" is usually contrasted with "inland," and does not mean what is or takes place on the sea.

[2] *Parliamentary Papers; Miscellaneous No.* 1 (1899), c. 9534: p. 349.

to be green in the case of military ones, red in that of private ones whether belligerent or neutral; and all must adopt measures with a view to making the colours in which they are painted sufficiently visible at night. All must also hoist the white flag with a red cross together with their national flag, and the vessels of neutral ownership must in addition fly from the mainmast the flag of the belligerent under whom they have been placed, the latter however to be lowered during any detention of them by the enemy. In the committee the Turkish delegation reserved the right of its country to use the crescent instead of the cross and the Persian that to use the Lion and Sun, and the British delegation accepted those reservations. At the full sitting Turkey withdrew her reservation.

Thus legitimated and distinguished, all hospital-ships "shall afford relief and assistance to the wounded, sick and shipwrecked of the belligerents independently of their nationality; the governments engage not to use them for any military purpose; they must not in any way hamper the movements of the combatants; during and after an engagement they will act at their own risk and peril; the belligerents will have the right to control and visit them, they can refuse to help them, order them off, make them take a certain course and put a commissioner on board; they can even detain them if important circumstances require it; as far as possible the belligerents shall inscribe in their sailing papers the orders they give them." The hospital-ships may use wireless telegraphy, subject to the right of a belligerent commander to require the removal of the apparatus, or its reduction so as to allow messages to be received but not sent. They may carry only such cannon as they need for signalling, but their *personnel* may be armed for their own defence and that of the persons under their care.

No neutral vessel, even though a casual volunteer, is to be liable for capture for picking up or carrying wounded, sick, or shipwrecked belligerents; and neutral mercantile vessels requisitioned or volunteering for hospital service under promise of immunity, after having committed infractions of neutrality, are freed from the penal consequences of such infractions to the extent of the promises made.

Art. 9 of the convention of 1899 provided that "the shipwrecked, wounded or sick of one of the belligerents who fall into the hands of the other are prisoners of war. The captor must decide according to circumstances whether it is best to keep them or send them to a port of his own country, to a neutral port or even to a hostile port. In the last case prisoners thus repatriated cannot serve as long as the war lasts." This is reproduced by Art. 14 of the form voted in 1907, and is therein supplemented by an Art. 12, proposed by the German delegation and supported by M. Renault, the French reporter of the draft, as carrying out the principle of the old Art. 9: "Every belligerent ship of war may demand the surrender to it of the wounded, sick or shipwrecked who are on board hospital-ships, whether military or belonging to red-cross societies or to individuals, merchantmen, yachts or boats, whatever may be the nationality of such vessels." The argument of M. Renault was that in the absence of a convention international law would allow a belligerent not only to seize enemy combatants found on board a neutral vessel, but also to capture and confiscate the vessel as having rendered an unneutral service to the enemy; and that if shipwrecked combatants, for example, escaped captivity by finding refuge on board a neutral vessel, belligerents would fend off the charitable action of neutrals which threatened them with irreparable damage. He also pointed out that belligerents cannot force a neutral merchantman to change her route and destination, as they are allowed to do for hospital-ships. Sir Edward Fry at the discussion in the committee placed on record that "the British government cannot acquiesce in the opinion expressed in the report as to the right of a belligerent ship of war to require the surrender of wounded, sick and shipwrecked combatants on board a merchant vessel sailing under a neutral flag. Failing a special convention, his government considers that the recognition of such a right cannot be based on the existing principles of international law." But this reservation was withdrawn at the full sitting of the Conference in which the form of the convention was voted, and the Art. 12 stands with no more question as a part of that form.

It is however scarcely the less necessary to form a judgment on the question of principle on which a difference of opinion between such authorities was expressed. To do so we must first remember one point on which the principles of neutral duty allow no controversy. If a neutral ship does not surrender to their enemy the combatants in a condition to fight again whom she has saved, she must carry them to her own country and they must there be interned. And this must equally be understood of those who may be expected to be again in a condition for fighting when their wounds have been healed. The real question is therefore whether the choice between the surrender and the internment of the persons concerned is to rest with the belligerent or the neutral. In favour of the neutral it may be urged that those who are under his flag at sea are constructively already in his country, and that their surrender can therefore no more be demanded than if they were physically in it. The belligerent may reply that the constructive identification of a ship with its country has not been admitted by the laws of war, as is proved by the right to take contraband goods, and formerly enemy's goods, from under the neutral flag; and that in the treaties stipulating the rule "free ships free goods," it is common to find it laid down that the freedom of the flag covers all persons on board except those in the enemy's military service[1]. To this it must be added that the belligerent commander cannot fairly be expected to trust the promise of a private shipmaster to carry his passengers to a port where they will be safely interned, especially since the performance of that promise might be defeated by other causes than bad faith. Our conclusion is that the reply is sufficient, and that Art. 12 of the draft convention of 1907 requires from a neutral no more than, in its absence, belligerents would insist on with good warrant. But we cannot agree that in the absence of the article a neutral shipmaster who had taken the persons in question on board would render his ship liable to confiscation for rendering unneutral service to the enemy. There would be no ground for presuming that he intended to restore them to the military service of their own side. If he had the correct intention to see to their safe internment, it is not clear what benefit the enemy would derive from internment being substituted for capture, and there would be no room for suggesting the existence of an improper arrangement between him and the enemy.

[1] See above, p. 262.

The duty of internment to which we have called attention is recognised by a provision that the shipwrecked, wounded or sick who are landed at a neutral port with the consent of the local authorities, or who are taken on board a neutral ship of war, must, failing a contrary arrangement between the neutral state and the belligerents, be guarded by the neutral state, so that they cannot again take part in the military operations; and that the expenses of entertainment and internment shall be borne by the state to which the shipwrecked, wounded or sick belong.

There are express provisions that the religious, medical or hospital staff of any captured ship is inviolable, and cannot be made prisoners of war, and that the belligerents must guarantee the enjoyment of their salaries to the staff which has fallen into their hands. Also that sailors and soldiers who are taken on board when sick or wounded, to whatever nation they belong, shall be protected and cared for by the captors.

Submarine Cables in War.

The Danish delegation, pursuing the line taken by their country in 1899, proposed at the Conference of 1907 the following addition to Art. LIII of the Hague Laws of War, second paragraph, given above, p. 102. "Submarine cables uniting an occupied or enemy territory to a neutral one shall not be seized or destroyed except absolute necessity requires it. They also shall be restored and the indemnities regulated at the peace." The laws of land war do not furnish an occasion for dealing with more than the shore ends of submarine cables, and these are plainly within the principles applied to land telegraphs in the second paragraph of Art. LIII. But the Conference failed to examine the subject, and we will place here what needs to be said on it.

On three points relating to submarine telegraph cables there is universal agreement. Such a cable connecting two neutral territories is inviolable. A cable connecting the territories of enemy belligerents, or two parts of the territory of one of them, may be cut in the territorial waters of either or in the open sea, but not in neutral territorial waters if it should happen to pass through them. And a cable connecting a neutral with a belligerent territory may be cut in the territorial waters of the latter, but not in those of the former. The question is whether a cable connecting a neutral with a belligerent territory may be cut in the open sea by the enemy of the latter. The three points agreed are covered without controversy by the principles that a belligerent may do acts of war in his own or his enemy's territory or territorial waters, but not in those of a neutral, nor in the open sea against neutral property not implicated in offences against the international rules of contraband or blockade. In this the term "property" is not limited to its sense in internal law. A telegraph cable cannot be attached to the shore except by the territorial sovereign or by virtue of a concession from him, granted from public motives and always subject to public control, so that it is a public institution belonging internationally to the state, even although it may in the narrower sense be the property of a company. If the cable connects different states it belongs to both, and if they are respectively neutral and belligerent it cannot be cut without violence being done to the neutral interest. That is justifiable in the territorial waters of the belligerent partowner, because property durably affixed to the soil must share the fate of the soil, as in liability to requisitions and contributions on land. It would not be justifiable to subject the neutral interest to violence in the open sea, and thus the principles which govern the undisputed cases dictate a negative answer to the question put in the fourth place, the decision in all being independent of the legal property in the cable being vested in a state or in a company.

Nevertheless the Institute of International Law in 1902 adopted resolutions with regard to submarine telegraph cables which, while otherwise in accordance with what we have said, laid down that "a cable connecting a neutral territory with the territory of one of the belligerents cannot be cut in the open sea unless there is an effective blockade, and then within the limits of the line of blockade, and subject to the duty of reestablishing the cable in the shortest time possible[1]." This was carried by a large majority, the reporter in its favour being the eminent Professor von Bar, and the equally eminent German and French jurists, Herr Perels and Mm. Renault and Lainé, voting in the minority only because they objected to the liberty of cutting the cable being restricted to the existence and line of a blockade. M. Renault invoked, not indeed the rules, but what he contended to be the principle of the law of contraband. Ships may be visited, and confiscated if they are found to carry contraband despatches: the right is used sparingly against postal packet-boats, but it exists. Despatches are now sent by telegraph, and "belligerents must find in the new situation an equivalent for the protection which they have lost." The new defence by cutting cables in the open sea must be admitted, "because otherwise there would no longer be any means of defence at all[2]." Herr Perels declined to concern himself with an enquiry into the principles of contraband, blockade or angary, "fearing lest such ideas should complicate the discussion by leading to endless

[1] 19 *Annuaire* 332. [2] Ib., p. 314.

developments......It is desirable to have free communications, but it is impossible to sacrifice the interests of belligerents. Military necessities must be reckoned with. We can in the Institute propose what we like, but the question is what governments can adopt[1]." General Den Beer Poortugael gave to these arguments the conclusive (as we think) answers that "there is no necessity of war against neutrals because there is no war against them"; and that unless you can sink a packet-boat because bad weather or the approach of an enemy prevents your verifying by a visit her having obnoxious despatches on board, cutting a cable when you cannot ascertain what despatches are sent by it has no analogy to the procedure in the case of contraband[2]. Professor von Bar, who also rejected both the doctrine of military necessity and the analogy to contraband, took the view, which the Institute appears to have adopted, that the principle of blockade is to prohibit all communication with the blockaded coast, and that communication by cable is a breach of that principle[3].

In truth, against all these attempts to impose fresh burdens on neutrals by extending the rules of blockade and contraband there lies the objection, deeper than that arising from the failure of any particular analogy, that those rules are not due to principle but to compromise, and therefore furnish no standing-ground on which a deductive extension can rest. Any extension must be the independent result of agreement, express or tacit, and in the latter case long and well tried. Meantime the general principles of neutrality, the only ones which as yet there are in the case, deny to a belligerent, blockade or no blockade, the right of cutting a neutral or neutral-belligerent cable outside territorial waters. It follows, if that is so, that a neutral may legitimately resent any such cutting of a cable in which he is interested, so long as no rules permitting it have received his assent, or have become a part of international law in the regular progress of its development.

We have seen that neutrals are not entitled to an indemnity for the damage suffered through lawful acts of war by the

[1] Ib., p. 310. [2] Ib., pp. 313, 316.
[3] Ib., pp. 16, 308, 316.

property which they have connected with a territory under military occupation by their residence or business in it[1]. On the same principles a neutral state or company, interested in a cable landed in belligerent territory, can claim no indemnity when the enemy cuts it in that territory or the waters belonging to it[2]. If international agreement should ever make it lawful to cut it in the open sea, justice would require that the same agreement should declare an indemnity to be due.

[1] Above, p. 117.

[2] In May 1898, during the Spanish-American war, Admiral Dewey cut at Manilla the telegraph cable from Hong Kong. The British Eastern Extension Australasia and China Telegraph Company claimed $36,000 damages from the United States, but on the ground here taken the Attorney-General of the latter advised his government that the claim was untenable. He added that the admiral's desire himself to use the cable, of which he buoyed the severed end, made no difference to the question of indemnity, considering that he did not use it. See the *Washington Evening Star* of 4 February 1899, as quoted with approbation, 7 *Revue Générale de Droit International Public* 270, by M. Renault, who adds that if Admiral Dewey had used the cable, not merely for official despatches but for despatches for which the company would have been paid, he should have considered that the profit ought to have been accounted for to the company. We agree. An example of an opposite kind was given by Chile in its war with Peru which ended in 1883. She had cut the cable of a British company connecting the two countries, and her government admitted and satisfied the claim of the company to compensation, without referring it to the mixed commission under the Anglo-Chilian convention of 1883. Letter in the *Times* of 1 June 1898, quoted 25 *Journal de D. I. P. et de la J. C.* 813.——The international convention of 14 March 1884 on submarine telegraph cables expressly reserved that its stipulations *ne portent aucune atteinte à la liberté d'action des belligérants.*

Neutrals in Belligerent Territory.

The four Articles following were adopted on the subject of Neutrals in Belligerent Territory at the full sitting of the second Hague Conference on 21 September 1907.

I. The persons considered as neutrals are the nationals of a state which does not take part in the war.

II. A neutral ceases to benefit by his character as such:

(*a*) If he commits hostile acts against a belligerent party;

(*b*) If he commits acts in favour of a belligerent party, for example (*notamment*) if he voluntarily takes service in the armed force of one of the parties.

In such a case the neutral shall not be treated more rigorously by the belligerent state against which he has abandoned neutrality than a subject of the other belligerent state could be treated by reason of the same fact.

III. The following shall not be considered as acts committed in favour of a belligerent party, in the sense of Art. II (*b*):

(*a*) Supplies furnished or loans made to a belligerent party, provided that the furnisher or lender is not an inhabitant of territory either belonging to or occupied by the other party, and that the supplies do not proceed from (*ne proviennent pas de*) territory of either description;

(*b*) Services rendered by way of police or civil administration.

IV. Railway plant[1] belonging to neutral states or to private companies or persons, and recognisable as such, cannot be requisitioned or used by a belligerent except when and so far as demanded by imperious necessity. It shall be returned to its original country as soon as possible.

The neutral state may equally in case of necessity retain and use a corresponding quantity of (*jusqu'à due concurrence*) the plant of the belligerent state found in its territory.

An indemnity shall be paid on either side in proportion to the plant used and the duration of its use.

The Argentine delegation reserved the consent of its government to Art. IV (*a*). The railways of Argentina are so largely in foreign ownership that that state appears to hesitate about entering into an agreement as to the use which may be made of their material in war. And this circumstance is further of interest, as indicating that Art. IV is intended, as might be inferred from the generality of its wording, to apply to the conduct of both belligerents and not only to that of the invader.

[1] *Le matériel de chemin de fer.* This is perhaps a larger expression than rollingstock.

At the same sitting the two following earnest desires (*vœux*), more or less germane to the position of neutrals in a theatre of land war, were unanimously expressed:

1. That in case of war the competent authorities, civil and military, shall make it a special duty to assist and protect the maintenance of peaceful relations, and in particular of commercial and industrial relations, between the inhabitants of the belligerent states and neutral states;
2. That the High Contracting Powers shall seek to establish, by agreements between them, uniform contractual provisions determining the relations, in respect of military obligations, of each state with the foreigners established in its territory.

We presume that the first of these earnest desires must be read as subject to military necessity. Since the object of an invasion is to cripple the invaded state, and the commercial and industrial relations between its inhabitants and neutral states are an important means of preventing its being crippled, it does not seem likely that invaders will exchange the practice of hindering those relations for that of fostering them. The second desire (*vœu*) is a very proper one, and will be understood when it is remembered that several of the Spanish American states, led by the great immigration into them to claim the children of immigrants as subjects by reason of their birth on the soil, have been engaged in controversies with European powers who have considered that the principle of nationality by parentage ought to exempt such children from military service[1].

Arts. II and III do not seem to contain any thing that is not an easy deduction from acknowledged principles. Art. IV coincides with the doctrine of H LIV of the Laws of Land War, 1899, as interpreted by us: see above, pp. 102, 118. And it expresses the invader's duty, which we had inferred, to pay an indemnity for the excess of neutral rollingstock which he detains and uses. It also expresses the duty of the neutral state or company to pay an indemnity for the excess of belligerent rollingstock detained and used on its part, and there cannot be a doubt but that the creditor to whom this latter indemnity will be due, at least primarily, is the belligerent state or company, owner of the rollingstock in respect of which it is due. But those who maintain an invader's right to exact payment of

[1] See our *International Law—Peace*, p. 218.

debts arising to his enemy in connection with the occupied district will probably hold that, if he has the physical means of paying himself the indemnity at the neutral's expense, he may employ them and oust the right of the true owner[1].

Art. I seems an unnecessary and not altogether suitable introduction to a scheme of such small dimensions as that formed by the whole body of four Articles which we are considering. The explanation is that originally it stood at the head of a scheme of twelve Articles proposed by Germany, of which the four contain all that after prolonged discussion obtained general agreement. The German scheme, which was supported by the United States of America, Austria-Hungary and Switzerland, attempted to upset the received theory and practice by which neutrals established in the territory of a belligerent state, and their property there invested, are exposed to the chances of war equally with the subjects of that state and their property[2]. It therefore began appropriately with a definition of neutral persons intended to make all rules about them turn on their permanent political character, and to place their property invested in belligerent territory in the position which we have claimed for that entering the territory in the course of a business carried on elsewhere, and which in the course of that business would soon leave it[3]. This revolutionary proposal could in the matter of legal reasoning only appeal to that kind which makes a merit of grouping every thing under the largest affirmations—here, for instance, making the political character of a person the test of every thing relating to him—with the addition by the German delegation that their view was imposed on them by treaties which their country had concluded. The United States and Swiss delegations pleaded that it was humane to exempt as many as possible from the evils of war. The

[1] See above, pp. 103, 104.

[2] See above, p. 117. The term "domicile" implies a certain legal relation which is not here in question, and had better not be used for the establishment by which a foreigner identifies himself with the fortunes of a country that may become a theatre of land war. At most the analogy is not to domicile in its proper sense, but to trade domicile in naval war. See above, p. 143.

[3] See above, p. 118.

received view was maintained by Great Britain, France, the Netherlands, Japan and Russia, whose delegations pointed out that immigrant settlers who have not changed their nationality may be called on to serve in the defence of their new countries—that if a neutral settler objects to such service, he has no right to be indemnified against the evils of war—that an invading general cannot distinguish neutral property—that a position good enough for the nationals of an invaded country is good enough for the foreigners who have established themselves there—that contributions are imposed *ratione loci* and not *ratione personæ* (M. Léon Bourgeois, representing France)—that many Far-Eastern countries do not possess any legislation on nationality, and in those parts there are numbers of persons whose nationality is uncertain, or can be changed at a moment's notice for interested reasons (Japanese delegation)—and that since no country distinguishes between its nationals and resident foreigners in granting relief on the occasion of a national calamity, as an inundation or a volcanic eruption, no distinction can justly be claimed by the latter with regard to the sufferings caused by war (General den Beer Poortugael, representing the Netherlands).

An International Prize Court.

The draft of a convention for the establishment of an international prize court was also adopted at the full sitting of the second Hague Conference on 21 September 1907, by 37 votes against that of Brazil as the sole dissentient; but ten states of the majority—China, Persia, and eight Spanish American ones, Chile, Colombia, Cuba, Ecuador, Guatemala, Haiti, Salvador and Uruguay—entered reservations concerning the nomination of the judges and their rotation, the provisions as to which were the ground of objection of Brazil. No part was taken in the vote by Russia, Turkey, Japan, Siam, Venezuela or San Domingo, but the three Russian delegates commissioned by Montenegro to exercise her vote gave it in favour of the draft. On the motion of Sir Edward Fry it was agreed that the draft should not be included in the general final act of the Conference, but should be the subject of a separate convention to be entered into by those powers which may determine to carry it into effect. The amount of approval to which the voting testified leaves little doubt but that such a convention will be concluded. The provisions which it will contain as to the nomination and rotation of judges may need adaptation to the list of powers which join, and even in other respect the signatories will not be bound by the vote of the Conference. But it is not likely that reconsideration will lead them to depart widely from provisions which, after much initial disagreement, were so successfully brought to the point of what may fairly be called general assent. A review of the principal of those provisions is therefore necessary.

We have seen that under the earliest custom which can be regarded as law even for a limited area of sea, the admiral determined what was to be done in relation to prizes taken by any ship under his command, and that this soon came to be the rule even when the authority which he represented was not that of a city but that of a monarchy, and the prizes of which he was the judge may be said to have been taken under his auspices but scarcely under his command[1]. From the point of view of

[1] See above, pp. 121–123.

his fellow-citizens or of his sovereign, to see that ships or goods were not wrongfully captured, and that the value of lawful captures came to the hands entitled to receive it as a regalian right or as prizemoney, belonged to the duty of the admiral as responsible for the discipline of the fleet or navy. From the point of view of foreigners, whether belligerents or neutrals, it was inevitable that they should have to deal in the first instance with some officer of the captors, who might as well be the admiral as any other judge. If they were dissatisfied with his decision, he wielded no authority which bound them, and their city or their prince might take up their cause. On this footing the matter has rested ever since. Questions of prize have always been matters of the domestic jurisdiction of the captor's country, commonly called the admiralty jurisdiction from its original form, by whatever name the branch exercising it may be known in any modern system of procedure. It is open to all those of any nationality whose interests may be affected by its decisions, and it is the duty of its judges, a duty in which they have seldom failed in any civilised country, to do justice to them all with strict impartiality[1]. In that sense a court of admiralty is an international one, but in that sense only, for the law which it administers cannot help bearing the impress of its own nationality.

A court must take its law from the authority under which it sits, and for a court of admiralty that authority has never been any other than that of its own country. It must apply any rules on international questions which it finds to be generally agreed on, a condition which involves the agreement of its own country with them. Where there is no general agreement and the supreme authority of its own country has not taken a decided line, the court must take that line which justice appears to it to require, whether favourable or not to a fellow subject being a party before it, or to what it may conceive to be the interest of its country. But where the supreme authority under which it sits has taken a decided line, a court of admiralty, like any other court, can only obey. Thus we have seen the English parliament and privy council determining

[1] See Chief Justice Marshall's appreciation of Lord Stowell, quoted above, p. 142, n. 1.

from time to time whether neutral goods in enemy ships should be deemed lawful prize, and the English admiralty deciding one way in 1357 and the other way two centuries and a half afterwards[1]. When the famous Orders in Council laid down rules as to neutral shipping for the then naval war which were certainly not justifiable otherwise than by way of retorsion against the Berlin and Milan decrees, the British admiralty did not and could not presume either to refuse execution to the orders, or to exercise an independent judgment as to their justification. And courts of admiralty have always held themselves bound to give effect to the treaties of their countries on points of international law, such treaties being another mode in which the will on those points of the authority under which they sit expresses itself.

This being so, it has followed that the decisions of courts of admiralty on prize law have never been considered to be binding on foreigners.

They are final as judgments, when carried up to the highest domestic court of appeal, because there has hitherto been no other court to which a further appeal could be made, and the individual losing party is therefore left helpless by them. But they have not been considered final settlements as against the government of the losing individuals, if it sees fit to espouse their cause, and on many occasions that government and the government of the prize court have entered into conventions under which the judgments complained of have been reviewed by mixed commissions, and damages have been paid by the state of which the prize court has thus been found to have pronounced erroneous judgments. A remarkable case is that of the treaty between Great Britain and the United States under which judgments of the Supreme Court of the latter, in prize cases arising during the War of Secession, were reviewed by a mixed commission on the complaint of subjects of the former. But the tardy justice done by mixed commissions, instituted after the close of a war with much diplomatic toil and as the result of much international friction, and then only when the grievances complained of by individuals amount to a sum sufficient to induce their government to seek an extraordinary

[1] See above, pp. 123–127.

remedy, has rather made apparent than effectually supplemented the inadequacy of the jurisdiction in prize cases. It is anomalous that the lawfulness of a capture should, so far as jurisdiction is concerned, be finally determined by the captor's state. And while neutral powers, for their own ease, leave to belligerents the repression of their subjects' enterprises in the matters of contraband and blockade, it is absurd that the one-sided character of the only jurisdiction existing should burden them, after all, with the diplomatic protection of their subjects against abuses of the power so left to belligerents.

Hence it has long been a desideratum that there should be established for prize cases a jurisdiction based on international authority, binding on all the parties to any suit, of which therefore the last word should be final even as against intervention by governments. Mixed commissions, resting in each case on the submission of the states who are parties to them, are arbitrations. What is wanted is not an arbitration, but something to which any party can address himself without being obliged to produce a submission from his antagonist, that is a jurisdiction. The question has been mooted both by individual thinkers and by private bodies like the Institute of International Law, and in 1907 received its first official recognition through the action of Great Britain and Germany, which submitted independent schemes to the Conference. To what extent these were respectively incorporated in the result arrived at will appear from the following review of the draft convention.

Art. 1. The validity of the capture of a merchant ship or of her cargo, whether neutral or enemy property is in question, is established before a prize jurisdiction conformably to the present convention.

The British plan restricted the International Court to matters affecting neutrals. The German plan comprised those affecting belligerents.

Art. 2. The prize jurisdiction is exercised initially by the prize courts of first instance (*tribunaux de prise*) of the capturing belligerent. The decisions of those courts are either given at a public sitting or officially notified to the neutral or enemy parties.

Art. 3. The decisions of the national prize courts of first instance may be the subject of appeal to the International Prize Court:

(1) When they concern the property of a neutral power or person;

(2) When they concern enemy property, and the case is one

(*a*) of goods loaded on board a neutral ship, or

(*b*) of an enemy ship captured in the territorial waters of a neutral power which has not made such capture the subject of a diplomatic demand, or

(*c*) of a demand founded on the allegation that the capture was made in breach of a convention in force between the belligerent powers, or of a law of the capturing belligerent.

The appeal from the national prize court of first instance may be on a question either of law or of fact.

These articles are in accordance with the German plan. The British plan allowed an appeal to the International Court only from the highest national court accessible to the neutral power or its subjects, and gave the right of appeal only to the neutral power and not to a private individual. The first of these restrictions would have protracted litigations through an unnecessary number of instances, and the second would have imposed on the neutral government the burden of deciding whether it should adopt the complaint of its subject, while, if its decision on that point was adverse, complete satisfaction would not be given. The German delegation in particular objected to a government's being enabled to withhold its cooperation for political motives.

Art. 4 distributes the right of appeal according to the interests affected, except that a neutral power may forbid its subject to appeal or may itself appeal in his place—which does not quite meet the German view mentioned—and that the appeal in the case of Art. 3, (2), (*b*) is given only to the neutral state.

Art. 5 is technical. Art. 6 provides that where the International Court is competent there can be only one national instance after the first, and that the International Court may be approached directly where a national decision has not been given within two years from the date of the capture.

Art. 7. If the question of law to be decided is provided for by a convention in force between the capturing belligerent and the power which or a subject of which is a party to the suit, the court follows the stipulations of that convention. In default of such stipulations the court applies the rules of international law. If there are no rules generally recognised, the court decides according to the general principles of justice and equity.

The above dispositions apply to what concerns the order of proofs as well as to the legal grounds (*les moyens qui peuvent être employés*).

If under Art. 3, (2), (*c*) the appeal is founded on the breach of a law of the capturing belligerent, the court applies that law. The court is at liberty to take no account of a party's being put out of court by the rules of procedure of the capturing belligerent, if it considers that such an effect is contrary to justice and equity.

The terms in which Art. 7 thus describes the law to be applied on the appeal require a careful examination. It is beyond question that relevant conventions must hold the first rank, and rules of international law which are generally recognised the second. But it is less clear in what sense all that is not concluded by one of those tests is referred to justice and equity. The school of "the Law of Nature and Nations," which succeeded to the school of Grotius and did not share that great man's reverence for facts, was ready to impose solutions of all international questions as the result of pure reason, and would have made short work of any dissents from its conclusions, even if supported by a considerable body of practice. It is true that this school is now much discredited, and in England especially, when reasoning has to be resorted to on the affairs of nations, the appeal is made to justice and the law of nature is rarely mentioned. Elsewhere however "the law of nature" or "the primary law" are still mentioned often enough to prevent one's feeling quite sure whether the notions once connected with them may not survive to such an extent as to influence the judgment about what justice and equity demand.

The subject is one which so imperatively demands frankness that we will illustrate it by examples, and they shall not be taken from topics covered by the Declaration of Paris, the rules of which may well be treated as now generally recognised. Is the notice of blockade, to which a ship desiring to enter a blockaded port is entitled, to be measured by the British or French rules? Is conditional contraband to be allowed? If not, can coal and provisions ever be absolute contraband? Does the declaration of the commander of a neutral convoy exclude the right of search? These and many others are questions on which it cannot be said that any rules are generally recognised. By leaving them to justice and equity, is it meant that they are left quite open for the International Prize Court to deal with as if they had never been raised before they came before it, as writers belonging to the school of the Law of Nature and Nations would have done? Or is it meant that a wholly different class of considerations may be taken into account? The appeal will lie from a national court bound by its sovereign's view of the law, and it is not just or equitable for a court of appeal to reverse a judgment which the court below was right in giving. The convention, if entered into, will not have been intended to transfer the jurisdiction from the national courts to the International Prize Court, but to afford a remedy for abuses in its exercise. Only in the case contemplated by Art. 6, where there will have been laches on the part of the proper jurisdiction, can the International Prize Court act as one of first instance. In every other case it will be dealing with a national pronouncement which justice and equity will forbid its reversing when it was founded on a view of international rights seriously entertained by the state in question, and not ousted by stipulation or general recognition to the contrary.

M. Renault, in the report which he presented on behalf of the sub-committee which prepared the draft (*comité d'examen de la seconde sous-commission*), fully admitted the strength of the latter view. "What," he said, "will happen if positive law, written or customary, is silent? The solution dictated by the strict principles of juridical reasoning does not appear doubtful. In default of an international rule firmly established, the international jurisdiction will apply the law of the captor. No doubt it is easy to object that we shall so have a very variable law, often very arbitrary and even such as to shock us, certain belligerents using to an excess the latitude left by positive law. That would be a reason for hastening the codification of the latter, in order to efface the gaps and uncertainties which are complained of, and which cause the difficult situation that has been pointed out." But he went on to say: "Nevertheless, after mature reflection, we think it our duty to propose to you a solution, bold without doubt, but of such a nature as seriously to ameliorate the practice of international law." Then he stated the formula adopted in Art. 7, and proceeded: "The court is thus called on to make the law (*faire le droit*), and to take account of principles other than those to which the national prize jurisdiction, of which the decision is attacked before the International Court, was subject. We are confident that the magistrates chosen by the powers will rise to the height of their mission, and will exercise it with moderation and firmness. They will point practice in the direction of justice without upsetting it. Let us then admit that a court composed of eminent magistrates shall be charged with supplying the insufficiencies of positive law, until the codification of international law, regularly pursued by governments, comes to simplify its task[1]."

It is therefore certain that the learned reporter intended, in default of stipulation and general agreement, to invest the International Prize Court with the mission claimed by a Pufendorff, only trusting to its moderation in exercising it. There are no doubt minor points on which the court might usefully build up a practice, or decide in particular cases where it would be difficult to embody a practice in terms of any generality. For instance, after what happened during the South African War a claim to search for contraband at any distance from the ship's destination cannot be said to be generally recognised[2], and the court might be trusted to decide whether any particular search was too remote, while if a rule of any generality resulted from such decisions it might be thankfully accepted. But in the light of M. Renault's report it is certain that the adopted draft of 1907 would be interpreted to put in the power of the court those major points of which we have given examples, and on which the inveteracy of the differences is proved by the failure of the same conference to settle them. We cannot therefore advise the conclusion of a convention in the terms of that draft unless the law of the captor be put in the last place in Art. 7, or at least unless Art. 7 be fenced by a proviso that the judgment of a court of any state shall not be reversed because it gives effect to a view of international law seriously maintained by that state. Under

[1] *Courrier de la Conférence*, no. 75, 10 September 1907.

[2] See above, p. 252.

such conditions an International Prize Court would still have great functions to perform, and would in our judgment be a valuable improvement on the present system.

The German draft did not declare what law was to be applied by the court of appeal which it proposed to institute, and the British draft (Art. 6) is not to be commended for lucidity on the point. Naturally, it placed relevant conventions first. Next, where the draft adopted by the Conference speaks of general recognition, there followed "the agreement of *all* civilised nations on a juridical point"; on which it may be asked, as the Conference seems to have asked, what if a single unimportant state should be the only one to dissent or hesitate? "Failing these conditions," the British draft continued, "the court shall decide by applying the principles of international law"—a direction which probably would have needed to be made more definite even if it had not been darkened by the previous reference to universal agreement.

Art. 8. If the court pronounces for the validity of the capture of the ship or cargo, it shall be disposed of according to the law of the capturing belligerent.

If the capture is declared null, the court orders the restitution of the ship or the cargo, and if there is occasion fixes the amount of the damages. If the ship or the cargo has been sold or destroyed, the court determines the indemnity to be allowed to the owner on that account.

If the capture had been declared null by the national jurisdiction, the court is only called on to fix the damages.

All that remains needing mention is the composition of the court. The British draft (Art. 4) had proposed a permanent court, of which each signatory power having more than 800,000 tons of merchant shipping should name a judge and a substitute (*juge suppléant*), each of whom was to be a jurisconsult of recognised competence in questions of maritime international law, and of the highest character (*jouissant de la plus haute considération morale*). All the judges so named except those named by the litigant powers were to sit in any case, their substitutes replacing them in their absence (Art. 12). The German draft proposed a court constituted for each war, and composed of two admirals named by the respective belligerents—two judges, named by neutral powers chosen by the respective belligerents, from among their respective members of the Hague Permanent Court of Arbitration—and a fifth judge, named from among its members of the same court by a third neutral power, chosen by the first two or in case of need by lot. The plan adopted by the Conference drew from the British draft the permanence of the court and the principle of not giving equal weight in it to all the powers, though not adopting mercantile tonnage as the test. From the German draft it drew the admission of belligerent judges. Its chief provisions were the following.

Art. 14. The acting court consists of 15 judges, of whom 9 are a quorum.

A judge who is absent or prevented sitting is replaced by his substitute.

Art. 15. The judges named by the following signatory powers—Germany, the United States of America, Austria-Hungary, France, Great Britain, Italy, Japan and Russia[1]—are always called on to sit.

The judges and substitute judges named by the other powers sit in turn according to the plan annexed to the present convention: their functions may be exercised successively by the same person. The same judge may be named by several of the said powers.

Art. 16. If a belligerent power has not in its regular turn a judge sitting in the court, it may claim that the judge named by it shall take part in judging all affairs arising out of the war. In that case it is determined by lot which of the judges sitting in regular turn must abstain. Such exclusion cannot be applied to the judge named by the other belligerent.

[1] This is the alphabetical order of their French names.

Contraband of War.

The fourth committee of the Hague Conference of 1907 was unable to frame any scheme relating to contraband of war which should unite sufficient suffrages to justify its being brought before a full sitting of the Conference. Our task therefore is only to register the most important views which received expression in the committee. First of these, as most radical, must be placed the following British declaration made at the opening of the Conference.

In order to diminish the difficulties encountered by neutral commerce in time of war, the government of H.B.M. is prepared to abandon the principle of contraband in case of war between the powers which may sign a convention to that effect. The right of visit would be exercised only in order to ascertain the neutral character of the merchantman.

In support of this declaration it was argued that profound doctrinal and practical differences exist as to contraband, especially as to the treatment of things which are not absolute contraband in the strictest sense, and that a codification of the law is hopeless—that the progress of science has increased the number of things which in certain circumstances are of use in war though not absolute contraband in the strictest sense—that the complaints of neutrals on account of interference with the trade in things of that class have consequently increased—that the complexity of the cargoes carried by modern merchantmen of large size makes the search in them for contraband goods difficult and vexatious—that further difficulties would arise if a ship accused of carrying contraband was allowed to proceed on her voyage, the alleged contraband being transhipped or destroyed—that the destination of contraband to the enemy is often difficult of proof, and that under the doctrine of continuous voyage a belligerent might almost entirely interrupt neutral commerce—that for all these reasons the principle of contraband is the source of great damage to trade in non-contraband goods, and that neutrals demand indemnities so large that prize courts refuse them—that during the Russo-Japanese war only the tact of the parties concerned prevented serious international results arising from the principle of contraband—that belligerents derive no compensating benefit from that principle—and that to abandon it would be a work of peace and justice[1].

We fully concur in these reasons, and may add to them that the practical difficulty which during the South African war was found in enforcing the right of search at a distance from the suspected ship's destination has much diminished the value of the principle of contraband to belligerents[2]. The extent to which these arguments prevailed is shown by the vote taken in committee on a resolution to the effect of the British declaration, which was affirmed by the delegations of the following 26 states: Argentina, Austria-Hungary, Belgium, Brazil, Bulgaria, Chile, China, Cuba, Denmark, Great Britain, Greece, Italy, Mexico, Netherlands, Norway, Paraguay, Peru, Persia, Portugal, Salvador, San Domingo, Servia, Siam, Spain, Sweden and Switzerland. Negative votes were given by the delegations of four great powers and one small state: France, Germany, Montenegro, Russia and the United States of America. And the delegations of four states abstained from voting: Japan, Panama, Rumania and Turkey.

The decision of the fourth committee not to pursue the matter further at the then Conference having been taken on 24 September, Sir Edward Fry on that day issued to the delegations which had supported the British proposal an invitation to a meeting on the 25th, accompanied by a draft to which he proposed that they should all adhere, declaring that in case of war between any two or more of the contracting powers, no non-contracting power being a party,

1. Goods belonging to a subject of a neutral contracting power on board neutral or enemy ships cannot be condemned as being contraband;
2. The flag of a neutral contracting power covers all the goods on board.

The meeting was held, all the delegations which had voted affirmatively except those of Belgium, Denmark, Mexico, Paraguay and Peru being represented, besides that of Venezuela, which seems to have been absent at the voting. But of the 21

[1] The fact was also cited that the abolition of contraband was proposed by Mr Secretary Marcy of the United States, in a note of 28 July 1856 to the minister of Russia at Washington.

[2] See above, p. 252.

delegations thus assembled besides the British, only that of Haiti supported the latter in being ready to sign. All the others supported or acquiesced in the view which M. de Kapos Mere (Austria-Hungary) and Count Tornielli (Italy) took the lead in expressing. Their votes had been given as a part of the proceedings of the Conference, of which the principle was that unanimity or an approach to it was necessary for a result[1]. To sign at the Conference a convention outside it would damage the Conference, and might prevent the powers from agreeing to another. Thus the partial realisation of the abolition of contraband, by agreement between the powers desiring it, was postponed to what we hope may be an early date, at which it may be attained by the ordinary methods of diplomacy.

But it is worth while to consider the reasons for declining to attain it at the Hague, during the Conference and through representatives at least primarily accredited to that body, although certainly not incapable of receiving instructions outside its scope. A practical remark is that a government may measure differently the concessions which it will make in order to bring about a vote of a conference on a question of general law, carrying vast weight even if not quite unanimous, and those for which it will consider itself to be repaid by an avowedly partial result. When the former fails, it may reasonably desire time for appreciating the amount and importance of the divergence disclosed, before accepting the latter result on the footing of the same concessions; and such appreciation cannot well be made during the sitting of a body which the government concerned is intent on watching, and of which the final attitude cannot be known till its close. Beyond this however, or rather implied in it, is the growing feeling that there is a real difference between conferences on international law and other diplomatic functions. In the twelfth and thirteenth centuries, in all Western countries, parliaments, great councils, or similar bodies under different names, with the king at their head, exercised legislative, judicial and administrative powers, the separation of which and their attribution to distinct organs was one of the earliest improve-

[1] *Qu'on ne saurait agir qu'à l'unanimité ou à la presqu' unanimité*: M. de Kapos Mere. *Courrier de la Conférence*, no. 89, 26 September, 1907.

ments in the art of government. The conferences on international law, far short as they fall of a true international legislature, are beginning to be felt as a step in that direction, and that their distinctness from all other international organs should be felt to be a condition of their usefulness is in accordance with the domestic experience of states.

The proposal next most radical after the British in the relief offered to neutral commerce was that of the United States, on behalf of which, contrary to the line they had taken at the commencement of the Conference, Admiral Sperry read in July a formal declaration that they were in favour of the complete abolition of conditional contraband. After this comes the Brazilian proposal, which qualified the abolition of conditional contraband by a permission to belligerents to sequestrate or preempt[1] certain named articles—victuals, coal, raw cotton and men's clothing—when destined either for an enemy port or for a neutral one clearly proved to be a stage (*étape*) towards an enemy destination. The German proposal maintained conditional contraband when diplomatically declared in advance by the belligerent government, as might have been expected from the line which we have mentioned as that of the late Dr Perels[2], but gave to the doctrine of continuous voyage only the limited support which it might derive from the admission of a peremptory presumption against the goods when addressed to the authorities of the enemy power or to a contractor with it (*fournisseur militaire*), or when destined for a fortified place of the enemy's country or some other place serving as a base (*point d'appui*) for his forces. The least favourable proposal to neutral commerce was that of France, which limited absolute contraband rather strictly, but while nominally proclaiming the freedom of neutral commerce in all things not absolutely contraband allowed to the belligerents the power of "restraining its freedom" by a diplomatic notification of the things which they intend to intercept, these to be confiscated if their hostile purpose (*but nettement hostile*) is proved, otherwise to be preempted. It may be said of this, as of the very similar

[1] We apologise for this word, which it is difficult to avoid without circumlocution.

[2] See above, p. 249.

proposal of the Institute of International Law[1], that the excessive interference with neutral commerce which it would authorise would not be compensated by an indemnity to be obtained only after delay and often also after litigation. From M. Renault's speech it appears that France maintains the doctrine of continuous voyage.

[1] See above, p. 249.

Blockade.

Blockade is another subject on which the Hague Conference of 1907 came to no conclusion, though it was mentioned at it. The Italian delegation proposed rules expressing the view held by the Armed Neutralities and usually by the continental powers of Europe, namely that a blockade must be maintained by stationary ships, but adding that "the blockade is not considered as raised if bad weather has compelled the blockading ships to leave their station for a short time[1]." The Brazilian delegation proposed the further rule that a blockade must be "limited to the ports, roads, anchorages, bays and other landingplaces on the coast of the enemy, as well as the parts giving access to them"; and that "the Conference should fix a number of miles, to be reckoned from the coast at low water or from an imaginary line joining the extremities of ports or bays, as the boundary within which the action of blockading shall be performed." These rules were explained by M. Ruy Barbosa as intended "to make blockade a simple operation of war, without any character vexatious for neutrals." We may however remark that, if it is desired to prevent commercial blockades, such a result can only be attained by limiting blockade to cases of real siege or attack. If the institution is to be used as a means of preventing the introduction of contraband into a country, which might perhaps be covered by the expression "a simple operation of war," it must interfere with other commerce as well[2].

Sir Ernest Satow, who had taken part in a discussion on these proposals in the fourth committee, shortly afterwards announced that he had been instructed by the British government to declare that there was so great a divergence of opinions that any discussion of it would be without result. The question of blockade was then allowed to drop.

[1] See above, pp. 229, 236.

[2] As to commercial blockades, see above, pp. 226–228.

Conversion of Merchantmen into Ships of War.

A regulation on the conversion of merchantmen into ships of war was adopted at the full sitting on 27 September of the Hague Conference of 1907, by 32 affirmative votes against no negatives ones, the delegations of Nicaragua and Paraguay being absent, that of Turkey expressing a reserve due to its not having received instructions, and those of China, Colombia, Ecuador, Guatemala, Persia, Salvador, San Domingo, the United States of America and Uruguay not voting.

Considering that many of the high contracting parties will desire in time of war to incorporate merchant ships in their fighting fleets;

That consequently it is desirable to define the conditions under which that can be done, so far as rules relating thereto are generally accepted;

That, the high contracting parties not having been able to agree whether the conversion of a merchantman into a ship of war may take place in the open sea, it is understood that the question of the place of conversion is untouched and is in no way affected by the enunciation of the following rules.

We pause at the close of the preamble. The general question is intimately connected with that of the conditions under which a ship originally private may be employed in war without violating the first article of the Declaration of Paris[1], and it was therefore very apposite that, at the sitting of the Conference at which the regulation we are dealing with was voted, the delegations of Spain and Mexico declared the adhesion of their governments to that Declaration in all its articles. Further, the question of place mentioned in the preamble has a peculiar significance in connection with the conventions which prohibit the passage of the Dardanelles and Bosphorus by ships of war while the Porte is at peace. During her war with Japan Russia caused the *Petersburg* and the *Smolensk*, vessels belonging to what is called her volunteer fleet, to pass the straits under her mercantile flag, which in the Mediterranean they discarded for the war flag. This was justly objected to as an unpermissible evasion of the conventions, but was more summarily condemnable if it can be maintained that the conversion of a merchantship into a ship of war cannot take place

[1] See the paragraph on *Privateers*; above, pp. 154, 155.

in the open sea. At the Conference Great Britain proposed the division of ships of war (*vaisseaux de guerre*) into the classes of fighting and auxiliary ships (*vaisseaux de combat* and *bâtiments auxiliaires*), defining the former as follows:

> The term "fighting ship" comprises every ship flying a recognised flag, armed at the expense of the state for attacking the enemy, and of which the officers and crew have been duly authorised for such attack by the government of the state to which they belong. It shall be prohibited for any ship to assume the foresaid character after her departure from a port of her state, or to lay it down except after reentering a port of her state.

The Italian and Dutch proposals were to the same effect as the British with regard to the place of conversion, but Japan proposed that a merchantman may be converted into a ship of war either in the ports or territorial waters of her state, or in those occupied by the military or naval forces of her state.

In the discussion which followed the German and Russian delegations maintained that conversion ought to be allowed in the open sea, as being a place subject to no jurisdiction foreign to that of the converting state, and that since it is permitted to turn captured ships into ships of war in the open sea, the same ought to be allowed for one's own merchantmen. In answer it was pointed out that neutrals would be exposed to the consequences of the change of a ship's character made in the open sea without their knowledge, and that a merchantman which had benefited by the hospitality of a neutral port ought not afterwards to abuse it by a conversion. The preamble having then been drawn up with the recital that there was no agreement as to conversion in the open sea, it was moved by the German delegate, M. Kriege, to cancel the last words on the ground that the disagreement extended to conversion in a neutral port. But Lord Reay successfully pointed out that there could be no disagreement as to conversion in a neutral port being an illegal augmentation of force there, or as to its facilitating fraudulent evasions of the limit of stay allowed to ships of war in a neutral port.

The operative part of the regulation adopted by the Conference does not call for remark.

Art. 1. No merchantman converted into a ship of war can have the rights and obligations attached to that character unless it is placed under the direct authority, immediate control, and responsibility of the state whose flag it carries.

Art. 2. Merchantmen converted into ships of war must bear the external signs distinctive of the ships of war of their nationality.

Art. 3. The commander must be in the service of the state and duly commissioned by the competent authorities. His name must appear in the official list of officers of the military fleet.

Art. 4. The crew is subject to the rules of military discipline.

Art. 5. Every merchantman converted into a ship of war must conform in its operations to the laws and customs of war.

Art. 6. The belligerent who converts a merchantman into a ship of war must mention the conversion as soon as possible in its navy list.

Enemy Merchantmen at the Commencement of Hostilities.

The practice as to enemy ships and cargoes in belligerent harbours at the outbreak of war has been stated above, p. 39. It is now placed on a surer footing by the following regulation, adopted at the full sitting on 27 September 1907.

Art. 1. When a merchantman of one of the belligerent powers is found at the opening of hostilities in an enemy port, it is desirable that it should be allowed to leave freely, either immediately or after a sufficient term of grace, and to proceed straight, after being furnished with a passport, to its port of destination or to such other port as may be named for it.

The same applies to a ship which left its last port of sailing before the commencement of the war, and enters an enemy port in ignorance of the hostilities.

Art. 2. The merchantman which owing to *force majeure* has not been able to leave the enemy port during the term of grace contemplated by the preceding Article, or which has not been allowed to leave, cannot be confiscated. It is only subject to be seized under an obligation to restore it after the war without indemnity, or to be requisitioned with indemnity.

Art. 3. Merchantmen which have left their last port of sailing before the commencement of the war, and which are met at sea while ignorant of the hostilities, cannot be confiscated. They are only subject to be seized under an obligation to restore them after the war without indemnity, or to be requisitioned or even destroyed with indemnity and under an obligation to provide for the security of the persons and the preservation of the papers on board.

After such ships have touched at a port of their country or at a neutral port, they are subject to the laws and customs of naval war.

Art. 4. Enemy goods found on board the ships contemplated in Articles 1 and 2 are also subject to be seized and restored after the war without indemnity, or to be requisitioned with indemnity either together with the ship or separately.

The same applies to goods found on board the ships contemplated in Art. 3.

Art. 5. This regulation does not concern merchant ships of which the construction indicates that they are intended to be converted into ships of war.

Postal Correspondence at Sea.

The practice as to neutral mail bags which was adopted in the American civil war has been sanctioned, and extended to belligerent mail bags, by the following regulation, passed at the same full sitting of 27 September 1907[1].

Art. 1. The postal correspondence whether of neutrals or of belligerents, and whether its character is official or private, found at sea in a neutral ship, is inviolable. If the ship is seized, it must be forwarded by the captor with the least possible delay, except in the case of a breach of blockade and the correspondence coming from or being destined to the blockaded port.

The dispositions of the preceding paragraph apply equally to postal correspondence found at sea on board an enemy ship.

Art. 2. The inviolability of postal correspondence does not exempt neutral mail boats from the laws and customs of war concerning merchantmen in general. Nevertheless, they ought to be searched only in case of necessity, and then with all the consideration and speed possible.

It must be mentioned to the credit of Germany that this beneficent regulation was proposed by her.

[1] See above, p. 265.

The Crews of Enemy Merchantmen Captured by a Belligerent.

The following regulation was also adopted at the full sitting of 27 September 1907.

Art. 1. When an enemy merchantman is captured by a belligerent, the men of its crew, being subjects or citizens of a neutral power, are not made prisoners of war.

The same holds for the captain and officers, equally subjects or citizens of a neutral power, if they promise formally in writing not to serve on an enemy ship during the war.

Art. 2. The captain, officers and members of the crew, being enemy subjects or citizens, are not made prisoners of war on condition of their engaging, under the faith of a formal written promise, not to take during the hostilities any service having relation to the operations of the war.

Art. 3. The names of the individuals left free in the conditions contemplated by Art. 1, second paragraph, and Art. 2 are notified by the belligerent captor to the other belligerent. The latter is forbidden knowingly to employ the said individuals.

Art. 4. The preceding dispositions do not apply to ships which take part in hostilities.

This regulation practically admits that, independently of it, the persons serving on board captured enemy merchantmen may be detained as prisoners[1].

[1] See above, p. 130.

Coast Fisheries and other Immunities.

Another regulation adopted at the full sitting of 27 September 1907 is the following.

Art. 1. Boats employed exclusively in coast fisheries or in local coast navigation are exempt from capture, as well as their tackle, rigging, gear and cargoes.

This exemption ceases as soon as they participate in any manner in hostilities.

The contracting powers oblige themselves not to profit by the inoffensive character of such boats, by employing them with a warlike purpose while preserving their peaceful appearance.

Art. 2. Ships charged with scientific, religious or philanthropic missions are equally exempt from capture.

This regulation, allowing for its brevity, agrees with what we have said about coast fisheries and about science and the like[1]. We assume, when it is said that the exemption of coast fishing boats ceases as soon as they participate in hostilities, that this does not mean that no particular boat can lose the immunity without having itself so participated, but allows the immunity to be withdrawn from the class on any part of the enemy's coast, when he there employs them or the fishermen with a warlike purpose.

[1] Coast fisheries, above, p. 133. Science &c., above, p. 138.

Enemy Private Property at Sea.

The Conference of 1907 was of course a field of battle for those who attack the existing system with regard to private enemy property at sea, either radically or only desiring some modification of it. Our own views on the subject have been given above, pp. 129–132. We will notice the proposals made at the Conference in the order in which they were radical.

First in that order, as most radical, stands the proposal made by Mr Choate in the name of the United States, that all private property shall be exempt from capture at sea except under the laws of contraband and blockade, an exception which may here be stated once for all as made, expressly or tacitly, in all the proposals for immunity brought forward at the Conference. This proposal received during the discussion the assent in general terms of the German and Swedish delegates, the former however, the baron Marschall von Bieberstein, declaring that in the opinion of his government the laws of contraband and blockade ought to be first settled, and the latter, M. Hammarskjöld, admitting that there would be difficulties in the application of the principle. The Danish delegation declared that their government was ready to recognise the principle of the inviolability of private property at sea if it should obtain the approbation of the Conference, but that if the time had not arrived for realising that humane idea by common accord, they would assist in the adoption of measures tending to limit the inconvenience of the existing practice. On the other hand the delegates of Colombia and Argentina maintained the capture of enemy property, as such, as necessary for the defence of powers weaker at sea[1].

Next in order come the proposals for a modification of the right of capture made in the names of Belgium and Brazil. The first clause of the Belgian proposal laid down that enemy

[1] A passage in the speech of the Colombian delegate M. Triana is worth quoting for the reply which it makes to the misuse of historical argument. "M. Choate," he is reported to have said, "*nous a dit que le droit actuel est un héritage de l'ancienne piraterie. C'est vrai, comme il est vrai que la guerre n'est que le meurtre organisé. Nous ne gardons ces droits que pour le moment où la normalité aura cessé.*"

merchantmen and enemy goods under the enemy flag can be captured and retained by a belligerent only subject to their restitution at the end of the war. Other clauses gave him the right to use the ships and cargoes for military purposes, to sell the ships when their repair or their keep would be out of proportion to their value, and to sell the cargoes if perishable; also he might destroy the ships if the circumstances or the approach of an enemy force prevented his carrying them *intra præsidia*. At the end of hostilities the property remaining in kind, the value of that destroyed, and the sale monies were to be restored to the owners by the captor's state, without any indemnity for deprivation of enjoyment, or for deterioration not caused by grave fault; but that state might shift the burden to the enemy state by the treaty of peace. The crews of the captured ships were to be disembarked as soon as circumstances permitted, and set free on their engagement not to serve against the captor's state during the war, which engagement was to be respected by their own government. The Brazilian proposal empowered a captor to destroy or take an enemy merchantman or all or any part of her cargo, even neutral cargo if the ship is taken, "when commanded to do so by the most imperious exigencies of war," on giving to the captain receipts as for requisitions, "with all possible details for ensuring to the interested parties their right to a just indemnity." Since the receipts which the Hague laws of land war, even as amended in 1907, require to be given for requisitions neither express nor involve a liability of any one[1], while it must be very difficult to put any real bounds to a plea of imperious exigency, this proposal, considered with regard to enemy property, was far more favourable to the captor's state than the Belgian one. Considered with regard to neutral cargo, which under it might be requisitioned without destroying the ship, it was contrary to the Declaration of Paris. But in another respect the Brazilian proposal was very favourable to the captured and their state, since it provided for the crew of the ship destroyed or taken being put on shore in a neighbouring port, "with the resources necessary for their return to their country," but did not provide for their not serving against the

[1] See above, pp. 99, 100, 270.

captor's state. There was also a proposal made by the Netherlands delegation, to the effect that the captor should set free those enemy merchantmen which he did not desire to use for military purposes, delivering to them a passport in which it should be declared that the enemy is not to use them for such purposes.

At the opposite extreme to the United States proposal among those submitted was the French one, which was as follows.

Considering that if the positive law of nations still admits the legitimacy of the right of capture applied to private enemy property at sea, it is eminently desirable that, until an understanding as to its suppression can be arrived at between states, its exercise should be subjected to certain regulations (*modalités*):

Considering that it is most important that, conformably to the modern conception of war which ought to be directed against states and not against individuals, the right of prize should appear solely as a means of coercion practised by one state against another:

That in that order of ideas all individual profit to the agents of the state who exercise the right of prize ought to be excluded, and that the losses incurred by individuals through captures ought to fall in the last resort on their state:

The French delegation has the honour to propose to the fourth committee that it should express the desire (*vœu*) that states which shall exercise the right of capture should suppress the shares of prize money assigned to the crews of the capturing ships, and should take the measures necessary in order that the losses caused by the exercise of the right of capture may not fall entirely on the individuals whose property has been captured.

A vote being taken in the fourth committee on the United States proposal, it received the voices of the 21 states which follow in the alphabetical order of their English names: Austria-Hungary, Belgium, Brazil, China, Cuba, Denmark, Ecuador, Germany (with reservations), Greece, Haiti, Italy, Netherlands, Norway, Persia, San Domingo, Siam, Sweden, Switzerland, Turkey, United States, Uruguay. It will be observed that the states which had made intermediate proposals, except France, testified by their votes that they had done so only in the hope of conciliation. The following 11 states voted against the United States proposal: Colombia, France, Great Britain, Japan, Mexico, Montenegro, Panama, Portugal, Russia,

Salvador, Spain. It is superfluous to name the states which took no part in the vote. It was then decided to consider the intermediate or subsidiary proposals, in order that the commission, before reporting, might discover whether a majority more nearly approaching unanimity could be reached. The first vote taken in pursuance of that decision was on a clause of the Brazilian proposal, by which the words "apart from cases governed by maritime law" were to be omitted from Art. LIII of the Hague laws of land war[1], as a step towards bringing naval capture under the principle of requisitions. This clause was rejected by 13 votes against 12, and the Brazilian proposal was thereupon withdrawn. The next vote taken was on the first clause of the Belgian proposal[2], and gave a majority of 14 to 9 in its favour; but the first Belgian delegate, M. Beernaert, thus finding that the opposition of the powers which sided with Great Britain for the maintenance of the present law was not broken, withdrew the whole proposal.

On a later occasion the French proposal was considered by the same committee, and the first part of it was adopted by 16 votes against 4 negative ones and 14 abstentions, after having been modified, in deference to the objection that prize money belonged to national and not to international legislation, by substituting, for the *vœu* originally expressed, an invitation to the powers which should maintain capture to consider the means of abolishing that reward. The second part, pointing to some indemnity to the persons whose property is captured, was defeated. There were 7 votes in its favour, among which was that of Sir Ernest Satow, against 13 negative ones and 14 abstentions.

The proceedings in committee do not seem to have been carried further with express reference to private enemy property at sea, but the Conference, at its full sitting on 27 September, unanimously expressed its desire (*vœu*) that the powers, while awaiting a special regulation, should as far as possible apply to naval war the principles of the convention of 1899 with regard to war on land, and that the drawing up a special regulation should be placed on the programme of the next Conference.

[1] See above, p. 102. [2] See above, p. 311.

Naval Bombardments.

A draft regulation on Bombardments by Naval Forces was adopted in the full sitting of the Hague Conference on 17 August 1907. See above, p. 76, for the corresponding regulation by land, H XXV.

Art. I. The attack or bombardment by naval forces of ports, towns, villages, habitations or buildings which are not defended is prohibited.

A locality cannot be bombarded for the sole fact that automatic submarine contact mines are moored before its port.

Refusals to accept the second paragraph were registered by Great Britain, France, Germany, Japan and Chile. They were right. A place cannot be deemed undefended when means are taken to prevent an enemy from occupying it. The price of immunity from bombardment is that the place shall be left open to the enemy to enter.

Art. II. Nevertheless, this prohibition does not include military works, military or naval establishments, stores of arms or of material of war, workshops and installations suitable to be used for the wants of the enemy fleet or army, or ships of war lying in the port; all which the commander of a naval force may destroy by cannon after a summons fixing a reasonable delay, if all other means are impossible and the local authorities have not proceeded to destroy them within the time fixed. In that case he incurs no responsibility for the involuntary damage which may have been occasioned by the bombardment.

If military necessities demanding immediate action do not permit the delay to be granted, it is understood that the prohibition of bombarding the undefended town remains as in the case of Art. I, and that the commander shall make all the dispositions required for causing the least possible inconvenience to the town.

The word "installations" used in the first paragraph was intended to include such as are not of exclusively warlike use, and in the report of the committee railways and floating docks were given as examples. But the word "provisions," which for example would include coal, was not admitted, since it was thought that the term "material of war" gave sufficient satisfaction to military requirements. As an example of the military necessities mentioned in the last paragraph it was pointed out that a naval commander must be allowed to open fire immediately on ships lying in a road, in order to prevent their joining an enemy fleet close at hand.

Art. III. Undefended ports, towns, villages, habitations and buildings may be bombarded after express notice, if the local authorities refuse to obey a formal summons to furnish requisitions of victuals or other provisions, necessary for the actual wants (*besoin présent*) of the naval force before the locality.

These requisitions shall be in proportion to (*en rapport avec*) the resources of the locality. They shall only be demanded on the authority of the commander of the said naval force, and shall as far as possible be paid for in ready money; if not, the fact of furnishing shall be recorded by receipts.

Art. IV. Bombardment of undefended ports, towns, villages, habitations or buildings, for the non-payment of contributions in money, is prohibited.

It will be seen that all the preceding Articles except the second paragraph of Art. I are in agreement with the doctrine which we have laid down on pages 77, 78, only we did not there consider the case of requisitions in kind, which Art. III allows on conditions similar to those laid down by H LII—above, p. 96—for requisitions on land. Attention may be drawn to one point in which the rule for naval forces is even more strict than that in land war, for while H LII allows requisitions for supplying the necessities of the army of occupation, of which only a small part may be in or near the place subjected to the requisitions, the naval Article allows them only for those of the force before the locality. A contribution in money for military necessities, which H XLIX—see above, p. 95—contemplates on land, is excluded by the naval Articles. And with reason, because the naval force has no other market at hand in which to supply itself with what the locality cannot furnish in kind, and the money, unexpended, would not relieve its necessities.

Art. V adopts H XXVII with the amendment adding historical monuments to the edifices protected—see above, pp. 78, 269—and substitutes the following for its second paragraph:

It is the duty of the inhabitants to point out these monuments, edifices and places where the sick and wounded are collected by visible signs, which shall consist in large rectangular panels, divided by a diagonal into two coloured triangles, black above and white below.

Art. VI. *Except when military exigencies would not permit it, the commander of the attacking naval force must, before commencing the bombardment, do all he can to warn the authorities.*

The difference between this Article and H XXVI—see above, p. 78—is due to the able representation of the possible exigencies of naval war, made by the British delegate Captain Ottley and the Japanese delegation.

Art. VII reproduces H XXVIII—above, p. 79.

Destroying Prizes at Sea.

The capture of enemy's property at sea ousts the enemy owner. The judgment of a prize court may be necessary for securing the discipline of the capturing country's fleet, or formerly of its privateers, and for seeing that neutrals are not unjustly despoiled, but it is not necessary against the enemy, nor does the latter's title await in suspended animation the chance of being restored by recapture. Therefore the enemy has no cause of complaint if his property is destroyed at sea instead of being brought in for adjudication. On similar principles a neutral has no cause of complaint if property of his is destroyed at sea which, if brought in, must have been condemned under the law of blockade or contraband. For him, too, the judgment would only have verified a forfeiture imposed by the facts. But when neutral goods not impeachable under the law of blockade or of contraband are found in an enemy ship, and the belligerent cannot tranship them and forward them to their destination, it might be thought that he must forego a right to destroy his enemy's property which he could not exercise without also destroying the property of an innocent owner, or at least, supposing the destruction to be justified by the plea of strong necessity, that he is bound to indemnify the neutral. And in any case of the destruction of a ship, enemy or neutral, it would be the destroyer's duty to save the men and to preserve all the papers and other evidence which might assist a neutral claimant in proving that innocent property of his had been destroyed.

But this obvious view has not in all points been generally received. During the Franco-German war two German ships, the *Ludwig* and the *Vorwärts*, were burnt by their French captors because the latter had so many prisoners on board that they could not safely spare a prize crew. The neutral cargo-owners, against whom no offence of contraband or blockade-running was alleged, claimed compensation, alleging the immunity of neutral goods under the enemy flag by the Declaration of Paris; and the decision was against them both in the court of first instance and in that of appeal[1]. It was said that the effect of

[1] Prize court at Bordeaux, 27 February 1871; *commission provisoire* in place of *conseil d'état*, 16 March 1872.

the Declaration is only that a neutral is entitled to the restitution of his goods embarked in an enemy ship, or to receive the sum for which they may have been sold, but not that he can demand an indemnity for damage caused either by a legally good capture of the ship or by acts of war which may have accompanied or followed the capture. And the decision is approved by Calvo, and apparently also by Hall, who however regrets that no limits were set in it to the right of destroying neutral property embarked in an enemy's ship[1]. The reasoning amounts to treating a neutral's shipping goods on board an enemy as an identification of himself *pro tanto* with the enemy, the very principle on which the ancient confiscation of such goods was based, and to treating the Declaration of Paris as only partially freeing the neutral from the consequences of the identification. It amounts to a rejection of the point of view from which the Consolat del Mar proceeded, namely that belligerent property and neutral property as such stand at sea on the same mutually independent footing. Such however as it is, the reasoning seems to have taken so great a hold that at the Conference of 1907 nothing was heard about an unoffending neutral's right to an indemnity for the destruction of his goods along with that of an enemy's ship, the effort made being only to prevent or limit the destruction of neutral ships and their cargoes without bringing them in to await adjudication.

The interest felt in that part of the subject was largely due to an incident of the Russo-Japanese war. The *Knight Commander* was on her way from Hoboken in the United States of America to Japan, with a miscellaneous cargo, when she was captured by a Russian cruiser, and sunk because it was extremely difficult to bring her into port and in the undoubting opinion of her captors she was carrying contraband of war. The British part of the crew was taken on to Vladivostok, and the native part was put on board another vessel which happened to be passing. Notwithstanding the absence of the ship her case was brought before the Russian prize jurisdiction, in which the condemnation pronounced at Vladivostok was reversed on appeal, but not on the ground of any illegality in her destruction.

[1] Calvo, 3rd edition, § 2817; Hall, § 269.

Great Britain, which had taken that ground in her correspondence with Russia, submitted at the Hague in 1907 a proposal to declare that "the destruction of a neutral prize by the captor is prohibited. The captor ought to release every neutral ship which he cannot bring before a prize court." The United States submitted a proposal to the same effect. The Russian counter-proposal was as follows:

Believing that the absolute prohibition to destroy neutral prizes would place powers having no maritime bases except on their home coasts[1] in a position of inferiority, and being of opinion that every international agreement ought to be founded on the principle of reciprocity and equal opportunity, the Imperial Russian delegation submits to the consideration of the fourth committee the following disposition which appears to it to take account of all the interests involved;

The destruction of a neutral prize is prohibited except if its preservation might compromise the security of the capturing ship or the success of its operations. The commander of the capturing ship must use the right of destruction with the greatest reserve, and must take care first to tranship the men and so far as possible the cargo, also in every case to preserve all the shipping documents (*papiers de bord*) and other elements necessary for an adjudication on the prize and for fixing the indemnities due to neutrals. It is well understood that, in case of the seizure or destruction of neutral prizes recognised by the prize court or the competent authorities to have been illegal, the interested parties have a right to sue for damages.

It will be observed that the Russian argument assumes that the prohibition to destroy neutral ships cannot be claimed as a neutral right, and is therefore a subject of bargain, in which character it was not unfair to connect it with the relative practical situations which it would create for a certain class of powers. Col. Ovtchinikoff, in the discussion in the fourth committee, observed that the position of inferiority referred to in the proposal would be aggravated if the regulation on the rights and duties of neutrals in maritime war, then before the third committee, should make it more difficult for belligerents and their prizes to avail themselves of neutral ports. In the same discussion Sir Ernest Satow, in support of the British proposal, maintained that the destruction of a neutral prize is always in contradiction with the principles on the subject of

[1] *Côtes de la métropole,* which it is intended to contrast with both colonial and foreign coasts.

neutrality, which we do not think can be consistently asserted by any one who does not hold that the same principles condemn the destruction of an enemy ship with neutral cargo on board. But Sir Ernest appears to us to have stood on surer ground when he denied the existence of any established international practice of destroying neutral prizes, and refused an internationally binding character to the maritime regulations of certain states enumerating the cases for destroying captured ships[1], even could it be assumed that their application to neutral ships results from their not naming enemy ones as their sole purport.

In consequence of what as above mentioned was said by Col. Ovtchinikoff, the drafting sub-committees (*comités d'examen*) of the third and fourth committees held a combined voting, the result of which was thus summed up by the reporter. "Free access to neutral ports for the prizes made by belligerents has a very weak majority[2]; the prohibition to destroy, made by most conditional on that free access, has a majority slightly more marked[3]; lastly, the right to destroy [as proposed by Russia] itself has a weak majority accompanied by many abstentions[4]." The question of destroying prizes was then allowed to drop.

[1] Such as the Japanese instructions of 1904 to naval commanders, which allow the destruction of a prize when owing to her unseaworthy condition or because of dangers at sea she cannot be navigated, when there is reason to fear that she will be retaken by the enemy, and when she cannot be navigated without causing a deficiency in the complement of officers and men requisite for the safety of the capturing ship. To an enumeration substantially the same, the Institute of International Law in 1882 added the case of the port to which it would be possible to take the captured ship being too distant: 6 *Annuaire* 221. But neither of these enumerations is applied expressly to neutral prizes, though in neither are they expressly excepted.

[2] It was 9 against 2, with 6 abstentions.

[3] It was 11 against 4, with 2 abstentions.

[4] It was 6 against 4, with 7 abstentions.

Floating Mines.

There is no certainty that floating mines, even if anchored at first, will not get loose, nor even much probability that a large percentage will not get loose[1]. Thus the employment by a belligerent, even in his own territorial waters or in those of his enemy which merchantmen may be expected to avoid during war, of contact mines which do not become innocuous as soon as they get loose, is a cause, lying well within the limits of human foresight, of slaughter and damage to peaceable neutrals engaged in their lawful occupations in waters where they have a perfect right to be. During all the two years which have elapsed since the close of the Russo-Japanese war, the seas of the Far East have continued to be the scene of disasters which the employment of such mines in that contest has caused to peaceful shipping and fishermen. Now the right of a state in the waters subject to its sovereignty can certainly not rank higher than that of a private owner in the land or water which is his property. Still less, if possible, can the right of a state in the open sea, which is free to the use of all, rank higher than that of property. But no principle is more firmly established in the science of law than that which says to an owner *sic utere tuo ut alienum non laedas.* The right of sovereignty therefore does not extend to employing anywhere what may be foreseen to be engines of slaughter and damage to unoffending foreigners. The foreign government whose subjects suffer from such engines does not need to enquire whether their use is prohibited by any positive rule of international law, whether resting on recognised custom or an agreement. They are indefensible in themselves,

[1] "Anyone who has seen what happens even in peace manœuvres, when mines are laid for a brief period in unenclosed water, will know the impossibility after only moderately bad weather of ensuring that the mines will remain in place. It is quite common to find that some have shifted their position considerably. Mines laid in the outer anchorage of Port Arthur or at Dalny, and in the bays of either side of the Liautung peninsula, whether by the defenders or the assailants, are likely enough to break adrift in such gales as are common in the spring in the locality in question; and some of them would probably drift out into the open sea." Admiral Sir Cyprian Bridge, in the *Times* of 30 May 1904. His prophecy has been amply fulfilled.

and the foreign government concerned will be justified, not only in taking up the cause of its injured subjects. It will not have exceeded its rights if it interferes in order to stop the offending methods of war.

At the Conference of 1907 Great Britain maintained these principles both as to the limit of the right of a belligerent to employ floating mines, and as to the rights of neutrals and their governments when damage is caused by a disregard of that limit. At the opening of the Conference she proposed that the employment of unanchored contact mines, or of any contact mines which do not become innocuous as soon as they get loose, shall be prohibited. And the proposal went on to allow the employment of no contact mines at all except before fortified naval ports, and then only in the territorial waters of a belligerent or his enemy, or at most within a distance of ten miles from the position of the guns on land. Japan and Italy pleaded the usefulness of loose contact mines for ships which are being pursued, and proposed that they should be allowed on condition of their becoming innocuous within a fixed time, which Captain Ottley gave full scope to a spirit of conciliation by accepting on behalf of the British delegation. Brazil and the Netherlands wished that neutrals should be allowed to protect their own waters by contact mines, but Captain Ottley replied that electric mines would suffice for that purpose.

The opposition to the proposal was led by Germany, but received support from Austria-Hungary, Russia and the United States. At one stage of the prolonged proceedings in committee Germany offered to agree to a prohibition of all use of floating mines for five years in place of any permanent rule. Great Britain did not accept the offer, which can scarcely be otherwise interpreted than as indicating an opinion that war within five years was not probable. Ultimately, at the full sitting of 9 October, an emasculated draft convention was adopted subject to various reserves by different powers, to be in force for some years or until the close of the third Peace Conference. By this it was nominally "prohibited (1) to place unanchored contact mines not so constructed as to become innocuous an hour at most after those who have placed them have lost control over them, (2) to place anchored contact mines which do not become innocuous as soon as they have broken their moorings, and (3) to employ torpedoes which do not become innocuous when they have missed their aim": Art. 1. But this was watered down by the provision that "the contracting powers which do not yet possess perfected mines such as are contemplated by the present regulation, and which consequently cannot at present conform to Articles 1 and 3[1], undertake to transform their mines as quickly as possible, so that they may satisfy the said requirements": Art. 6. Sir Ernest Satow then read on behalf of the British delegation a statement which we insert at length, so important is its affirmation that the international law on the subject does not depend for its existence on any stipulations.

Having voted for the Mines Convention which the Conference has just accepted, the British delegation desires to declare that it cannot regard this arrangement as furnishing a final solution of the question, but only as marking a stage in international legislation on the subject. It does not consider that adequate account has been taken in the Convention of the rights of neutrals to protection, or of humanitarian sentiments which cannot be neglected. The British delegation has done its best to bring the Conference to share its views, but its efforts in this direction have remained without result. The high seas, gentlemen, form a great international highway. If in the present state of international laws and customs belligerents are permitted to fight out their quarrels upon the high seas, it is none the less incumbent upon them to do nothing which might, long after their departure from a particular place, render this highway dangerous for neutrals who are equally entitled to use it. We declare without hesitation that the right of the neutral to security of navigation on the high seas ought to come before the transitory right of the belligerent to employ these seas as the scene of the operations of war.

Nevertheless, the Convention as adopted imposes upon the belligerent no restriction as to the placing of anchored mines, which consequently may be laid wherever the belligerent chooses, in his own waters for self-defence, in the waters of the enemy as a means of attack, or finally on the high seas, so that neutral navigation will inevitably run great risks in time of naval war and may be exposed to many a disaster. We have already on several occasions insisted upon the danger of a situation of this kind. We have endeavoured to show what would be the effect produced by the loss of a great liner belonging to a neutral power. We did not fail to bring for-

[1] Art. 3 did not contemplate any case additional to those mentioned in Art. 1, but made belligerents undertake to provide as far as possible for the anchored contact mines employed by them becoming innocuous after a certain lapse of time.

ward every argument in favour of limiting the field of action for these mines, while we called very special attention to the advantages which the civilized world would gain from this restriction, since it would be equivalent to diminishing to a certain extent the causes of warlike conflicts. It appeared to us that by acceptance of the proposal made by us at the beginning of the discussion, dangers would have been obviated which in every maritime war of the future will threaten to disturb friendly relations between neutrals and belligerents. But, since the Conference has not shared our views, it remains for us to declare in the most formal manner that these dangers exist, and that the certainty that they will make themselves felt in the future is due to the incomplete character of the present Convention.

As this Convention, in our opinion, constitutes only a partial and inadequate solution of the problem, it cannot, as has already been pointed out, be regarded as a complete exposition of international law on this subject. Accordingly, it will not be permissible to presume the legitimacy of an action for the mere reason that this Convention has not prohibited it. This is a principle which we desired to affirm, and which it will be impossible for any state to ignore, whatever its power[1].

Baron von Marschall immediately made for the German delegation the following reply, which embodies what we have mentioned and discussed—above, p. 115—as being the affirmative answer usually made in Germany to the question whether the laws of war are liable to be overridden by necessity.

That a belligerent who lays mines assumes a very heavy responsibility towards neutrals and towards peaceful shipping is a point on which we are all agreed. No one will resort to this instrument of warfare unless for military reasons of an absolutely urgent character. But military acts are not solely governed by stipulations of international law. There are other factors. Conscience, good sense, and the sense of duty imposed by principles of humanity will be the surest guides for the conduct of sailors, and will constitute the most effective guarantee against abuses. The officers of the German navy, I loudly proclaim it (*je le dis à haute voix*), will always fulfil in the strictest fashion the duties which emanate from the unwritten law of humanity and civilization. I have no need to tell you that I entirely recognize the importance of the codification of rules to be followed in war. But it would be a great mistake to issue rules the strict observation of which might be rendered impossible by the law of facts. It is of the first importance that the international maritime law which we desire to create should only contain clauses the execution of which is possible from a military point of view—is possible even in exceptional circumstances. Otherwise the respect for law would be lessened and its

[1] *Courrier de la Conférence*, no. 100: translation as in the *Times* of 10 October 1907.

authority undermined. It would also seem to us to be preferable to maintain at present a certain reserve, in the expectation that seven years hence it will be easier to find a solution which will be acceptable to the whole world. As to the humanitarian sentiments of which the British delegate has spoken, I cannot (concluded Baron von Marschall, raising his voice to an appropriate pitch), I cannot admit that there is any country in the world which is superior to my country or my Government in the sentiment of humanity[1].

Thus Germany claims the right to destroy neutral shipping and fishermen, if absolutely necessary in order that she may win in a war: Great Britain declines to be bound by Germany's necessity to win. We must repeat our conclusion that to deny the sufficiency of the British answer cannot be reconciled with there being a law between states as equals.

Another point which arose in connection with floating mines was their employment for the purpose of blockade. An Article of the British proposal specifically prohibited the use of contact mines for establishing or maintaining a commercial blockade, which prohibition would also have resulted from the Article which refused to allow them except before naval ports. Germany, Russia and France opposed, it being urged on the part of Germany that mines might be necessary in order to prevent the enemy's ships of war from entering such of his ports as were not attacked. The draft convention voted by the full Conference prohibited by its Art. 2, subject to reserves by Germany and France, "placing contact mines before the coasts and ports of the enemy with the sole object of intercepting commercial navigation." Such an Article is futile, whether from the point of view of commercial blockades, which it would always be easy to establish by mines while pretending some other object, or from that of the danger which the mines would cause to innocent shipping in other waters. It must be added to the provisions of the draft about mines in general, as justifying Sir Ernest Satow's strong condemnation of its inadequacy as an exposition of the law.

[1] *Times* of 10 October 1907.

Neutrals in Naval War.

At the full sitting of the Conference on 9 October 1907 a draft convention was adopted, previous to the reading of which Sir Edward Fry made the following declaration:

For the reasons given at the sitting of the committee on 4 October, the British delegation reserves to its government the right to form an opinion on the draft convention regarding the rights and duties of neutrals in maritime war. It will abstain from voting on each separate article[1].

A similar general reservation was made by Mr Tsudzuki for Japan, and by the representatives of Spain and Portugal; while the United States, on the ground of requiring time for comparing the draft with their existing treaties, the Greek delegation on the ground of the want of instructions, and Cuba, made up the number of seven total abstentions from the vote, in addition to the reservations made on certain clauses by powers which voted affirmatively on the whole.

The reasons for the stand thus taken by Great Britain and Japan may be summed up in the fact that the draft convention failed to apply the strict principles of neutrality, in obedience to what we have described as "the desire of governments to retain in their hands the power to oblige their friends, and to avoid establishing a rule which may one day tell against themselves[2]." The line which the draft takes in that respect is foreshadowed to any careful reader by the introductory paragraphs of the report of M. Renault, from whom we cannot express dissent without paying a warm tribute to his learning and ability[3]. It was there said that the reception of a belligerent ship in a neutral port presents a different question from that of tolerating belligerent land forces in neutral territory, because ships of war are usually allowed to enter neutral ports in time of peace and are free to choose when they will leave; and it was asked whether a neutral state can suddenly break off that custom, which was described as a duty of hospitality. This argument is parallel to that

[1] *Courrier de la Conférence*, no. 100, 10 October 1907.

[2] Above, p. 210.

[3] The report is given in the *Courrier de la Conférence*, nos. 94, 95, 96; the draft convention in no. 91.

which would claim immunity for the traffic in contraband of war because the traffic in the same things is free in time of peace. It was further said, with reference to the fact that the rules laid down in different countries vary, as also do those laid down in the same country at different times, that "the essential thing is that all should know what to expect, and that there shall be no surprise." This treats as practically unessential the abstention from rendering aid to a belligerent, which the reporter consistently mentions elsewhere merely as a duty to be reconciled with the duty of hospitality. Again it was said that "the starting point of a regulation must be the sovereignty of the neutral state, which cannot be affected by the sole fact of a war to which it intends to remain a stranger." The only possible meaning of sovereignty in such a connection is freedom of choice not seriously restricted by rules, a sense which, if it were admitted, would make all international law an infringement of sovereignty. These principles are familiar to us in international action, and are by no means unknown in the penumbra of diplomatic expression. Indeed they are the relics of the time before the theory of neutrality had begun to be elaborated. Not the less is their present appearance in a scientific form, backed beyond all question by sincere scientific conviction, an important fact to be noted. We can now review rapidly the chief details which our readers will have been enabled to understand in their inner significance. Much about which there is no controversy need not be mentioned.

Art. 3. When a ship has been captured in the territorial waters of a neutral state, that state, if the prize is still within its jurisdiction, must take the necessary measures for obtaining the release of the prize with its officers and crew, and for interning the prize crew put on board of it.

If the prize is out of the jurisdiction of the neutral state, that state may address itself to the belligerent government, which must release the prize with its officers and crew.

With regard to the second paragraph, Great Britain, Japan, Spain and Brazil voted in committee for its being obligatory on the neutral state to address the belligerent government.

Art. 7. A neutral state is not bound to prevent the export or transit, for the account of either belligerent, of arms, munitions of war, or any thing that can be useful to an army or a fleet.

This is valuable, as repelling the novel obligation which some theorists would impose on neutrals[1].

Art. 12. In default of different special regulation by a neutral state, belligerent ships are prohibited remaining in the ports, roads or territorial waters of such state for more than 24 hours, except in the cases provided for by this convention.

This repudiates the rule of 24 hours' stay as one of general law, and places the length of stay of belligerent ships of war in the discretion of the neutral state, so long as that discretion is exercised by general laws or ordinances (*législation*, which we have translated "regulation") and not by individual permits. A German proposal of conciliation, supported by Russia but not accepted by Great Britain, was that the rule of 24 hours' stay should be obligatory in neutral ports and waters "situate in immediate proximity to the theatre of war," that term being understood to mean "the space of sea on which an operation of war has just taken place (*vient de se faire*), or on which such an operation may take place (*pourra avoir lieu*) in consequence of the presence or the approach of armed forces of the two belligerents." Elsewhere it would not be necessary for neutrals to keep their ports and roads watched. Germany and Russia reserved their consent to Art. 12 as adopted.

Art. 15. A neutral state should (*doit*) fix in advance the maximum number of ships of war of a belligerent which may be at the same time in one of its ports. If not so fixed, the number shall be three.

Art. 16. When ships of war of the belligerent parties are at the same time in a neutral port or road, at least 24 hours must elapse between the departure of a ship of one belligerent and that of a ship of the other.

The order of departure is determined by that of arrival, unless the ship first arrived is entitled to a prolongation of her legal stay.

A belligerent ship of war cannot leave a neutral port or road less than 24 hours after the departure of a merchantman carrying the flag of her enemy.

The order of departure was the subject of discussion in committee, and in consequence of the decision come to on it Great Britain, Japan and Portugal voted against Art. 16 as a whole. The same three powers, with Germany and the United

[1] See above, pp. 167, 258.

States, voted in the majority against a proposal that "if a belligerent ship of war is preparing to enter a neutral port or road where there is a ship of war of her enemy, the local authority must as far as possible notify her of the enemy ship's presence."

Art. 19. Belligerent ships of war cannot revictual in neutral ports or roads except to complete their stores normal in time of peace.

Such ships also cannot receive more fuel than is necessary for gaining the nearest port of their own country. They can however (*d'ailleurs*) receive the fuel necessary to fill their bunkers properly so called, when they are in neutral countries which have adopted that measure of the fuel to be furnished.

Revictualling gives no right to prolong the legal length of stay. Nevertheless, if by the law of the neutral state ships cannot receive coal till 24 hours after their arrival[1], that length is prolonged by 24 hours.

Great Britain, Japan and the United States formed in committee a minority of three against the second paragraph of Art. 19. The limitation in the first sentence of that paragraph to the fuel necessary for gaining the nearest port of the ship's country was the British proposal, and the reporter, M. Renault, stated: "The meaning of that proposal was clearly defined by Sir Ernest Satow in answer to a question of M. Hagerup. The rule is one simply for calculation, and does not create for the neutral any obligation to watch over the destination of the ship which asks for the fuel. We allow ourselves to add that it does not imply any obligation for the ship to betake herself to any particular destination. In this way disputes which sometimes arise would be avoided." It will be observed that Sir Ernest Satow disclaimed responsibility to third parties for the proceedings of the assisted ship, and in this he was certainly correct, since to follow and watch her would be a duty too onerous to be imagined. M. Renault's opinion that the assisted ship will be under no obligation to the country in which she has coaled must be compared with what we have said above, p. 211.

Art. 20 adopted the rule of three months' interval between coalings—above, pp. 211, 212—Germany reserving her consent at the full sitting. Sir Ernest Satow proposed in committee to add to it a rule based on but carrying still further the British instructions of 8 August 1904—above, p. 212—to the effect that

[1] As by the Italian Code of merchant shipping, Art. 249, paragraph 2.

no munitions, victuals or fuel are to be allowed to a belligerent, "for going to meet the enemy or for engaging in operations of war." For this only Great Britain, Japan and Spain voted.

Art. 23. A neutral power may admit prizes to its ports or roads, whether they are escorted or not, when they are brought there in order to be left under sequestration pending the decision of the prize court. It can cause the prize to be conducted to another of its ports.

If the prize is escorted by a ship of war, the officers and men put on board her by the captor are allowed to pass to the escorting ship.

If the prize sails alone, the prize crew is left at liberty.

Great Britain and Japan were the only powers which voted in committee against this great assistance which it was proposed that neutrals might give to belligerents. The reason alleged for it was to prevent the destruction of prizes or render it less frequent.

INDEX.

The numbers are those of the pages.

CAMBRIDGE: PRINTED BY J. CLAY, M.A. AT THE UNIVERSITY PRESS.

Printed in Dunstable, United Kingdom

91219492R00198